917.64 Bro
Brown, Amy K.,
Backroads & byways of Texas : dri
ves, daytrips & weekend
$21.95   on1048041105

D0290130

BACKROADS & BYWAYS OF

TEXAS

DISCARD

BACKROADS & BYWAYS OF

TEXAS

Drives, Day Trips &
Weekend Excursions

THIRD EDITION

AMY K. BROWN

THE COUNTRYMAN PRESS
A division of W. W. Norton & Company
Independent Publishers Since 1923

Copyright © 2019, 2012, 2008 by The Countryman Press

All photographs by Amy K. Brown
Maps by Michael Borop (sitesatlas.com)

All rights reserved
Printed in the United States of America

For information about permission to reproduce selections from this book, write to
Permissions, The Countryman Press, 500 Fifth Avenue, New York, NY 10110

For information about special discounts for bulk purchases, please contact
W. W. Norton Special Sales at specialsales@wwnorton.com or 800-233-4830

Manufacturing by Versa Press
Series book design by Chris Welch
Production manager: Devon Zahn

The Countryman Press
www.countrymanpress.com

A division of W. W. Norton & Company, Inc.
500 Fifth Avenue, New York, NY 10110
www.wwnorton.com

978-1-68268-180-0 (pbk.)

10 9 8 7 6 5 4 3 2 1

Contents

INTRODUCTION

I have said that Texas is a state of mind, but I think it is more than that. It is a mystique closely approximating a religion. And this is true to the extent that people either passionately love Texas or passionately hate it and, as in other religions, few people dare to inspect it for fear of losing their bearings in mystery or paradox. But I think there will be little quarrel with my feeling that Texas is one thing. For all its enormous range of space, climate, and physical appearance, and for all the internal squabbles, contentions, and strivings, Texas has a tight cohesiveness perhaps stronger than any other section of America. Rich, poor, Panhandle, Gulf, city, country, Texas is the obsession, the proper study and the passionate possession of all Texans.

—John Steinbeck, 1962

Texas is the perfect backdrop for adventure. With vast spaces, diverse cultures, and shoot-from-the-hip sincerity, the Lone Star State is the ultimate road trip fantasy. To travel Texas is to experience the open road, with the wind in your hair and convention at your back. Texas has plenty of destinations—exquisite San Antonio, lively Austin, and fascinating Fort Worth, among many others—but there is, as a glance at the map makes clear, a whole lot of in-between. The routes outlined in the following pages offer a sampling of this huge state and the essence of the regions they traverse. For this book I've gone slightly off the beaten path, highlighting places of natural beauty, cultural heritage, and historical significance, in the hopes that your trip through Texas, like mine, will become a journey.

Though each of the routes suggested is accessible from at least one major Texas city, the cities themselves are not generally included. While Texas' cities are certainly worth visiting, they are also books unto themselves (See Countryman's *Explorer's Guide Austin, San Antonio & the Hill Country* for just a few examples). I may dart into several cities along the way to visit a museum or historical site of particular interest, but I never tarry long.

Distances in Texas can be deceptive. Driving in the Hill Country, just west of Austin and San Antonio, it is easy to make stops every 30 minutes or so, while in West Texas you can drive for hours with the distinct feeling that you are getting nowhere fast. To help you keep perspective and better plan your excursion, I have noted the mileage of the segments and the whole of each route. Whether you are planning to drive the coast for the day or take the family camping in Big Bend, this book will be a knowledgeable and helpful companion.

Founded on ambition, guts, and sheer force of will, Texas is the only state in America to enjoy a history of sovereignty, and, in many ways, Texas is as independent, wily, opinionated, self-sufficient, and wide open now as at any time in its past.

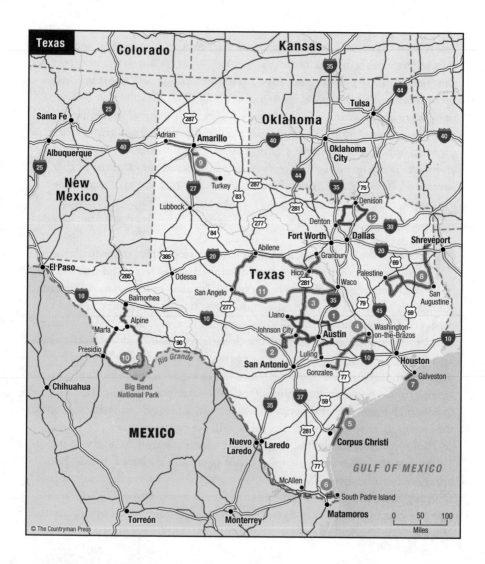

Evidence places human habitation in the region as far back as 11,000 years. Until the sixteenth century, Texas was sparsely inhabited by various groups of Native Americans, who lived as a mix of settled groups and nomadic tribes. The arrival of the Spanish marked the beginning of colonization, and in 1519, Spain claimed Texas as part of its massive holdings in Mexico. However, the country's rule existed primarily on paper and it failed to establish a lasting presence or control over the region.

TEXAS PRIDE

In 1685, the French attempted to expand the western border of Louisiana by claiming Texas as their own, a stand foiled almost immediately by the Spanish, who in 1690 reclaimed the land they'd lost. This time, serious about expanding its empire, Spain set about establishing *misiones* (missions) to convert Native Americans to Christianity and the ways of Spanish citizenship, and *presidios* (forts) to protect these fledgling communities. While the missions did have a huge impact on the lives of Native Americans, Spain was unable to keep its foothold in the new land. When Mexico won independence from Spain in 1821, Texas passed to Mexican rule and into an era of pioneer life, as hopeful immigrants tried their hand at claiming the frontier.

Since the seat of Mexican authority was distant, the new Texans enjoyed a measure of self-rule. When Mexican general Santa Anna set aside the Mexican Constitution in the 1830s, in effect declaring himself king, the seeds of the Texas Revolution were planted. Texas Revolutionaries sparred with Mexican troops in Gonzales, the Alamo in San Antonio, and, finally, in San Jacinto. This final battle, on April 21, 1836, won the state its independence, and the Republic of Texas was born.

Texas' sheer size, wealth of resources, and status as a border state all contributed to its attractiveness as an acquisition by world powers. On December 19, 1845, Texas joined the United States of America, passing from a nation to a state. Sixteen years later, the Civil War tore the unstable nation apart and Texas, though advised by Governor Sam Houston to remain neutral or reestablish a Republic, sided with the Southerners. The flag of the Confederacy flew over Texas from 1861 to 1865, to be replaced in 1865 by the flag of the United States.

With 268,601 square miles, Texas is ranked behind Alaska as the second largest of the states in the Union. Home to well over 20 million people, it is the second most populous state after California, and with Houston, it can claim the fifth-largest city in the country. Much of the population of Texas clusters along I-35, running from Dallas through Austin and San Antonio on

Pests

For whatever reason, pests love Texas and thrive in its temperate climate despite efforts to control them. The truth is that many serve an important ecological function and most are harmless, but there are a few pests that should have you watching where you sit, step, or stand.

FIRE ANTS

The biggest pests in Texas are the fire ants, for which you will frequently see warning signs posted. Fire ants tend to make their mounds in sunny open fields and parks, by the side of the road, and at the bases of trees and other objects, such as picnic tables. When their nest is disturbed, they swarm and deliver many simultaneous stings, which are similar to bee stings in look and feel. Usually no medical intervention is required, but as with bee stings, a small percentage of the population may have a severe allergic reaction, in which case emergency medical care is essential. The only prevention is avoidance, so watch where you sit and stand and be especially aware with small children.

SNAKES

Snakes are common in Texas, but of the seventy-two native species and sub-species, only fifteen pose any threat to humans. Generally, snakes keep to themselves and do not tend to initiate interactions. If you have the unfortunate experience of being bitten, seek medical attention.

SPIDERS

Of the 900 species of spiders present in Texas, only two groups pose any threat to humans: the recluse and widow spiders. In many cases, if you are bitten by one of these, you may not notice until the appearance of a suspicious wound coupled with fever, chills, nausea, pain, vomiting, or weakness, among other symptoms. In all cases, swab the wound with alcohol, relieve swelling and pain with ice, and call your doctor or, depending on the severity, visit the emergency room.

Weather

When it gets hot in Texas, it gets really, really hot. When it gets humid in Texas, it gets really, really humid. Since dehydration and heatstroke are not uncommon conditions, it's important to be aware and prepared. Sunglasses, sunscreen, a light cotton long-sleeved shirt, a wide-brimmed hat, an umbrella, or even a small spray bottle filled with water for misting can help provide protection and relief. Staying hydrated is essential; steering clear of sodas and alcoholic beverages in favor of water, sports drinks, and juices is considered wise.

STORMS

Arriving sometimes without warning, summertime thunderstorms can bring torrential rain and flash floods. When flash flood warnings are issued, it is best to exercise caution and avoid creeks, drainage ditches, and low-water road crossings, as signs in these areas will indicate. Tornadoes frequently accompany thunderstorms, so it is best to listen to or watch the news for any words of caution. A tornado or severe-thunderstorm "watch" serves as an alert that conditions are favorable for either event, while a tornado or severe-thunderstorm "warning" means that either event has been detected on radar and danger may be imminent. In this case, it is best to seek cover in a substantial building, away from windows. In cooler weather, ice

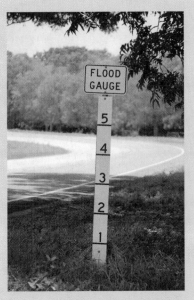

THE STATE'S BACKROADS OFFER ADVENTURE

storms can occur, and since Texas does not maintain a large fleet of sand or salt trucks, the roads can become treacherously slick and hazardous. Texas drivers are inexperienced with slick or icy roads, and during storms accidents tend to be frequent.

WILDFIRES

According to the Texas Forest Service, approximately 90 percent of wildfires in the state are caused by people. As you travel the backroads of Texas, please check local restrictions on campfires and grilling and be mindful of dry, windy conditions.

its way to Mexico. But Texas' urban history, the rise and growth of its cities, is largely a story of the twentieth century. The deeper roots of the state's history, peoples, and culture are firmly planted in the rural landscape that is its greatest hallmark.

From the quiet, shaded Pineywoods of East Texas to the mountains, deserts, and stunning sunsets of West Texas, the plains and canyons of the Panhandle to the sandy dunes of the Gulf Coast, the diversity of Texas will astound you. With its vivid wildflowers, poky armadillos, prickly pear cacti, migrating monarch butterflies, and earnest roadrunners, the land is chock-full of the classic icons of the American West. Barbecue, sweet tea,

Travel Tips

Texas can get very rural very quickly. Some points to consider before starting your trip:

- The first thing you will want to do is purchase some good, updated maps, both of the state in general and the specific region you'll be exploring.
- Be sure your vehicle is in good working order. At minimum, check the air in the tires and the fluids, and consider arranging for a tune-up.
- Pack supplies. Be sure to include extra water, both for the engine and for drinking, a flashlight with fresh batteries, a small first aid kit, a blanket, matches, and snacks such as energy bars and dried fruit.
- Fill up with gas frequently. Even if your tank is half full, be sure to top it off if you can rather than risk running out of gas.
- Generally speaking, expect spotty and unreliable cell phone service and plan accordingly. Do not rely on your cell phone to bail you out of an emergency. Call your cell phone provider and check their range of service.
- Be sure to bring sunscreen and, again, plenty of drinking water. The Texas heat is legendary, and dehydration, sunburn, and sunstroke are very real possibilities.

STATE PARK PASS
If you are planning to visit several of the regions outlined in this book, it might be to your advantage to purchase a Texas State Parks Pass, which will give you free entrance to all the state parks in Texas and discounts on camping fees. Visit the Texas Parks and Wildlife Department at www.tpwd.texas.gov for details.

INTERNET RESOURCES
Two particularly good websites for exploring Texas are www.traveltexas.com and www.texasoutside.com.

A WARM TEXAS WELCOME

and chicken-fried everything speak to the influences of the American South, and savory enchiladas, sizzling fajitas, and nourishing tortilla soup are just some of the Tex-Mex staples that have kept the region's bellies full and souls nourished for centuries.

So, go ahead. Set out on an adventure. Use the routes I've suggested or veer off on your own. Ask the folks you meet where they like to eat, drink, and relax and you will discover something different on the road less traveled. Wherever you roam—no matter how varied the landscape, people, or traditions—rest assured, you are still very much in Texas. The state's prized natural wonders, historical sites, and cultural treasures are its legacy—gifts from Texans to their fellow Americans. Taken together, they are our "passionate possession," and we're happy to share.

Key to pricing

Lodging
$ Inexpensive (Up to $125 per couple)
$$ Moderate ($126–$175 per couple)
$$$ Expensive ($176–$250 per couple)
$$$$ Very expensive (more than $250 per couple)

Dining
$ Inexpensive (Up to $10 per person)
$$ Moderate ($11–$30 per person)
$$$ Expensive ($30–$60 per person)
$$$$ Very expensive (more than $60 per person)

1

THE BEST BBQ IN TEXAS

DRIFTWOOD, LLANO, GEORGETOWN, TAYLOR, ELGIN, LOCKHART, LULING

TOTAL DISTANCE: 250 miles.

HIGHLIGHTS: Folks come to Texas hungry for barbecue, and Central Texas serves it up hot and juicy from old-style, family-owned pits. There are countless ways to get it, and everyone has their favorite. From huge mess halls to local gas stations, the barbecue joints in these parts aren't just places to stop in for a bite; they are places to stop in and experience a little history.

Most classic barbecue spots are no-frills establishments, serving up piping-hot meat with exacting precision, but very little attention gets paid to ambiance. The truth is, eating at well-worn communal tables with little more than butcher paper for a plate, a roll of paper towels by your side, and juice dripping down to your elbows is just the sort of atmosphere folks have come to expect. In Texas, barbecue is the great equalizer; from bikers to bankers, everyone loves good 'cue, as a lunchtime visit to any of the joints below will attest.

While there is plenty of great barbecue in Texas' big cities, fantastic barbecue is worth leaving the city limits behind you. This route visits several small towns—**Driftwood**, **Llano**, **Taylor**, **Elgin**, **Lockhart**, **Luling**, and **Georgetown**. Within striking distance from Austin, this is a backroad route hiding in plain sight.

GETTING THERE: From Austin, take MoPac (Route 1) south to TX 45, turning west, then south onto FM 1826, following it for 8 miles to Driftwood. From Driftwood, follow FM 150 northwest for 5 miles and pick up RR 12. Continue for 10 miles until it dead-ends into Hamilton Pool Road/RR 3238. Turn left and follow signs 6 miles to the park. Leaving the park, take FM 962, US 281, then TX 71 55 miles to Llano.

In Llano, turn right onto TX 16, taking it north through town, then right onto E. Young Street/TX 29, following TX 29 30 miles east to Burnet and an additional 35 miles to Georgetown. From Georgetown, remain on TX 29,

LEFT: HOWEVER YOU SPELL IT, IT'S GOOD

heading east until it dead-ends into TX 95 after 15 miles. Turn right, traveling south the remaining 5 miles to Taylor on TX 95. From Taylor, it's a straight shot on TX 95 16 miles south to Elgin and another 18 miles south to Bastrop. Heading back to the west, follow TX 21 23 miles until it intersects US 183, and take US 183 10 miles south to Lockhart. Double back north on US 183 and 30 miles later, you'll find yourself back in Austin.

While you can follow this route in either direction, I have chosen to leave Austin and head northwest before arching to the east, and finally south. If you are coming from San Antonio, it's an easy 73-mile drive northeast to Lockhart, where you can begin the route and follow it in reverse. From Llano, you can return to San Antonio, 107 miles to the south, via TX 16 and then I-10/US 87.

INTERSECTIONS: Chapters 2, 3, and 4

There are different ways to approach this route. You can easily take in one or two of the restaurants and recommended sites in a day trip from Austin or San Antonio. Folks from Dallas or Houston will find the route a pleasant weekend getaway. But however you tackle it, there is always the issue of eating. The only way to find out what you like best is to try it all. So, throw caution, calories, and cholesterol counts to the wind and follow the smoke from the pits. Since great barbecue is admittedly a matter of opinion, I'll introduce you to the classics and let you decide. This route covers a dozen or so barbecue spots, each a legend in its own right, and several diners, eateries, and even a vineyard; all I can say is if you go, go hungry.

While you may see it spelled "barbecue," "bar-b-que," "barbecue," or "BBQ," in Texas it's all good. The roots of the name have been lost to history, though some believe it may have come from the Spanish version of an indigenous tribe's word, *barbacoa*. One thing is sure, pit cooking is popular in many forms and methods the world over, as this method renders even the toughest cuts of meat moist and juicy. From clambakes to pig roasts, every culture has its version.

In the United States, the style and flavor of barbecue depend on the region. In the Southeast, folks love to drown their pork barbecue in a sweet tomato sauce with a vinegary twang, while the Southwest favors its meat dry-rubbed without any sauce at all. Chicago barbecue is heavy on both the sauce and the pepper. Generally speaking, the farther north you go, the more chicken dominates the menu. But in Texas, it's all about the beef, usually brisket, served straight from the pit. Typically, the meat is dry rubbed, smoked, and served with a side of very optional sauce with various signature concoctions that run the gamut from sweet and smoky to hot and spicy.

A simple Internet search will reveal the depth of opinion and conviction when it comes to Texas barbecue. I don't want to influence your palate unduly, but there are some indisputably great choices, and I present them to you here, unranked and uncategorized. As you make your way through Central Texas, mopping up the juices with sliced white bread and paper towel, you can rest assured that you are eating some of the very best barbecue the state has to offer.

No need to leave Austin for some of the best barbecue in Texas. While the city's East Side isn't exactly a backroad, it's a part of town locals gravitate to for experiences like lunch at **Franklin BBQ**. Started as a food truck in 2009, Franklin has outgrown its charming mobile digs, just recently graduating to a brick-and-mortar storefront. 'Cue is served from "11 AM until out of food," which tends to happen quickly. The line forms mid-morning and never lets up, and the succulent meats, purple cabbage slaw, and mustard-y potato

The Best BBQ in Texas

© The Countryman Press

PULLED PORK SANDWICHES AT
FRANKLIN'S IN AUSTIN

salad are gone in the blink of an eye. No matter how much meat they smoke, the folks at Franklin can't seem to keep up with the insatiable consumer demand—they've sold out every day they've been open. Sadly, in the summer of 2017, Franklin sustained heavy damage in a fire and was forced to close in order to rebuild. This didn't stop Aaron's creativity, though. He threw his energy behind numerous projects: the Hot Luck Food and Music Fest (www.hotluckfest.com), inspired by tailgates, backyard cooking, and family shrimp boils; a new partnership with Austin Chef Tyson Cole to launch a Japanese smokehouse; and support for the local community and causes. Dubbed a "BBQ genius" by *Bon Appétit* magazine, Aaron has legions of Franklin BBQ fans who eagerly queue up for the next delicious brisket.

No matter how much great barbecue there is in Austin, there always seems to be room for more. **La Barbecue** slices and serves tender meats from its food truck in East Austin, each with the perfect balance of dark, burnt bits (also known as bark) on the outside and juicy goodness inside. Give El Sancho Loco a try; that's a trio of pulled pork, chopped brisket, and house-made sausage piled high on a bun with a scoop of pickled red onions on top. The 'cue here rivals the best around, and eating it outside at the communal picnic tables seems to make it just that much tastier. Lines start early and grow long; free beer is often on offer.

Head south out of Austin on MoPac/Loop 1, passing the Lady Bird Johnson Wildflower Center (page 35); turn west on TX 45, then south on FM 1826 for 8 miles to Driftwood, where **The Salt Lick** has been drawing meat-lovers from far and wide for years. Located on the edge of the Hill Country, The Salt Lick cooks their meat over a blazing hot oak fire in a huge, 40-year-old stone pit, but the secret to the delicious barbecue seems to be in the sauce. The meat is basted in a tomato-less sauce with just a pinch of sugar to help it stay fresh and bright as it caramelizes over the heat, resulting in juicy goodness every time. The family-style meal option features big bowls of coleslaw, potato salad, and beans for passing and slices of bread to sop up the juices. You can't beat the Salt Lick's setting. The grounds surrounding the restaurant feel almost ranch-like, with wooden picnic tables nestled under the big oak trees and live music. BYOB and cash-only. Across the street from a Fall Creek Vineyard winery and tasting room. Stop in here or continue with the route and visit the vineyard in Tow (page 20).

Take FM 150 north out of **Driftwood**, turning right onto RR 12 toward Dripping Springs, then picking up Hamilton Pool Road/RR 3238, passing by **Hamilton Pool Nature Preserve**. A rugged trail leads from the parking lot to the clear natural pool, cool grotto, and 45-foot waterfall. There are no lifeguards and you'll need to carry in your own food, water, and other necessities, but this place is a very popular swimming spot on hot Texas days. Once the lot is full, parking is first come, first served, and the line can get long. You may even be turned away due to overcrowding, so come with a Plan B and prepare to be flexible. Back on the road, continue north on FM/RR 962, cross over US 281 (see Chapter 3), and cruise into Llano on TX 71. The trip from Driftwood to Llano is just over 70 miles.

ON THE TABLE: SAUCE, SALT, PEPPER, AND TOOTHPICKS

Llano (pronounced LAY-no) is a former frontier town in the northern reaches of the Texas Hill Country. Located on the Llano River and TX 71, Llano is a jumping-off point into the Highland Lakes region (page 57). This unassuming slip of a spot also just so happens to be home to one of Texas' culinary gems—**Cooper's Old Time Pit Bar-B-Que**, located on W. Young Street, just west of the intersection of TX 16 and TX 29. The first things you'll notice when you pull up to Cooper's are the huge outdoor pits organized under a corrugated metal roof. Step up to place your order, and the pit masters will open the heavy metal counter-weighted lids wide, inviting you to get a good look inside—the smell of sizzling meat in your nose and tangy mesquite smoke in your eyes—and point to exactly what you'd like. Once you've made your choice, the pit master will ask if you'd like your selection dunked into a huge vat of peppery red sauce before you take it inside for slicing. The dining room at Cooper's has long communal tables and walls adorned with heads of bobcats, deer, and other animals you won't find being slow-cooked. Curiously, many of the other barbecue joints in this chapter share this taxidermy theme. Cooper's has expanded, with pits in Austin and

New Braunfels, but a pilgrimage to the original is rewarding. Speaking of cooking over an open flame, if you are in Llano on a weekend or maybe on your way to Enchanted Rock (Chapter 2), stop by **Tommy's Mesquite Flamed Pizza** for some zesty, yeasty, cheesy goodness.

A great place to cleanse your palate on this route is **Fall Creek Vineyards**, perched on the north shore of **Lake Buchanan**, part of the chain of Highland Lakes described on page 57. Its origins go back to 1973, when local ranchers Ed and Susan Auler took a trip to France and quickly noticed the similarities between their Texas landscape and the French wine region. Back at home, they took a chance on the location's magical combination of soil, sunny days, and lake breezes and established a vineyard. The oldest and perhaps best-known of the Texas vineyards, Fall Creek paved the way for winemaking in the state, and they now have plenty of colleagues throughout the Hill Country (page 41). While renowned for their super-premium red wine, Meritus, the vineyard consistently garners praise for all the wines they produce. Try them at their daily wine tastings. To get there, leave Llano, traveling east on TX 29, then north on RR 2241, through Bluffton, to Tow, then south on CR 222; the winery is located 2.2 miles past the Tow post office. To reconnect with the route, retrace your steps to Bluffton and take TX 261 south to rejoin TX 29 and continue eastward, skirting the southern tip of the lake. Additional tasting room in Driftwood, across from the Salt Lick (page 18).

TEXAS BLUEBONNET

The spring-fed Fall Creek, for which Fall Creek Vineyards is named, ambles through that vineyard before cascading into Lake Buchanan in the form of the 90-foot **Fall Creek Waterfalls**. Also of interest on the lake is the **Canyon of the Eagles**, where in the winter and early spring some two dozen majestic American bald eagles nest and live. The **Vanishing Texas River Cruise**, a beautiful and educational ecologically themed boat cruise, takes in both sights. The cruise leaves from the **Canyon of the Eagles Resort**, on the east side of Lake Buchanan, practically across the lake from Fall Creek Vineyards. The resort is a recreation and retreat center and lodge with fairly basic hotel-room

Bluebonnets

Burnet has been designated as the Bluebonnet Capital of Texas, and you can print a map of the self-guided Bluebonnet Trail from the Chamber of Commerce website, www.burnetchamber.org, to use for maximum bluebonnet viewing in the springtime.

style accommodations, cabins, a campground, restaurant, and swimming pool spread. Most of the 940 acres of this property is a nature preserve with 14 miles of hiking trails, perfect for nature lovers who enjoy canoeing, kayaking, camping, or star gazing. The resort is a lovely spot from which to explore the lake, making this detour a backroad to tranquility. From the intersection of TX 29 and RR 2431, drive 3 miles west of Burnet and turn north onto RR 2431, following it 14 miles to the resort entrance.

Leaving Burnet (detailed in Chapter 3) and heading east on TX 29, you'll travel approximately 50 miles to the community of Liberty Hill. Just north of the intersection with RR 1869 and a stone's throw from TX 29, **Dahlia's Café** serves breakfast, lunch, and dinner to what seems like almost everyone in town. From morning omelets to evening desserts, Dahlia's offerings are consistently delicious, but if you have to choose just one thing, make it the juicy chicken-fried chicken with the homemade signature jalapeño gravy. The restaurant looks small from the front, but it is wide open in the back, with space for live music on weekends. Great country cooking and an amiable atmosphere make Dahlia's a great stop if you'd like to break up this section of the route.

Continuing east, the small college town of **Georgetown** is one of the most sensible and pleasant places on this route to spend the night. Home to Southwestern University, the oldest university in the state, Georgetown also has a particularly lovely downtown, with neatly renovated historic buildings surrounding the town square, a courthouse at its center, and stately homes from the 1880s.

Located in a lovely restored 1918 bungalow, **The Sweet Lemon Inn** is a bright green and yellow boutique bed & breakfast and cafe just off the Georgetown Square. Rooms are fresh and airy, with pretty furniture, bedding, and whimsical accents. When you wake, slip downstairs to the **Sweet Lemon Kitchen**. Try a cinnamon roll or a sweet or savory *kolache*, a Czech pastry popular in Central Texas. For lunch, the turkey and brie sandwich is made special by their homemade spiced jam and locally-baked poblano sourdough bread. Be sure to leave room to taste their buttery lemon cookies and lemon squares.

Across the street, John Mueller's **Black Box Barbecue** smokes and serves some fantastic brisket, beef ribs, and more out of their busy food trailer. Son of smoked meat legend Louie Mueller (see below), John brings his own taste and techniques to Black Box, routinely selling out before lunch is over. On Austin Avenue, in a little commercial strip anchored by a gas station, you'll find **Hello Sweetie**, a hidden gem of barbecue. This tiny spot turns out big flavor including delicious pulled pork, snappy jalapeño sausages, and creamy potato salad. The owner, Allen, is a treat.

Given that you will eat your fill of barbecue on this route, Georgetown is also a good place to sample something different. The **Monument Café**, located on S. Austin Avenue, has created a hit with its formula of combining comfort foods made from scratch using stellar ingredients—often organic and locally grown—with a 1940s diner atmosphere. Since everything is delicious, just ask folks on their way out the door what their favorite is and order accordingly. Seriously consider saving room for a sliver of their signature chocolate pie. The thick, nutty crust is made from toasted pecans and topped with a chocolate mousse filling and whipped cream—silky, creamy creation that melts in your mouth.

If the hot, humid Texas weather is getting to you, then head into **Inner Space Cavern**, where the air is clean, clear, and a constant 72 degrees. The cavern, located underneath bustling I-35, was discovered in 1963 during drilling through 40 feet of solid limestone for highway construction. While there are numerous caves and caverns in the area, this is one of the more accessible ones, with a cable car, paved trails, and an informative tour that lasts just over an hour; just the thing if you've forgotten the difference between stalactite, stalagmite, and spelunker. You'll find the cavern just a minute south of Georgetown at exit 259 on I-35.

Heading out of Georgetown east along E. University Avenue will take you past pretty Southwestern University; the road becomes TX 29, dotted with little homes, pastures, and low water crossings, which dead-ends approximately 16 miles later into TX 95, at which point you will head south, following signs to **Taylor**.

This small town on the San Gabriel River certainly looks as if it's seen better days, but some local antique shops and an old theater showing first-run movies for $2.50 hold their own. Then there's **Louie Mueller Barbeque**. Folks come from up the street and as far away as Asia to darken the door of Louie Mueller's. This place is the perfect mix of everything you might want in a barbecue joint. The inside is charred to a thick gray-black, and the air is tinged with smoke from the pits behind the counter. There are plenty of well-worn wooden tables, each with its own selection of mismatched wooden chairs.

Step up, take a look at the menu written on butcher paper and taped to the wall, and order. Whether you select brisket or spare ribs or homemade jalapeño sausage, Mueller's staff will grab your selection fresh from the pit

FRAMED ACCOLADES AT LOUIS MUELLER BARBEQUE IN TAYLOR

and lop off a slice for you to taste before carving it up in a flash. While they offer a tangy tomatoey sauce, few people even give it a glance. The meat's just that good.

Salt, pepper, and an oak-fueled fire are all that make up this fantastic 'cue. It sounds simplistic—but only in the same way you might say that all paintings are made of just canvas and paint. The finished product depends on the skill of the handlers, and these folks are masters. Judging from the knives, the wear and tear on the cutting block, and just simply everything in this place, Mueller's motto seems to be "If it ain't broke, don't fix it." If Louie Mueller's never changes another thing, they are still well within perfect.

Leaving Taylor, head south again, traveling approximately 16 miles on TX 95 to **Elgin** (pronounced EL-gin). If you like sausage, you will have plenty of chances to eat your fill here; the town is home to three of Texas' best-loved sausage makers, earning it the distinction of the Sausage Capital of Texas.

After entering town, **Southside Market and Barbecue** is the first spot you'll come across, located on US 290, just south of where TX 95 dead-ends into it. The family that originally owned Southside started making sausage in 1882; the current owners took over in 1968, carrying on the very same tradition. This spot started as a meat market, but they added an eating area for people who just couldn't wait to get home before digging in. Whether you choose a single link or take a couple of pounds home to freeze, Southside's sausages are always juicy with just a little bit of a kick.

Loosen your belt and head east on US 290 to **Meyer's Elgin Smokehouse**. The folks here have been making sausage since 1949, using an old family recipe brought to this country from Germany. Until 10 years ago, Meyer's was exclusively a wholesale operation, but sausage lovers demanded more, so the company added a dining area. Now you can enjoy sausage, along with pork ribs, turkey breast, and brisket on site. Order the "three meat combo" for a taste of almost everything. The decor is basic, food comes on butcher paper, and the rolls of paper towels set out on the tables are meant to be used.

The route continues to **Lockhart**, where the triumvirate of **Kreuz Market**, **Smitty's**, and **Black's** rules the smoking pits that put this town on the map.

The oldest of the Lockhart barbecue joints, **Kreuz** (pronounced KRITES) began as a meat market and grocery in 1900. As was the custom at the time, the market cooked meat as a way of staving off spoilage, and customers often bought pieces hot off the grill for a quick meal. By the 1960s, Kreuz sold barbecue exclusively, serving it on butcher paper, with saltines, bread, pickles, onions, and, uniquely, cheese. In 1999, the business picked up and moved, bringing its 99 years of experience to the brand-new building it inhabits today. While they've expanded the menu somewhat, adding a few newfangled items, thankfully they didn't touch the barbecue, which is just as hot and juicy as it's always been. A trip to Kreuz's usually means spending some time in line. Once inside the front door, you are encouraged to wash your hands at the freestanding sink (consider this a subtle reminder that Kreuz doesn't hand out forks with their barbecue), and then wait to be herded into

Saturdays Only

Overshoot Taylor and head south on FM 112 until you come to the little town of Lexington, home of **Snow's BBQ**. If you want to taste the barbecue here, you'll need to hustle—Snow's opens at 8 AM on Saturdays, and they only serve until noon, unless of course they sell out first, which happens a lot. Something this hard to get had better be special, and Snow's is. The brisket is perfectly cooked, a little crisp and salty on the outside and melt-in-your-mouth on the inside, thanks to the efforts of Tootsie Tomanetz, a tiny whirlwind of a woman who's been smoking meats since the late 1960s and is clearly an expert. You might not even end up saucing anything, since the meats are that flavorful on their own. The ribs are outstanding, though the sides aren't particularly notable. Snow's is housed in a bitty shack of a place with an attached covered outdoor eating area. To pick up the route again, travel 20 miles west on FM 696 and 4 miles north on US 290 north to Elgin.

the cavernous pit room. You place your order, by the pound, at the counter, exit through the double doors, choose your sides, pay, and find yourself a spot to sit down and dig in.

Located just off the town square, these days **Smitty's** minds the pits at what used to be Kreuz. In fact, Smitty's is named for Edgar "Smitty" Schmidt, the founder of Kreuz, whose daughter opened this old-style joint in 1999 after Kreuz moved to its current location. While a disagreement may have fragmented the family, many of their old barbecue traditions survived intact. The menu here is what you'd expect—beef, pork chops, sausage—all served sauceless, on brown paper. Outside, Smitty's looks like little more than a dirty and tattered set of double doors. Once you get inside, you'll realize that it's dirty and tattered all the way to the billowing open fires funneling smoke and heat into the pits. In this case, however, the residue is best described as a patina—

COMMUNAL DINING TABLES AT KREUZ IN LOCKHART

that finish that you get through years and years of good use. The dining area is a bit more generic, with tables pushed end to end and fluorescent lights, but each time the doors swing open and you get a glimpse of the pits, it's like love at first sight all over again.

Black's is altogether different. Located a block or two off the square and in business since 1932, Black's claims to be the "oldest and best major barbecue restaurant continuously owned by the same family." While this may seem like splitting hairs, the point is well taken. Recipes and techniques handed down within the family, not to mention years and years of practice, have produced excellent results, and the proof is in the eating. President Lyndon Johnson once had them cook up a mess of sausage to be sent to the capital. Secret Service and Department of Agriculture employees came to oversee preparation, but, to date, Black's trade secrets have remained safe with them.

The ordering experience here is less communal; diners never pass by the pits, but instead go through a cafeteria-style line, sit at four-person tables, and enjoy a view of trophy heads and hunting pictures. The atmosphere doesn't detract from the food, which is, after all, why you are here in the first place. Folks say that the brisket is the best around, smoked over post

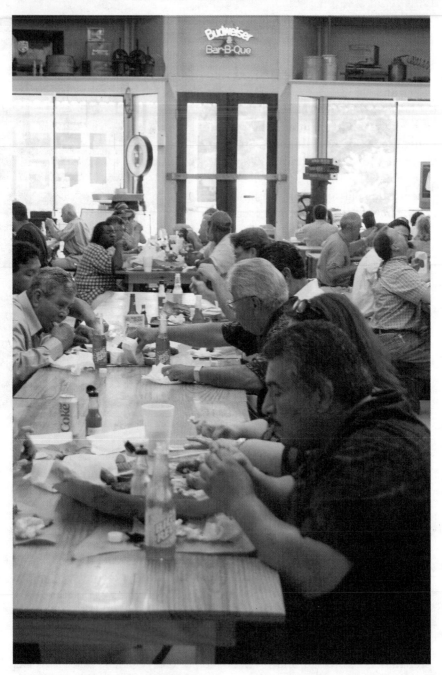

A PACKED DINING ROOM AT SMITTY'S IN LOCKHART

FRANKLIN BBQ IN AUSTIN

oak until succulent. Pork, ham, chicken, and sausage are also on the menu, and the thick sauce makes plenty of diners happy. While at most barbecue places the available sides consist of potato salad and onions, Black's offerings are more wide-ranging. From green pea salad with ham to hard-boiled eggs, Black's keeps 'em coming back for more . . . year after year after year. They've even opened an additional pit in Austin.

Back on US 183, follow the signs another 15 miles or so to the small town of **Luling**. In town, the highway becomes Magnolia Street, then veers sharply to the east and continues south to Gonzales (see below). Just a block west of the highway, at 633 E. Davis Street, sits **Luling City Market** ("City Market," for short) surrounded by an aura of mesquite smoke that's been there since it opened in the late 1950s. The place isn't much to look at—by now you've noticed most aren't—but step inside and it's all business. The pit is indoors, at the back of the restaurant, enclosed on all sides, with windows and doors for access. Once in this barbecue antechamber, order up and watch as your meat is handpicked, carved, and passed over the counter. Grab a pickle, some onions, saltines, and maybe some beans, and sidle up to the tables to find yourself a seat. One thing that really sets City Market apart is its sauce. The fact that it has any at all is distinctive, but it is surprisingly tasty, with just enough sweetness and heat to complement the tender and slightly salty meat. Everyone loves the pork ribs, sausages, and, of course, brisket.

BARBECUE WITH ALL THE FIXIN'S AT LULING CITY MARKET IN LULING

The route properly ends here, and I-20 and US 183 are handily located to take you to your destinations, but for those who'd like a little more, travel just a few miles south to **Gonzales**, the spot where the first battle cries of the Texas Revolution were heard. Park yourself in a seat at either the **Gonzales Food Market** or **Baker Boys BBQ** and get ready for more fantastic barbecue, served by some of the friendliest folks in Texas. If your travels take you to Brenham, stop in at **Truth Barbeque** and let them set you straight on matters of delicious barbecue. (Gonzales Food Market, Baker Boys BBQ, and Truth Barbecue are reviewed and detailed in Chapter 4.)

If you finish this route with a heavy heart as well as a full stomach, take comfort in the fact that if you just had some of the best Texas brisket you've ever tasted, you'll never really have to go without. If you live in the area or find yourself passing through, all of these places would love to have you back anytime. And if you live afar, just call up and place an order; most of the places on this route will be happy to ship you whatever you desire. Rest assured, these are the folks who understand the need for great Texas barbecue.

IN THE AREA

BLACK'S, 215 N. Main Street, Lockhart, 78644. Call 512-398-2712. Closed Mondays. Great brisket, ribs, and serve-yourself sides in this stalwart of Texas barbecue. Additional restaurant in Austin. Website: www.blacksbbq .com. $$.

BLACK BOX BARBECUE, 201 E. 9th Street, Georgetown, 78626. Call 512-635-6024. Closed Monday–Wednesday. More great barbecue from a Mueller family member, served at picnic tables beside their food trailer and smoker. Website: www.blackboxbbq.com. $–$$.

CANYON OF THE EAGLES RESORT, 16942 RR 2341, Burnet, 78611. Call 512-334-2070. Basic hotel-room style accommodations, cabins, a campground, restaurant, and swimming pool on the shores of Lake Buchanan. Website: www.canyonoftheeagles.com. $–$$.

CITY MARKET, 633 E. Davis Street, Luling, 78648. Call 830-875-9019. Try the pork ribs or snappy beef sausage at this old-school mainstay. Closed Sundays. Cash only. $–$$.

COOPER'S, 604 W. Young Street/TX 71/29, Llano, 78643. Call 325-247-5713. Closed Mondays. Renowned barbecue served straight from the outdoor pits to your plate. Additional restaurants in Austin and New Braunfels. Website: www.coopers bbq.com. $$.

DAHLIA'S CAFÉ, 2450 RR 1869, Liberty Hill, TX 78642. Call 512-515-7772. Closed Sundays and Mondays. Delicious home-cooked country-style meals in a true community restaurant. Website: www.dahliacafe.com. $–$$.

ELGIN CHAMBER OF COMMERCE, 114 Central Avenue, Elgin, 78621. Call 512-281-5724. Website: www.elgintx.com.

FALL CREEK WINERY AND VINEYARDS, 1820 County Road 22, Tow, 78672. Call 325-379-5361. Website: www.fcv.com.

FRANKLIN BARBECUE, 900 E. 11th Street, Austin, 78702. Call 512-653-1187. Amazing meats from the man dubbed a "BBQ genius" by *Bon Appétit* magazine. Website: www.franklinbbq.com. $–$$.

GEORGETOWN VISITOR INFORMATION CENTER, 103 W. Seventh Street, Georgetown, 78626. Call 1-800-436-8696. Website: www.visit.george town.org.

HAMILTON POOL NATURE PRESERVE, 24300 Hamilton Pool Road, Dripping Springs, 78620. Call 512-264-2740. Website: www.co.travis.tx.us.

HELLO SWEETIE, 2200 S. Austin Avenue, Georgetown, 78626. Call 512-869-3304. Closed Sunday. Succulent barbecue and a warm welcome await at this hole-in-the-wall surprise. Website: www.hellosweetiebbqandmore.com. $–$$.

INNER SPACE CAVERN, 4200 S. I-35, exit 259, Georgetown, 78626. Call 512-931-2283. Seasonal hours. Fee. Website: www.myinnerspacecavern.com.

KREUZ MARKET, 619 N. Colorado Street/US 183, Lockhart, 78644. Call 512-398-2361. The large restaurant was built in the 1980s, but houses the same pits they've been using for 100 years to smoke fantastic barbecue. Website: www.kreuzmarket.com. $–$$.

LA BARBEQUE, 2027 E. Cesar Chavez Street, Austin, 78702. Call 512-605-9696. Closed Mondays and Tuesdays. Juicy barbecue from this East Austin food truck is some of the best around. Website: www.labarbecue.com. $–$$.

LLANO COUNTY CHAMBER OF COMMERCE, The Railyard Depot, 100 Train Station Drive, Llano, 78643. Call 325-247-5354. Website: www.llano chamber.org.

LOCKHART CHAMBER OF COMMERCE, 702 S. Commerce Street, Lockhart, 78644. Call 512-398-2818. Website: www.lockhartchamber.com.

LOUIE MUELLER BARBECUE, 206 W. Second Street, Taylor, 76574. Call 512-352-6206. Closed Sundays. James Beard Foundation "American Classics" winner for consistently fantastic barbecue. Website: www .louiemuellerbarbecue.com. $$.

LULING AREA CHAMBER OF COMMERCE, 421 E. Davis Street, Luling, 78648. Call 830-875-3214. Website: www.lulingcc.org.

MEYER'S ELGIN SMOKEHOUSE, 188 Highway 290, Elgin, 78621. Call 512-281-3331. Excellent sausage made from an old German family recipe since 1949. Website: www.meyerselginsausage.com. $–$$.

MONUMENT CAFÉ, 500 S. Austin Avenue, Georgetown, 78627. Call 512-930-9586. Serving eggs with homemade biscuits and jam for breakfasts and burgers, King Ranch casserole, daily specials, and famous chocolate pie for lunch. Website: www.themonumentcafe.com. $$.

THE SALT LICK, 18300 FM 1826, Driftwood, 78619. Call 512-894-3117. Tasty barbecue smoked and served in a huge stone restaurant in a pretty part of the Hill Country. Website: www.saltlickbbq.com. Cash only. $–$$.

SMITTY'S, 208 S. Commerce, Lockhart, 78644. Call 512-398-9344. Hot and smoky barbecue served straight from the time-tested pits. Website: www.smittysmarket.com. $–$$.

SNOW'S, 516 Main Street, Lexington, 78947. Call 979-542-8189. Saturdays only, 8 AM until it's gone. Taste the legendary barbecue that's worth the drive, the wait, and the getting up early. Website: www.snowsbbq.com. $$.

SOUTHSIDE MARKET AND BARBEQUE, 1212 Highway 290, Elgin, 78621. Call 512-281-4650. Hot, peppery beef sausage links in six different flavors. Additional restaurants in Bastrop. Website: www.southsidemarket.com. $–$$.

THE SWEET LEMON INN, 812 S. Church Street, Georgetown, 78626. Call 512-270-0812. Gorgeous rooms tucked into the second floor of a 1918 bungalow just a block off the square. Website: www.sweetlemoninn.com. $$$$.

THE SWEET LEMON KITCHEN, 812 S. Church Street, Georgetown, 78626. Call 512-270-0812. Closed Sundays and Mondays. Straight-from-the-oven breakfast treats, fresh and healthy lunches, and lemon squares for dessert. Website: www.sweetlemonkitchen.com. $$.

TAYLOR CHAMBER OF COMMERCE, 1519 N. Main Street, Taylor, 76574. Call 512-365-8485. Website: www.taylorchamber.org.

TOMMY'S MESQUITE FLAMED PIZZA, 633 E. Davis Street, Luling, 78648. Call 830-875-9019. Piping hot pizzas right out of a homemade, wood-fired oven. Cash only.

VANISHING TEXAS RIVER CRUISE, 16942 RR 2341/443 Waterway Lane, Burnet, 78611. Call 512-756-6986. Website: www.vtrc.com.

A President does not shape a new and personal vision of America. He collects it from the scattered hopes of the American past.

Lyndon B. Johnson

2

LYNDON AND LADY BIRD'S
HILL COUNTRY

JOHNSON CITY, STONEWALL, FREDERICKSBURG, LUCKENBACH

TOTAL DISTANCE: Approximately 90 miles

HIGHLIGHTS: Though several US presidents have hailed from Texas, at his best, President Lyndon Baines Johnson (LBJ) embodied the grand spirit of the state. LBJ's boyhood in rural Texas in the early 1900s planted the seeds of compassion and sense of duty that informed the revolutionary social changes he ushered in during his presidency. Start at the **Lyndon Baines Johnson Library and Museum**, pay a visit and your respects to former first lady Lady Bird Johnson, at her **Wildflower Center** in Austin, and continue west into the Hill Country to see the **Lyndon B. Johnson National Historical Park** and the **LBJ Ranch**. Sample Texas wines and peaches as you make your way to **Fredericksburg**. Enjoy beautiful vistas and abundant wildflowers on the **Willow City Loop**, **Enchanted Rock State Natural Area**, and along the backroads between **Comfort**, **Sisterdale**, and **Luckenbach**. **Detour:** Willow City Loop (see pages 42–44).

GETTING THERE: The Lyndon Baines Johnson Library and Museum is located on Red River Street in Austin, along the eastern edge of the University of Texas campus. From there, take Red River three blocks south, pick up San Jacinto and follow it south, skirting the Texas State Capitol complex. Turn right on 11th Street and left onto Congress Avenue, using the Ann Richards/Congress Avenue Bridge to cross Lady Bird Lake. From there, turn right into Barton Springs Road, following it to MoPac/Route 1. Take MoPac/Route 1 south to La Crosse Avenue, following signs to the Lady Bird Johnson Wildflower Center, a total of 13 miles from the LBJ Library. Leaving the Wildflower Center, double back to MoPac/Route 1, this time heading west on Slaughter Lane. Follow Slaughter for 2.5 miles, turning left onto US 290 and following it west for 31 miles. US 290 will merge with US 281, so follow the route north to Johnson City. From Johnson City, take US 290 16 miles west to Stonewall and an addi-

LEFT: PRESIDENT LYNDON BAINES JOHNSON

tional 14 miles west to Fredericksburg. From Fredericksburg, double back on US 290 and take RR 1376 south to Luckenbach.

INTERSECTIONS: Chapters 1 and 3

This part of Texas, so close to the urban centers of Austin and San Antonio, still retains a rural look and feel. Pastures of cows and sheep, ripening vineyards and peach orchards, lazy creeks, and wildflowers along the roadways paint a picture of a bucolic Texas worthy of postcards and calendars. Driving along the backroads of this region makes for a terrific weekend trip. You can certainly do parts of this trip in a day, and three full days would be ideal. The Hill Country is already a popular getaway, so be sure to book accommodations plenty of time ahead and consider an off-season, midweek trip, which is almost always more relaxing.

Starting in Austin, stop in at the well-curated **Lyndon Baines Johnson Library and Museum** on the University of Texas campus for an overview of the life and times of Lyndon Baines Johnson, former Texas state representative and 36th president of the United States. The museum offers changing exhibits on such topics as the Vietnam War, all interesting and all a part of the larger story of the politically charged 1960s, when heady idealism and harsh realities divided the country's citizens.

Leaving the LBJ Library and Museum, swoop down Congress Avenue to **Lady Bird Lake,** the reservoir on the Colorado River which separates downtown Austin from South Austin, and enjoy a stroll. When the Colorado River was dammed in 1960, the resulting lake was named Town Lake. Though it was intended to provide beauty and recreation for Austinites, the lake became overgrown, polluted, and dangerous. After a decade of neglect, Lady Bird stepped in to form the Town Lake Beautification Committee and set about clearing, cleaning, planting, and adding 10 miles of hiking and biking trails along its shores. After her death, the city renamed the lake in her honor (a gesture she had resisted during her lifetime) in recognition of her diligent restoration work. Lady Bird Lake is now a hub of outdoor activity in Austin and the site of many cultural, musical, and athletic events.

Head west to Route 1, known within the city limits as MoPac, a reference to the Missouri Pacific Railroad, which runs alongside it, and then south to the **Lady Bird Johnson Wildflower Center.** This lovely piece of Central Texas countryside is hemmed in by the ever-expanding Austin suburbs, but the grounds themselves are spacious and private. An environmentalist long before "going green" was popular, Lady Bird Johnson is directly responsible for the many azaleas and dogwood trees dotting the Washington, DC, parks. Back in Texas, in 1982, she transformed her simple idea that "a little beauty can create harmony" into the Wildflower Center, opening it along with her friend, the actress Helen Hayes, on her 70th birthday. The center was designed to protect and preserve North America's native foliage, and in doing so has become a foremost authority on the subject, with an encyclopedic website that is sure to be of interest to gardeners from every region. When Lady Bird died in 2007, she left a powerful legacy of conservation and environmental custodianship well represented by the Wildflower Center.

While spring and summer are the most vivid seasons at the center, there seems to be a native flower or plant in bloom almost year-round, making it a wonderful place for nature photography. After a stroll around the grounds, visitors enjoy browsing in **Wild Ideas,** the on-site gift shop, or relaxing over a drink at the **Wildflower Café,** which you'll find tucked into a corner of the hacienda-style main building.

Leaving the Wildflower Center, double back slightly, then turn left at Slaughter and north on US 290, following it to its merger with US 281 in Johnson City, for a total of 40 miles. As you come into Johnson City, US 281 will continue north, following the route laid out in Chapter 3, while US 290 will continue to the west, taking you through the rest of this chapter.

If you are visiting at mealtime, **Johnson City** has some folksy restaurants to stop in for a laid-back meal. Across from the courthouse, the **Pecan Street Brewing Company** offers burgers, rustic pizzas, freshly brewed beers, and

HILL COUNTRY WILDFLOWERS

a surprising number of local wines. Housed in an old lumberyard, the **East Main Street Grill** is a welcome stopping point for classics like chicken-fried steaks and creative dishes such as pork ribeye with chipotle plum sauce, both served with a heaping scoop of homemade garlic mashed potatoes. **Bryan's on 290** is a delicious detour, the sort of restaurant where half a chicken with smoked gouda macaroni and cheese shares the menu with Asian-glazed pork belly pineapple fried rice.

The next stop on this route is the **Lyndon B. Johnson National Historical Park**. The visitor center, complete with maps and restrooms, is located beside the parking lot, and from there it is just a short walk to either the **Johnson Settlement**, with a log cabin, windmill, and barns dating back to the 1860s and owned by LBJ's grandparents, or **LBJ's boyhood home**. The Johnson family moved to this neat and tidy Folk Victorian in town from a farm in Stonewall in 1912, just before a young LBJ turned 5 years old. Today the site is owned by the National Park Service and has been restored in mid-1920s style. This restoration was no small feat; it took three years of hard work for historians, architects, carpenters, and stonemasons to give the property the historically accurate look and feel it has today. As you tour the home, take note of the details, particularly the woodstove in the kitchen, which speaks volumes about life in the Hill Country in those days, when the region was still without access to electricity. Life in the Texas Hill Country in the 1930s was like reliving the 1830s. While much of the rest of the country lived in cities with access to refrigeration, electric stoves, ovens, irons, and indoor plumbing, folks in the Hill Country struggled to meet their most basic needs in the absence of these amenities through backbreaking work and determination. Farms limped along without electricity. Hulking woodstoves were kept burning all year long regardless of the heat. Women (almost exclusively) had to carry water from nearby rivers and streams. Milking was done by candlelight—a dangerous inconvenience in hay-filled barns.

This was the environment in which the young Lyndon Johnson grew up, and he understood all too well its hardships. The work of the people to meet their most basic needs was neverending, and Johnson hated the idea of people suffering needlessly when the innovations that could ease their work were so readily available elsewhere. In fact, he saw this disparity as an injustice. Northeastern electric companies consistently balked at bringing electricity to rural Texas, declaring that folks living on farms and in the country wouldn't be able to pay their utility bills. When he became a congressman, Johnson set out to change things. Thinking that if they couldn't convince the big companies to help, then they had best help themselves, Johnson brought the idea of starting a power cooperative to his neighbors throughout the Hill Country, who, after some initial skepticism, signed on.

In 1935, President Franklin D. Roosevelt unveiled the New Deal, with rural electrification as an integral part of post-Depression economic recovery, and by the 1940s the lights were on in the Texas Hill Country and all across rural America. This simple fact had a social, cultural, and economic impact so profound that it is difficult to grasp today, but as Johnson himself wrote in 1959, "I think of all the things I have ever done, nothing has ever given me as much satisfaction as bringing power to the Hill Country of

Sunday Houses

Devoutly religious Germans settled on farms and ranches outside Fredericksburg, committed to working the land but also determined not to miss church services on the Sabbath. Weather, distance, and road conditions made getting to church difficult, so they built tiny houses on small bits of land in town to use for shopping on Saturday and church on Sunday. Known as Sunday houses, these were wood structures, with steep roofs and a sprinkling of decorative millwork and with little lean-to kitchens tacked on the back, and sometimes a staircase to a second floor running along an outside wall. The houses were popular between 1890 and 1910, and small groups of them survive today along West San Antonio Street, near St. Mary's church, on W. Main Street and S. Milam Street.

Texas." So, as you make your way through the countryside outlined in this route, every once in a while let your imagination drift back to a time not so long ago, when the entire region was in the dark. Those numerous utility poles marring the otherwise pristine Hill Country views are the hard-won results of teamwork, diligence, and perseverance.

Leaving Johnson City and heading west on US-290 will take you the 13 miles to **Stonewall**, home of the **LBJ Ranch**, which is operated by the National Park Service. The ranch is a collection of buildings, including the home Johnson was born in, the "Texas White House," and the Johnson Family Cemetery; the Pedernales River, in which Johnson was baptized, flows through the property.

Though Johnson's birthplace was razed in the 1940s, what you will see is a meticulous reconstruction, based on photographs of the original. The reconstructed home has running water, electricity, and other modern amenities that would not have existed at the time, as well as donated antique furniture in much better condition than what Johnson would have seen as a child, but the design of the house, in the regional "dog-trot" style, is just

OUTHOUSE AT THE LBJ RANCH

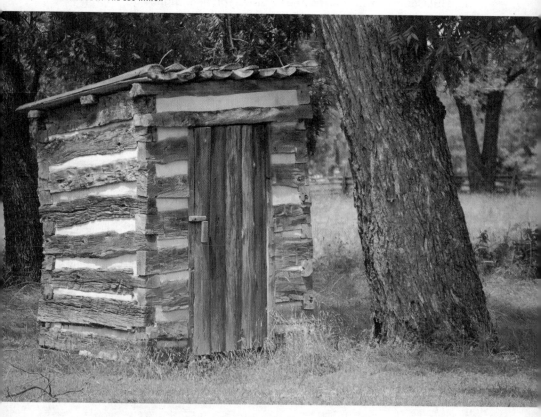

as it would have been. This utilitarian house plan separated the stifling hot kitchen from the rest of the house by a long thin hallway.

The **Texas White House** is so called because Johnson spent so much time here while in office—490 days, a quarter of his presidency. The house became the Johnsons' home after he left office, and Lady Bird lived here until her death in 2007. Both are buried in the **Johnson Family Cemetery** on the property. The ranch, while a national historic site, is also private property; the only way to see it is to take one of the National Park Service's bus tours.

Stonewall is also home to an exquisite bed & breakfast, **Rose Hill Manor**, a Charleston-style home with wide porches and large windows overlooking the Hill Country countryside. The main house has four rooms, each with queen-sized beds, sun porches, sitting areas, or access to the veranda and thoughtfully decorated with a restrained use of floral prints. Additionally, the cottages on the property offer rooms as spacious and spotless as those in the main house, though newer, with vaulted ceilings, warm wood floors, and king-sized beds. A full gourmet breakfast is served each morning. For an evening meal, Rose Hill Manor serves a seasonal and fundamentally French five-course prix fixe menu by reservation only. An impressive wine list, crisp table linens, candles, and stunning views of the Hill Country make Rose Hill Manor so special that some folks stay the whole weekend in Stonewall.

Looking for lunch while flying along US 290 between Johnson City and Stonewall? Make a pit stop at **Hye Market**, housed in the old Hye General Store and Post Office, built in 1904. The building provided a poignant back-drop when President Johnson announced his appointment of Lawrence F. O'Brien as United States Postmaster General from it's front porch in 1965. Still the center of the community, Hye's makes tasty deli sandwiches featuring local meat, cheese, and produce, served alongside libations and, sometimes, a side of live music.

Venturing on to Fredericksburg along US 290, you'll come upon **Wildseed Farms**, a thriving plant nursery surrounded by fields exploding with color in the spring and summer. Wildseed Farms provides both native and non-native plants and seeds, workshops, tips for growing and identifying native plants, and a "Butterfly Haus" filled with butterflies. While there is a fee to stroll "The Meadows," the distant view is free and you are welcome to meander through the rows and rows of plants for sale, taking photos to your heart's content. A small café serves refreshments, sandwiches, and a selection of Texas wines.

Back on US 290, the road between here and Fredericksburg, several miles to the west, is dotted with wineries (see box on page 41) offering a nice sampling of Texas wines. Stop in and try a few, or branch off this route entirely and spend the day driving among the Hill Country vineyards outlined on www.texaswinetrail.com.

Fredericksburg is named for Prince Frederick of Prussia. The city was founded in 1846 by John O. Meusebach and a group of 120 German immigrants who came to the area from New Braunfels as participants in the *Adelsverein*, a planned German settlement of Texas. But the region was also home to Native Americans, namely the Comanche, who were not keen on letting in outsiders. In 1847, against all odds, Meusebach and the Native Americans hammered out the details of an agreement, the Meusebach-Comanche Treaty, establishing peace in their shared valley—a remarkable feat given the times and circumstances—and the town prospered.

These days, Fredericksburg is the hub of tourism in the Hill Country. Located approximately 75 miles from both Austin and San Antonio, Fredericksburg is just close enough to make a comfortable day trip. People come for the food, the boutique shopping, and most of all, the thrill of driving the winding backroads en route. Folks flock here for romantic weekends at the area's dozens of bed & breakfasts, guest houses, and boutique hotels, and it is essential to book a room in advance.

The rooms at **Hoffman Haus** are each unique, but consistently luxurious. Crisp linens, rough-hewn beams, wood floors, understated furniture, and lovely window treatments create an atmosphere that is both rustic and sophisticated. The bed & breakfast is not one house, but several buildings arranged on a nicely landscaped piece of property with breakfast delivered straight to your door each morning in a wicker basket. For an extra cozy feel, **Two Wee Cottages** are as adorable as they sound. The charming old-fashioned Granny Hein House and the bright and cheerful My Little House are tucked behind the owner's home on Morse Street, eight blocks north of Main Street. Private hot tubs, hammocks, and homemade baked goods add to the experience. **Magnolia House** is more intimate. The home is full of 1920s charm and is expertly managed by gracious owners, who woo guests with homemade cookies and delicious breakfasts made from locally sourced ingredients. Warm and homey, this bed & breakfast is tucked away on a quiet side street several blocks from the center of town and makes a relaxing getaway. **Hangar Hotel**, adjacent to the small Gillespie County Airport on the edge of town, feels a bit more masculine; the furnishings and decor suggest the South Pacific, circa 1940s. For a real taste of Texas, stay at the **Chuckwagon Inn Bed & Breakfast**, where innkeepers Sam and Becky Higgins have used cherished family recipes and years of culinary expertise to create mouthwatering gourmet breakfasts. The "inn" is a collection of accommodations—some restored structures from the property's past as a dairy farm, plus a nineteenth-century Texas cabin brought to the site log-by-log and reassembled—and each is as charming as the next. Located a few minutes outside of Fredericksburg, with miles of Hill Country views and an extra serving of Texas hospitality. If you're unable to find a room, try calling the **Main Street Bed and Breakfast Reservation Service** or **Gastehaus**

Schmidt, two local reservation services that handle a wide variety of accommodations in the area.

There are plenty of pricey places to eat in Fredericksburg, but in keeping with the back-to-basics nature of this chapter, I've chosen to highlight several casual favorites.

For treats and snacks on E. Main Street, stop in at **Clear River Pecan Company** for ice cream, or **Rustlin' Rob's** to sample some of the dozens of Texas-made jams, jellies, preserves, salsas, and even jalapeño peanut butter. The **Fredericksburg Pie Company** on E. Austin Street tempts those who dare to stray from the well-trodden path with homemade marvels such as the bourbon orange pecan or the fresh peach pie. They tend to sell out fast, so plan on pie for a morning snack.

For lunch, the **Peach Tree Tea Room** is a perennial favorite. The fried green tomato BLT and ham and Swiss on raisin bread are two good examples of the dainty southern luncheon fare this casual spot specializes in. It

Vintage Texas

The Texas Hill Country is also becoming increasingly well known for its wines. The region's limestone outcroppings, rich alluvial soil, and hot, sunny days mimic the more famous wine-growing areas of France, and for the past 40 years vintners in Texas have cultivated, nurtured, and coaxed their vineyards to bear fruit in the Lone Star State. Success has come steadily; there are now close to two dozen vineyards in the Hill Country. All offer tastings; some are complimentary and others charge a small fee, between $1 and $5. Connoisseurs may want to mine the comprehensive website of the **Texas Hill Country Wineries** (www.texaswinetrail.com) for details about festivals, special events, a list of all member wineries, and the printable Texas Hill Country Wineries Trail Map.

As you travel the route laid out in this chapter, you will be within easy striking distance of the seven wineries that cluster along TX 290 between Johnson City and Fredericksburg. One mile east of Johnson City, **Texas Hills Vineyard** is on RR 2766, also known as "the road to Pedernales Falls State Park." **Becker Vineyards**, **Grape Creek Vineyards**, **Torre di Pietra Vineyards**, and **Woodrose Winery** are all located just south of TX 290 approximately 3 miles west of Stonewall and 9 miles east of Fredericksburg; just follow the signs. **Fredericksburg Winery** has wines for sale right on Main Street in Fredericksburg, but to sample products from **Chisholm Trail Winery**, you'll need to head back out of town, travel 9 miles west on TX 290, then 2.4 miles south on Usener Road. **Singing Water Vineyards**, **Bending Branch Winery**, and **Sister Creek Vineyards** are all in or near Comfort (page 45).

is located on Adams Street, just south of its intersection with Main, cleaving the thoroughfare into East and West.

Housed in a little bungalow on Adams Street, the **Sunset Grill** is a charmer that manages to be modern and cute at the same time. The dining room is casual, open and bright, with orange walls and fun accents, and the shaded patio is adorable. The smoked salmon Benedict is a creamy, smoky, salty, fluffy wonder atop a toasted English muffin, sprinkled with capers and bits of red onion, then covered with an herb-infused hollandaise—a menu standout. Paninis, burgers, and enormous salads are on the menu for lunch. The Grill stays open for dinner on Friday and Saturday nights.

Gourmet burgers are on offer at **Hondo's**. Hondo, the "clown prince" of Luckenbach, was a local character with a capital *C*. Though he passed away in 1976, his legend, humor, and free-spirited approach to life live on

HILL TOP CAFÉ OUTSIDE OF FREDERICKSBURG

in this part of the Hill Country. The burgers here are tailored to your whims. Made in the shape of a doughnut and grilled over a mesquite fire, they can be customized with irreverent ingredients like goat cheese and poblano peppers.

Some of the most eclectic eating around Fredericksburg is actually about 10 miles outside town at a little spot called the **Hill Top Café**. The Hill Top is located atop a truly hilly section of TX 87, 10 miles west of Fredericksburg next to . . . well, nothing, actually. This little restaurant sits all alone, and if you didn't know to stop, you might drive right on by and miss out on the Cajun-spiced frog legs, pan-seared quail, and *kefalotiri saganaki*, an appetizer of flaming Greek cheese. If the menu sounds a little chaotic, check out the decor. Old signs, posters, license plates, and all sorts of other mementos and memorabilia fill almost every inch of wall space and the evenings are filled with live blues, jazz, and boogie-woogie.

If you are out and about on a beautiful day, consider driving the **Willow City Loop**, a backroad trail well worth a detour. From Fredericksburg, head 13 miles north on TX 16, then right on RR 1323, and left following signs for

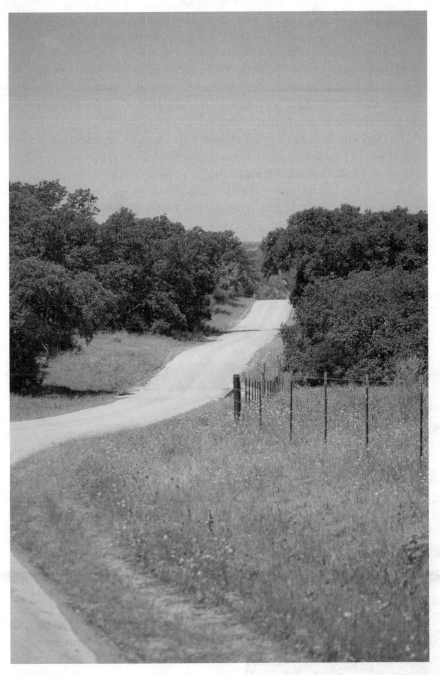

WILLOW CITY LOOP

Willow City and the Willow City Loop. The small country road will loop around for 13 miles, climbing in and out of valleys with plenty of scenic overlooks before rejoining TX 16. This route is very popular during the height of wildflower season in the spring, but it is a slice of unspoiled Texas all year long. Much of the route is on private land with loose livestock, and while visitors are welcome to drive through and take photos, please be respectful and refrain from hiking or picnicking.

The loop will return you to TX 16, and you can either turn south and head back toward Fredericksburg or north approximately 20 miles along FM 965 to **Enchanted Rock State Natural Area** (see box on page 47).

Leaving Fredericksburg, take the scenic route—east on US 290 for 3 miles, then south on Old San Antonio Road, aka Old No. 9, traveling for 10.5 miles and following signs to Old Tunnel Wildlife Area until you reach the **Alamo Springs Café**. Known for its outstanding old-fashioned burgers, Alamo Springs is the real deal. Try one of the enormous green chile cheeseburgers served with grilled onions and avocado, or order their most popular burger, a massive patty with cheddar cheese, grilled onions, and mushrooms on a jalapeño cheese bun. The café is located beside the **Old Tunnel Wildlife Management Area**; its caves, from March through October, are home to some 3 million bats, which funnel into the sky and fan out over the Hill Country each night at dusk; an amazing spectacle.

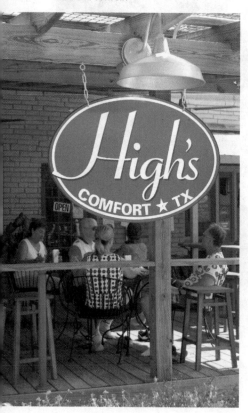

HIGH'S IN COMFORT

Continue on Old No. 9 to the hamlet of **Comfort**. While it's not much more than a few blocks long, what makes Comfort unique is that almost the entire downtown is on the National Registry of Historic Places. It feels like everyone in town stops by **High's** at some point during the day; maybe it's to grab a muffin and coffee for breakfast, maybe for a turkey sandwich with pepper jack cheese and cilantro-orange-chipotle cabbage slaw for lunch, or a homemade key lime tart with a graham cracker crust in the middle of the afternoon. The food at this casual eatery is outstanding, matched only by the friendliness of High's lovely owners and staff. If the slow pace of this little town appeals, spend the night at **Meyer Bed**

and Breakfast, a complex of buildings dating from the 1800s to early 1900s, on High Street overlooking Cypress Creek. Also along the creek you'll find the stylish **Camp Comfort**, a circa-1860s German social club now repurposed as a boutique retreat. A strong sense of design and a laid-back vibe make this "camp" a popular choice for a feel-good getaway. At the center of town, the **Hotel Faust** was built to last; constructed of 21-inch limestone blocks, it is now over 130 years old. Guests can also choose to stay in a pioneer log cabin relocated from Kentucky, a two-bedroom cottage which was once the innkeeper's residence, and a carriage house which contained the hotel's original kitchen and dining room.

Comfort offers a chance to taste Hill Country wines (page 41). **Singing Water Vineyards** and **Bending Branch Winery** each have intimate tasting rooms, lovely grounds, and friendly, knowledgeable staff. Hop

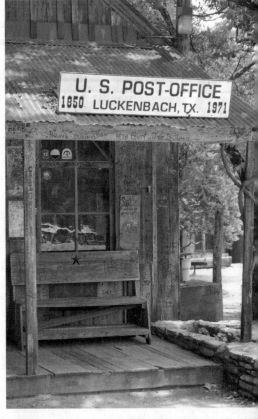

LUCKENBACH

back on the road and head east along rustic RM 473 to **Sisterdale**, home of **Sister Creek Vineyards**. Housed in a restored 1800s-era cotton gin, Sister Creek has earned kudos for their moscato, a sweet and refreshing sparkling white wine.

From Sisterdale, it's a straight shot 16 miles up RR 1376/Sisterdale Road to little **Luckenbach**. If you have heard of Luckenbach, you may think of it as a kind of archetypal small town, but it is really just a cluster of worn wooden buildings nestled in the shade under the sprawling oak trees beside Grape Creek. You'll have no problem finding **The General Store**, the all-purpose store, bar, post office, and hot spot doing business since 1848. The place is old and creaky, with an uneven front porch and holes in the floor made from the boots of thousands of visitors. Want more details? Check out the town's sleek website, www.luckenbachtexas.com. Despite its size, Luckenbach has a reputation that has long preceded it. Immortalized in a Waylon Jennings song, "Luckenbach, Texas (Back to the Basics of Love)," the site of Willie Nelson's legendary Fourth of July parties, and host to the annual town "Hug In" in February, Luckenbach is a destination unto itself.

The route ends here, in the rural roots of the Hill Country. Luckenbach's motto, "Everybody is somebody," seems to echo LBJ's sentiments toward his Hill Country neighbors, fellow Texans, and all Americans. A little food for thought as you head back to your city, big or small.

IN THE AREA

ALAMO SPRINGS CAFÉ, 107 Alamo Road, Fredericksburg, 78624. Call 830-990-8004. Closed Tuesdays. Popular spot for a burger eaten al fresco under the Hill Country trees. $$.

AUSTIN VISITOR CENTER, 602 E. Fourth Street, Austin, 78701. Call 512-478-0098. Website: www.austintexas.org.

BECKER VINEYARDS, 464 Becker Farms Road, Stonewall, 78671. Call 830-644-2681. Website: www.beckervineyards.com.

BENDING BRANCH WINERY, 142 Lindner Branch Trail, Comfort, 78013. Call 830-995-2948. Closed Monday through Wednesday. Website: www .bendingbranchwinery.com.

BRYAN'S ON 290, 300 E. Main Street, Johnson City, 78636. Call 830-868-2424. Closed Sundays and Mondays. Fine dining featuring Hill Country cuisine and wines; a Johnson City gem. Website: www.bryanson290.com. $$–$$$.

CAMP COMFORT, 601 Water Street, Comfort, 78013. Call 830- 995-2356. Stylish "camp" style accommodations. Website: www.camp-comfort.com. $$$.

CHISHOLM TRAIL WINERY, 2367 Usener Road, Fredericksburg, 78624. Call 830-990-2675. Website: www.chisholmtrailwinery.com.

CHUCKWAGON INN BED & BREAKFAST, 1156 FM 2093, Fredericksburg, 78624. Call 830-990-2777. Warm welcome, hot gourmet breakfast, and Hill Country views at this unique "inn" a few miles from town. Website: www .chuckwagoninn.com. $$–$$$.

CLEAR RIVER PECAN COMPANY, 138 E. Main Street, Fredericksburg, 78624. Call 830-997-8490. Ice cream, baked goods, and deli sandwiches. Website: www.icecreamandfun.com. $$.

Rock Climbing and Barbecue

I t is no surprise that the huge pink granite dome of **Enchanted Rock State Natural Area** is the subject of lore and legend among the Tonkawa Indians. As the tale goes, long ago a Spanish conquistador escaped captivity and eluded recapture by hiding near the rock, where he was swallowed and reborn as a Tonkawa, communing with the many spirits thought to inhabit the region around the rock. The rock still casts a spell over the many visitors who come to hike and camp. The park is so popular, especially on weekends, that it often reaches capacity and is forced to close. So, if you come for a hike, you might find yourself out of luck, but you can certainly enjoy good views from several miles away, or from the park's parking lot.

If you're visiting around mealtime and you get a craving for barbecue, consider driving another 20 miles north—first on FM 965, then north at the merge with TX 16—to sink your teeth into some of the finest mesquite smoked brisket in Texas at **Cooper's** (page 19) in **Llano**. You will be leaving this route and picking up the Best BBQ in Texas route featured in Chapter 1.

EAST MAIN STREET GRILL, 209 E. Main Street, Johnson City, 78636. Call 830-868-7710. Comfort food, including chicken-fried steak, served in a repurposed lumberyard. Website: www.theoldlumberyard.weebly.com. $$.

ENCHANTED ROCK STATE NATURAL AREA, 16710 Ranch Road 965, Fredericksburg, 78624. Call 325-247-3903. Website: www.tpwd.texas.gov.

FREDERICKSBURG PIE COMPANY, 108 E. Austin Street, Fredericksburg, 78624. Call 830-990-6992. Closed Sunday through Tuesday. Wide variety of pies, including seasonal flavors. Website: www.fredericksburgtexas shopping.com. $.

FREDERICKSBURG WINERY, 247 W. Main Street, Fredericksburg, 78624. Call 830-990-8747. Website: www.fbgwinery.com.

GASTEHAUS SCHMIDT, 231 W. Main Street, Fredericksburg, 78624. Call 866-427-8374. Website: www.fbglodging.com.

THE GENERAL STORE, 412 Luckenbach Town Loop, Fredericksburg, 78624. Call 1-888-311-8990 or 830-997-3224. Website: www.luckenbachtexas.com.

GRAPE CREEK VINEYARDS, 10587 E. US 290, Stonewall, 78671. Call 830-644-2710. Website: www.grapecreek.com.

HANGAR HOTEL, 155 Airport Road, Fredericksburg, 78624. Call 830-997-9990. Watch air traffic come and go from this comfortable and unique 1940s WWII Army Air Corps-themed hotel. Website: www.hangarhotel.com. $$.

HIGH'S, 726 High Street, Comfort, 78013. Call 830-995-4995. The community's go-to spot for coffee, sandwiches, or just to check in and say "Hi." Website: www.highscafeandstore.com. $$.

HILL TOP CAFÉ, 10661 US 87, Fredericksburg, 78618. Call 830-997-8922. Closed Mondays. Eclectic atmosphere and menu make this eatery and music venue a one-of-a-kind Hill Country experience. Website: www.hilltopcafe .com. $$.

HOFFMAN HAUS, 608 E. Creek Street, Fredericksburg, 78624. Call 830-997-6739. Gorgeous accommodations in several limestone and rough-hewn wood buildings on a landscaped property in town. Website: www .hoffmanhaus.com. $$–$$$.

HONDO'S, 312 W. Main Street, Fredericksburg, 78624. Call 830-997-1633. Closed Mondays and Tuesdays. Fun spot for burgers; named after one of Fredericksburg's most beloved characters. Website: www.hondosonmain .com. $$.

HOTEL FAUST, 717 High Street, Comfort, 78013. Call 830-995-3030. Solid limestone inn has been hosting guests in style since the end of the 1800s. Website: www.hotelfaust.com. $$–$$$

HYE MARKET, 10261 W US Hwy 290, Hye, 78636. Call 830-868-2300. Closed Mondays. Tasty deli offerings served in the town's historic post office building. Website: www.hyemarket.com. $$.

LADY BIRD JOHNSON WILDFLOWER CENTER, 4801 La Crosse Avenue, Austin, 78739. Call 512-232-0100. Fee. Website: www.wildflower.org.

LYNDON BAINES JOHNSON LIBRARY AND MUSEUM, 2313 Red River Street, Austin, 78705. Located one block west of I-35, between MLK and 26th Street. Call 512-721-0200. Fee. Website: www.lbjlibrary.org.

LYNDON B. JOHNSON NATIONAL HISTORICAL PARK, 100 Ladybird Lane, Johnson City, 78636. Call 830-868-7128. Website: www.nps.gov.

Festivals

Oktoberfest (830-997-4810; www.oktoberfestinfbg.com) and the **Fredericksburg Food and Wine Festival** (830-997-8515; www.fbgfoodandwinefest.com) keep visitors busy in October, and the Weihnachten, or Christmas festival and market, helps make December fun. The **Easter Fires Pageant** commemorates the Meusebach-Comanche Treaty, which brought peace to the region, and the **Stonewall Peach Jamboree** (www.stonewalltexas.com) in mid-June is a sweet start of summer. Throughout the spring and summer, additional festivals of lavender, wildflowers, and wines abound; details online at www.visitfredericksburgtx.com.

MAGNOLIA HOUSE, 101 E. Hackberry Street, Fredericksburg, 78624. Call 1-800-880-4374. 1920s charm throughout this spotless property and breakfasts worth waking up for. Website: www.magnolia-house.com. $$.

MAIN STREET BED AND BREAKFAST RESERVATION SERVICE, 337 E. Main Street, Fredericksburg, 78624. Call 1-888-559-8555 or 830-997-0153. Website: www.travelmainstreet.com.

MEYER BED AND BREAKFAST, 845 High Street, Comfort, 78013. Call 830-959-2304. A variety of individually-decorated rooms and cottages, spread along a lovely stretch of Cypress Creek. Website: www.meyerbedandbreakfast.com. $$–$$$.

OLD TUNNEL WILDLIFE MANAGEMENT AREA, 10619 Old San Antonio Road, Fredericksburg, 78624. Call 866-978-2287. Website: www.tpwd.texas.gov.

PEACH TREE TEA ROOM, 210 S. Adams Street, Fredericksburg, 78624. Call 830-997-9527. Light lunch fare in a cute cottage dining room. Website: www.peach-tree.com. $$. *Permanently closed 1-21*

PECAN STREET BREWING COMPANY, 106 E. Pecan Drive, Johnson City, 78636. Call 830-868-2500. Burgers, wood-fired pizzas, and house-brewed beer in a casual setting on the square. Website: www.pecanstreetbrewing.com. $$.

ROSE HILL MANOR, 2614 Upper Albert Road, Stonewall, 78671. Call 830-644-2247. Choose from a room in the elegant inn or several charming cottages, all in beautiful pastoral setting. Website: www.rose-hill.com. $$–$$$.

RUSTLIN' ROB'S, 121 E. Main Street, Fredericksburg, 78624. Call 830-990-4750. Website: www.rustlinrobs.com.

SINGING WATER VINEYARDS, 316 Mill Dam Road, Comfort, 78013. Call 830-995-2246. Closed Monday through Wednesday. Website: www.singingwatervineyards.com.

SISTER CREEK VINEYARDS, 1142 Sisterdale Road, Sisterdale, 78006. Call 830-324-6704. Website: www.sistercreekrvineyards.com.

SUNSET GRILL, 902 S. Adams Street, Fredericksburg, 78624. Call 830-9975904. Colorful and casual spot serving bistro fare for breakfast and lunch. Website: www.sunsetgrilltx.com. $$.

Peachy

Ask anyone in Texas where the best peaches in the state grow and they'll point you in the direction of Gillespie County, specifically the stretch of US 290 between Stonewall and Fredericksburg. Forty percent of the peaches grown in Texas are grown right here, and if your trip coincides with peach season, the opportunities to sample are abundant.

From May through July, peach stands spring up along US 290. If you turn north off US 290 onto Gellerman Lane, just west of Stonewall (approximately 13 miles east of Fredericksburg), and continue to the intersection with FM 2721, turn west, continue to FM 1631, and go straight until you reach Main Street in Fredericksburg, approximately 35 miles later, you will pass plenty of rural stands with peaches and other Texas produce. For a complete list of area orchards, with opening hours, telephone numbers, and directions, check the Hill Country's Fruit Council's website, www.texaspeaches.com. Stonewall hosts the Peach Jamboree during the third week in June, so if you are in town, be sure to swing by.

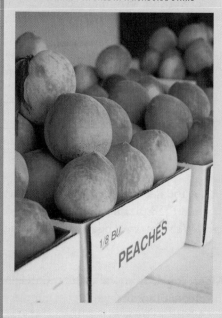

TEXAS PEACHES FOR SALE AT A ROADSIDE STAND

TEXAS HILL COUNTRY WINERIES. Call 872-216-9463. Website: www
.texaswinetrail.com.

TEXAS HILLS VINEYARD, 878 RR 2766, Johnson City, 78636. Call 830-
868-2321. Website: www.texashillsvineyard.com.

TORRE DI PIETRA VINEYARDS, 10915 E. US Hwy 290, Fredericksburg,
78624. Call 830-644-2829. Website: www.torredipietra.com.

TWO WEE COTTAGES, 108 E. Morse Street, Fredericksburg, 78624. Call
830-990-8340. Cute-as-can-be-cottages, made even sweeter with the addition of freshly baked homemade treats. Website: www.2weecottages.com.
$$–$$$.

WILDSEED FARMS, 425 Wildflower Hills, Fredericksburg, 78624. Seven
miles east of Fredericksburg on US 290. Call 1-800-848-0078. Website: www
.wildseedfarms.com.

WOODROSE WINERY, 662 Woodrose Lane, Stonewall, 78671. Call 830-
644-2539. Website: www.woodrosewinery.com.

donkey for sale

FRESH FUDGE

WE MAKE OUR OWN FUDGE

3

SCENIC US 281 BETWEEN SAN ANTONIO AND FORT WORTH

BLANCO, JOHNSON CITY, BURNET, MARBLE FALLS,
HAMILTON, HICO, GLEN ROSE, GRANBURY

TOTAL DISTANCE: 270 miles

HIGHLIGHTS: From San Antonio, follow your nose to **Blanco**, home of the annual **Blanco Lavender Festival**, and press on to **Johnson City**, home of President Lyndon Baines Johnson, and **Marble Falls**, the jumping-off point into the **Highland Lakes** region. Grab a bite to eat in **Hamilton**, poke around in the charming town of **Hico**, and sip a Dublin Dr. Pepper in **Dublin**. Check out the dinosaur tracks at **Dinosaur Valley State Park** or the endangered animals at **Fossil Rim Wildlife Center**, both in **Glen Rose**, and treat yourself to a night at a bed and breakfast in **Granbury**. **Detour:** The Highland Lakes (see page 57).

GETTING THERE: This route will take you from San Antonio to Fort Worth or vice-versa. From San Antonio, take TX 281 north to Blanco, a distance of approximately 51 miles. Continue north on TX 281 for another 14 miles, passing through Johnson City (see page 56), then an additional 23 miles to **Marble Falls**. From Marble Falls, travel 13 miles to Burnet (see page 56), then 68 miles to **Hamilton**, and 21 miles to Hico. At this juncture, you can take TX 6 west for 21 miles to detour to Dublin or continue along the route outlined below by following TX 220 north an additional 22 miles to **Glen Rose**, where it is just an easy 16.5-mile drive northwest along TX 144 to **Granbury**. Fort Worth is only a 41-mile drive north on US 377.

INTERSECTIONS: Chapters 1 and 2

When driving between San Antonio and Dallas/Fort Worth, many travelers choose I-35. While the highway promises speed, inevitably congestion, fender benders, and breakdowns hold up the show. Those in the know choose US 281, a route that expands and contracts—here it's a two-lane highway, there it's a small-town Main Street—as it runs from the US-Mexican border

in Texas to the US-Canadian border in North Dakota. The International Peace Garden, straddling the border, marks its northernmost point. US 281 bypasses the sprawl of cities, trading a landscape of big-box stores and chain restaurants for oak trees and pastures. This route offers up a selection of classics—diners, roadside cafés, greasy spoons, bed & breakfasts, and inns— where you can grab a bite or spend the night. Far from the hustle and bustle of the interstate, traveling the Texas backroads is a pleasure.

Leaving San Antonio, it's a breezy 50 miles north on US 281 to **Blanco**. This small ranching and trade town got its start in 1858; it was the county seat until 1890, when the title shifted to nearby Johnson City. Blanco is a typical little Hill Country hamlet, with a courthouse in the middle, shops all around, and hillside surrounding. As US 281 funnels into town, you would be likely to drive right past the **Blanco Bowling Club**. Since they've already got their hands full with locals, the folks here don't feel the need to put on a pretty face to pull potential diners in from the highway. Regulars stop in for a hot cinnamon roll to go with their morning coffee, keeping the seats warm and the Formica tables occupied. The bowling lanes are in constant use, too. Whether you start with a burger, a hot roast beef sandwich, chicken-fried steak, or a Mexican entrée, all meals should end with a piece of one of the Bowling Club's meringue pies.

The Hill Country is one of Texas' wine-growing regions (see box on page 57), but **Real Ale Brewing Company** in Blanco has also put down some serious roots, offering beer tastings on Fridays from 2 to 5 PM. Fireman's #4 is often cited as a must-try. Beer aficionados might like to take a brewery tour (Fridays, 3 and 4 PM) and learn all the details of modern brewing from the folks who are passionate about it. Can't make it to the source? You'll find their beer throughout Texas, or just a short drive away at the **Redbud Café Market and Pub**. This delightful café is located across from the courthouse in the center of town and is owned and operated by local potters Jon and Jan Brieger. In fact, their pottery shop is right next door. The menu is fresh, thoughtful, and healthy. You'll find tasty chicken salad, hot pastrami Reubens on marble rye, pimento cheese sandwiches, homemade soups, quiches, and several delicious vegetarian options including a grilled Portabella mushroom burger and an avocado and vegetable sandwich. After a meal, consider stretching your legs at **Blanco State Park**. With over 100 acres of land on either side of a bend in the Blanco River, this park is one of the oldest in the state, known for great trout fishing, shaded campsites, and river tubing (a favorite Central Texas pastime) on warm Texas days. The park is located an easy four blocks south of the Blanco town square on Park Road 23. Inquire at the park store about tube, canoe, and kayak rentals and water safety tips. There are several other state parks within striking distance of US 281, and each offers a close-up look at a piece of the Texas landscape A complete listing and maps can be found online at www.tpwd.texas.gov.

Before heading out of Blanco, stop at the only street light in town and set your odometer to zero. Drive exactly 3.5 miles north and you will find yourself at **Pink Tractor Farms**, located on the east side of the highway. (If you are coming from the north, look for the farm 4 miles south of the US 281/US 290 intersection.) This small farm stand sells locally grown produce, cheeses, and eggs, and locally made jams and preserves as well as pies, cookies, and *kolaches* they bake in their own little bakery. In the fields behind the farm stand you'll find **Hill Country Lavender** (page 65), a great place to stop in and get a good whiff of the Hill Country.

After leaving Blanco, proceed another 14 miles on US 281 to **Johnson City**, where you'll have no trouble finding the **Lyndon B. Johnson National Historical Park**. Stop in its informative visitor center and see the **Johnson Settlement**, which features several buildings dating back to the 1860s and **LBJ's boyhood home**, a tidy house that illustrates life in rural Texas in the 1920s. The **Johnson Ranch**, which includes the "Texas White House," is 13 miles west on US 290 in **Stonewall**. Lodging and dining options in Johnson City, Stonewall, and the surrounding area are discussed in Chapter 2. Press on from Johnson City 23 miles northward to **Marble Falls**. Just north of town, on RM 1431, sits what is left of Granite Mountain. Despite its impressive name, the huge dome of pink and red granite was quarried to the ground over time, some of it going directly to Austin, where it was used to construct the Texas Capitol. A plaque across the road from the site tells the tale.

If you pull into town on a weekend and don't notice the **Bluebonnet Café**'s rather small red and white sign, you'll be sure to notice the line of hungry diners snaking out the door and down the porch steps. With a reputation for one of the best honest-to-goodness breakfasts in Texas, the Bluebonnet also keeps customers coming with classic southern comfort foods such as fried okra, catfish, chicken-fried steaks, pot roast, and chicken and dumplings. If you choose nothing else at Bluebonnet, do as the sign on the wall says and "try some pie." From cream to meringue, the Bluebonnet makes plenty of pies each day; your waitresses can recite the long list with impressive efficiency. The Bluebonnet is a perennial Texas favorite.

Speaking of bluebonnets, the next stop on the route is **Burnet**, 13 miles farther north. The Bluebonnet Capital of Texas, Burnet is host of the **Bluebonnet Festival** (www.bluebonnetfestival.org), complete with a parade, carnival, food, and music, in April. Between April and June, the proliferation of bluebonnets in this region, not to mention other native Texas wildflowers, can be absolutely stunning. Visit the Burnet Chamber of Commerce and ask for a "Scenic Drive and Wildflower Trail Map," or print one at www.burnet chamber.org.

The highway passes through a nondescript commercial section of Burnet, but just a few blocks away **Mama's Home Cooking** is more memorable. One of the newer restaurants in Burnet, Mama's lives in the bright blue building perched on a small hill in Hamilton Creek Park, surrounded by shade trees and with a lovely view of the small creek, ducks, and geese. There's chicken-fried chicken, chicken-fried steaks, creamed spinach, fresh rolls, and a chalkboard full of specials and desserts.

Leaving Burnet, it's an easy 22 miles to Lampasas, where you can detour

The Highland Lakes

Both **Marble Falls** and **Burnet** are access points to the region's chain of six lakes, known collectively as the **Highland Lakes**.

During the early 1800s, the Colorado River was prone to flooding, and resulting logjams made the river impassable, cutting off trade and transportation to and from riverside communities. Finally, in 1935, technology caught up to the problem; the Lower Colorado River Authority (LCRA) constructed a series of six dams along the river to control flooding, creating the Highland Lakes. Here are the lakes listed from north to south.

Lake Buchanan is the largest and northernmost lake, and a known nesting place of the American bald eagle. **Canyon of the Eagles Resort**, in Burnet, has a lodge, campgrounds, cabins, and a restaurant, all in the middle of a 1,000-acre park and preserve. The **Vanishing Texas River Cruise**, also located in Burnet, hosts ecological cruises on the lake. At night, stargaze with the Austin Astronomical Society at the **Eagle Eye Observatory** (www.austinastro.org).

Inks Lake is best known for its location beside the popular **Longhorn Cavern State Park**. The park features tours of a large river-formed cavern, once a meeting area for Comanche Indians and a hideout for Confederate soldiers.

Lake LBJ has more humans than wildlife and gets crowded on warm, sunny days. Homes line the lake's shores, with the resort development of Horseshoe Bay anchoring its southern edge; boaters crisscross the waters all weekend long. The rich soil surrounding the lake benefits **Spicewood Vineyards**, a short drive south along TX 71.

Lake Marble Falls feels more like a wide spot in the river than a lake, and its steep rocky shores do little to change the impression. The town is a good place to refuel, get supplies, or enjoy a meal.

Lake Travis is very close to Austin. Crammed with numerous day-trippers and party boats, expect exuberance. Pleasant parks and numerous funky eateries keep things mellow.

Lake Austin is well within the city limits and rife with kayakers, cruises, restaurants, and live music, all with a uniquely Austin vibe. You can head online to www.highlandlakes.com, www.lakesandhills.com, www.lcra.org, or www.texasoutside.com for all the details.

into the Lampasas Square for some home-style German cuisine at Eve's Café. They are proud to serve *wurst* smothered in sauerkraut and sautéed onions and crisp breaded *schnitzel*, each served with fluffy *spätzle* on the side. There are deli-style sandwiches on rye bread, a few German beers, and homemade cheesecakes to choose from, too. Eve's is an unexpected, folksy place perfect for sampling Central Texas' German heritage.

It takes close to an hour and a half to drive the 67 miles north from Burnet to Hamilton, but the time passes quickly as you watch the rugged terrain soften into green hills. **Hamilton** got its start in the mid-1800s when the first settlers arrived, but the town wasn't incorporated until 1911, after the railroads came through. The town was known for its cotton gins, as well as numerous saloons, which until Prohibition lined an entire side of the town square.

These days, Hamilton is a little less rough around the edges and makes a pleasant place to stop for a bite to eat. Just off the square, **Wenzel Lonestar Meat Company** features the playfully named "Bite My Butt Fridays," featuring barbecued pulled pork sandwiches to welcome the weekend, and deli items all week long.

Take US 281 north out of town. In a few miles (just follow the directions on the billboards) you'll find the **Dutchman's Hidden Valley Country Store**. Started as a roadside pecan and produce stand decades ago, this rambling

DUTCHMAN'S HIDDEN VALLEY COUNTRY STORE IN HAMILTON

shop now sells hundreds of items, ranging from Reuben sandwiches and homemade fudge and candies to bison jerky and handcrafted candles. Dutchman's is a welcome throwback to a time when vacationing families would steer the station wagon into the parking lot and unload for ice cream. During hunting season, Dutchman's will process deer meat for a reasonable fee.

Travel 21 miles farther and you'll find yourself in **Hico**, which you'll notice right away differs from its neighbors. The town is not situated around a courthouse, but laid out as a small boulevard, with grass, benches, and walkways in the center. Originally, the town was a little settlement located a few miles away on Honey Creek, but when the Texas Central Railroad came through the region in 1880, the citizens relocated to be beside the tracks. Just a decade later, a fire destroyed close to half of the town, and a few weeks later a second fire destroyed almost all of what remained. The town rebuilt, this time in stone; the sturdy buildings you see now are from that era.

Address hunger at **Eis**, where you'll find ice cream, sodas, snacks, and homemade sandwiches. The difference here is that ingredients are very local—breads from a Sulak's Czech Bakery in Clifton, cheeses from Velduzien's in Dublin, and so on. The restaurant and adjacent Pecan Street Drink Shoppe, featuring Texas-made libations, share the building with the **Upstairs Inn**. Housing three beautifully renovated and appointed rooms, the inn is a wonderful chance to live as a local for as long as you'd like.

The **Koffee Kup Family Restaurant** is just past the merger of US 281 and TX 6. The menu here is simple, well-priced, and to the point, but it's the pies that make the difference. A dozen different kinds of pies piled high with meringues and whipped cream keep locals and out-of-towners stopping in day after day. Downed the last bite of pie, but your sweet tooth is still aching for more? Mosey next door to **Wiseman House Chocolates** for a treat. Located in a lovely Queen Anne Victorian, the shop is fancy and the chocolates are scrumptious. The Snack Pack won't force you to choose between sweet, salty, or creamy; it includes two peanut butter meltaways, two almond toffee squares, and one pecan caramel cluster.

Hico has a charming, small-town western atmosphere, making it unique to the region. Strolling around town, you'll find Pecan Street to be lined with boutiques and antiques shops selling nostalgia, artwork, and Texana. Take a peek in **Blue Star Trading**, a place that bills itself as a "ranch outfitter," but is much more. From home furnishings to jewelry to artwork by some of Texas' rising stars, along with utilitarian ropes and knives for working horses and hunting, Blue Star sells it all in their lovingly restored 1890s storefront. A block away, the small collection at the **Billy the Kid Museum** has a tale to tell. As the story goes, in 1950, as local resident Brushy Bill Roberts lay dying, he professed to be Billy the Kid. Thus Hico was linked to the

Detour to Dublin

What is a "Dublin Dr. Pepper"? While most consumers recognize the Dr. Pepper brand, the addition of "Dublin" may leave you scratching your head.

Dr. Pepper was invented at the Old Corner Drug Store in Waco, Texas, in 1885 by a pharmacist fiddling with soda flavorings. The drug store owner named it Dr. Pepper and sold it at the soda fountain to an enthusiastic public. In 1891, a Texas businessman tried the fizzy concoction, loved it, and set up the first Dr. Pepper bottling plant franchise, Dublin Bottling Works, in the tiny town of Dublin, Texas, 80 miles west of Waco, and serviced the three counties around it. In 1904, Dr. Pepper made its national debut at the St. Louis World's Fair. Though its roots remain in Texas, its countrywide popularity has grown ever since. These days, the Dr. Pepper we know as the national brand is still headquartered in Waco, and there devotees can visit the Dr. Pepper Museum (www.drpepper museum.com).

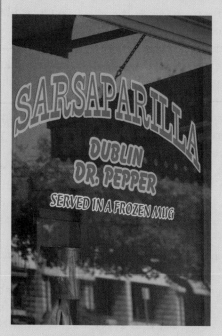

TRY A TASTE OF AN OLD-FASHIONED FAVORITE

What makes Dublin Dr. Pepper different is the Dublin Bottling Works commitment to Imperial Pure Cane Sugar. When the price of sugar rose in the 1970s, other plants replaced the sugar in the original recipe with corn syrup, but the Dublin plant stuck with pure sugar. It's the essence of "dancin' with who brung ya." The sugar gives the drink its distinctive taste; considering that Dr. Pepper itself is already something different in a world dominated by two other sodas, Dublin Dr. Pepper is something really special.

These days, "Dublin Dr. Pepper" is no longer associated with the national brand, but Dublin Bottling works still makes all kinds of sodas sweetened with cane sugar. Stop in the company's soda fountain and museum, **Old Doc's Soda Shoppe**, to sample some amid the collection of soft drink nostalgia. Details online at www.dublinbottlingworks.com.

outlaw legend. Fact or fiction, you decide, but be sure to order a Dublin Dr. Pepper to sip at the counter while you sit and ponder.

Moving along north, it is a short, 20-minute drive to **Glen Rose**, once a successful mill town, a moonshiner's paradise during Prohibition, and now a spa town for those seeking the healing effects of its mineral-rich waters. These days most visitors come to ogle at the fantastically well-preserved dinosaur tracks in **Dinosaur Valley State Park**. While local fishermen reported seeing the tracks in the Paluxy River bottom as early as 1910, it wasn't until the 1930s that scientific investigations and inquiries earned them worldwide recognition. The park opened in 1972 and has been a popular tourist attraction, perhaps best known for its two huge dinosaur statues just inside the entrance.

DINOSAUR VALLEY STATE PARK

The Tyrannosaurus and Brontosaurus, both recycled from the Sinclair Oil Company's exhibit at the 1964 World's Fair, stand side by side. Be sure to read all about one sculpture's identity crisis as was revealed along the way: one of the sculptures isn't anatomically correct. From Glen Rose, take FM 205 west to TX 59, following the signs for a total of 5 miles.

Another natural draw near Glen Rose is the **Fossil Rim Wildlife Center**, which has over 60 species of animals, some exotic and many endangered, roaming freely throughout a 2,700-acre spread. A paved 9-mile road winds through the peaceful wooded valley; visitors are encouraged to drive through at a leisurely pace while the giraffes, zebras, ostriches, emus, deer, and antelope roam. Allow at least an hour and a half to complete the circuit. To get to the preserve from Glen Rose, take US 67 to CR 2008 and follow signs; the trip is approximately 5 miles in total. Alternatively, drive past the entrance to the park on CR 2008, continue a mile or so uphill, take a right at the fork onto CR 2009, and follow signs to the overlook, where you can park for free and spend some time enjoying the valley views from the deck.

Back in town, **Hammond's** has been feeding Glen Rose since 1966. If you find it hard to believe the building is that old, it's not. Hammond's has burned to the ground and been rebuilt. Twice. A classic small-town barbecue joint, the restaurant is painted bright red on the outside and filled with old license plates and knickknacks inside, including a huge sign that welcomes diners with a jovial "Howdy Folks." The brisket, turkey, ribs, and sausage are favorites, and the fact that the sauce is served hot in a little jar on the side makes the meal. Stop in for a piece of pie at the **Pie Peddlers**. The two friends who own this darling shop are recently retired kindergarten teachers who used to teach on weekdays and bake pies on weekends. Trading the patience and creativity needed in the classroom for piecrusts has meant good news for Glen Rose.

Though the town is small, accommodations run the gamut here in Glen Rose. In the early 1900s, the **Inn on the River** was part of a compound known as Dr. Snyder's Drugless Health Sanitarium; the serenity of the inn

Chicken-Fried Anything

You cannot travel the Texas backroads without coming across more than your fair share of food "chicken-fried." While the term clearly denotes chicken, the subject of the chicken-frying itself is often steak—remember, you're still in Texas. You'll encounter it everywhere, and may wonder just exactly what it is. The lineage of culinary oddities is not always clear, and it can be difficult to pin down details. However, here are two keys to understanding chicken-fried steak: tough meat and Germans.

Tough meat is an age-old, universal problem, and many home cooks have devised ingenious ways to solve it. From stews to barbecue, the cooking is crucial. Time and heat are the key components to juiciness, and while slow cooking often does the trick, so does a fast hot sear. All across the South, cooks fried chicken. Dredging the meat in salt, seasonings, and flour and setting it in a pan of hot grease meant that the meat inside the coating cooked up hot and quick, sealing in juices and steam. Somewhere along the way, perhaps during the Depression, someone figured, "Why not beef?" Whether it was a home cook in the Texas Hill Country or a cowboy cook with his chuck wagon, a steak got a dip in flour, some time in the pan, and was served up with gravy. That, come to think of it, sounds a whole lot like Wiener schnitzel.

In the late 1800s, Germans immigrated to Texas, particularly Central Texas, in record numbers, and brought their recipes with them. Schnitzel is the generic German word for cutlet; Wiener schnitzel is a cutlet, breaded, fried, and served with a squirt of lemon. While in Germany, this technique was usually reserved for veal and sometimes pork, in America beef took precedence. *Rahmschnitzel* is similar, with a cream gravy in place of the lemon.

This brings us to a dining ritual peculiar to Texas. Ordering a meal here means answering a series of questions. Order chicken-fried steak and they'll ask "White or brown?" by which they mean gravy. Order tea and you'll be asked, "Regular or sweet?" Even dessert prompts a question: "Blue Bell on top?" (page 75). Confused? Just answer yes, and you'll always be right.

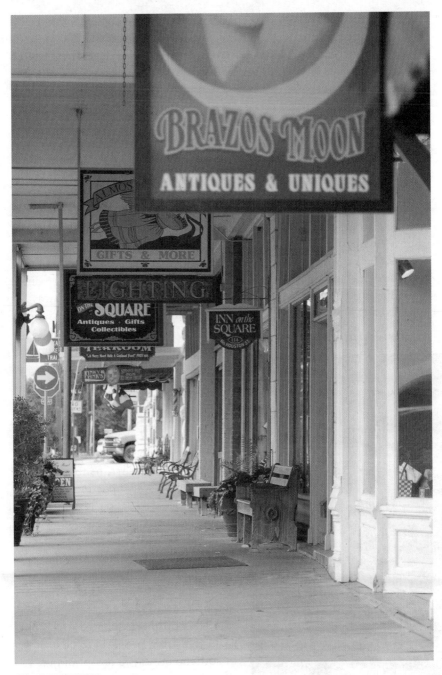

DOWNTOWN GRANBURY

still draws those in search of repose. The rooms are snug, decorated with soothing muted colors, ample linens, and delicate antiques. The grounds are spacious, with a pool, large oak trees, and Adirondack chairs scattered about. The on-site restaurant serves an outstanding four-course prix fixe dinner on weekends, with seatings at 6 and 8 PM. If the surroundings haven't helped you relax and reenergize, the meal just might. The **Country Woods Inn** is consistently lauded for being one of the area's most child-friendly establishments, and it's easy to see why. At the Country Woods, you can spend the night in one of 12 cabins or a restored Santa Fe Railroad car, stroll the inn's 40 shaded acres along the Paluxy River, feed the horses, tell stories around a campfire, and eat breakfast in the barn; it's a true backroads experience. At the other end of the spectrum, you can pamper yourself at the **Rough Creek Lodge**, 10 miles west of Glen Rose on County Road 2013. There is no roughing it here; the rooms, grounds, spa, and on-site restaurant are all well-appointed and impeccably maintained. Because of its fairly remote location and the fact that it is so self-contained, the lodge is a popular corporate retreat center and weekend getaway for folks from the big city. At Rough Creek, hunting and fishing go hand in hand with aromatherapy and massage and the pseudo-rustic decor—primarily leathers, woods, and rich fabrics.

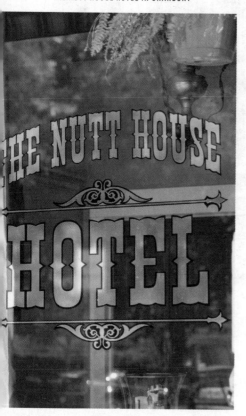

THE NUTT HOUSE HOTEL IN GRANBURY

Another 16 miles north on TX 144 is the historic town of **Granbury**. In 1969, a dam was built across the Brazos River, forming Lake Granbury and the waterfront property that is the town's hallmark. These days, fishing, boating, and golf are popular pastimes for locals and visitors alike, and the town strikes a nice balance between hometown and vacation spot. The town's charm, coupled with its location on the shores of Lake Granbury, just 40 miles southwest of Fort Worth, make Granbury popular for weekend retreats. In 1866, the Nutt brothers donated a parcel of wild riverfront property to be used for a settlement; one soon sprang up and it became a trading center. Livestock auctions and tons of peanuts, pecans, peaches, grain, and cotton passed through the town and the coming of the railroad boosted development to an

Lavender

Pull into Blanco at the right time of year and you might detect a hint of lavender in the air. Blanco and the surrounding area are home to over a dozen lavender farms, with new ones opening each year, thanks to the observant eye of lavender pioneer Robb Kendrick. It was Kendrick who, while on a photo shoot in Provence, noticed the similarities between the soil and climate of the South of France and the Texas Hill Country. Lavender blooming season usually stretches from May through July, with the annual **Blanco Lavender Festival** held in the peak month of May. Visit www.blancolavenderfest.com for details and to download a map of farm tours held throughout the growing season.

The conditions that favor lavender also favor grapes, a fact that the Beckers noticed when they visited France at about the same time as Mr. Kendrick. They returned home to open Becker Vineyard, one of the now many vineyards in Central Texas; see page 41 for a partial listing. Print a map from the **Texas Hill Country Wine Trail's** website (www.texaswinetrail.com) or pick one up on your travels. Driving to and from the many lavender farms and vineyards will take you along some of the most peaceful and scenic backroads in the Hill Country.

unprecedented level. Lining the town square today are several dozen of the solid, two-story limestone buildings built in the 1880s, the height of Granbury's prosperity. The Old Opera House and the red brick train depot, now a museum, are two examples.

The historic **Nutt House Hotel** is a great example of late-nineteenth-century Texas architecture and a good place for folks who like a well-seasoned hotel and a location right on the square. The Nutt House dates back to late 1893, when it was constructed to house overnight guests shopping at the mercantile store owned by the Nutt brothers. The seven suites have been remodeled, with antiques, photographs, and artwork representing the hotel's history; modern touches such as rich colors and cozy European linens give it an updated feel.

Then, of course, there is the lake. Lake Granbury has several nice places to stay surrounding it. A favorite of honeymooners and anniversary celebrators is the **Inn on Lake Granbury,** one of those decadent places that makes special occasions even more special. In many ways the inn feels more like a resort, with two acres of manicured lawn, a flagstone pool, lake views, and wonderfully appointed rooms decorated in soothing, earthy colors with thick window treatments and rugs. Some have fireplaces, others access to outdoor sitting areas, but all are entirely relaxing. Guests rave about the breakfasts.

Make reservations well in advance; this one fills up quick. **Baker Street Harbour Waterfront Bed & Breakfast** is another favorite, with fantastic views of the grounds and lake beyond. Shiny wood floors, spotless bathrooms, and quirky room layouts, some with beds tucked under the eaves, give the rooms here a cozy, romantic feel, which may explain why so many guests come to celebrate anniversaries.

The fresh and crispy fish tacos and Saturday-night shrimp boil at **Stumpy's Lakeside Grill** make for good waterside dining in Granbury. Located a few minutes' drive from town, Stumpy's is casual and family-friendly, with a spacious outdoor patio overlooking the boat-filled marina.

The route ends here, where you are poised to follow US 377 to either Dallas (73 miles) or Fort Worth (42 miles). As the population of Central Texas grows, US 281 is somewhat endangered, becoming entangled in highway exchanges in some places and widened for more traffic in others. So drive it while you can, and spend a dollar or two along the way to support all those local spots providing the simple thrills that make the journey worthwhile.

IN THE AREA

BAKER STREET HARBOUR WATERFRONT BED & BREAKFAST, 511 S. Baker Street Granbury, 76048. Call 817-579-8811. Website: www.bakerst harbour.com. $–$$.

BILLY THE KID MUSEUM, 114 N. Pecan Street, Hico, 76457. Call 254-796-2523. Fee. Website: www.billythekidmuseum.com.

BLANCO BOWLING CLUB, 310 4th Street, Blanco, 78606. Call 830-833-4416. Burgers, plates lunches, and bowling in this laid-back local hangout. Website: www.blancobowlingclub.com. $–$$.

BLANCO CHAMBER OF COMMERCE, 300 Main Street, Blanco, 78606. Call 830-833-5101. Website: www.blancochamber.com.

BLANCO STATE PARK, 101 Park Road 23, Blanco, 78606. Call 830-833-4333. Fee. Website: www.tpwd.texas.gov.

BLUEBONNET CAFÉ, 211 US 281, Marble Falls, 78654. Call 830-693-2344. Diner-style menu and atmosphere and, of course, pie. Closes early on Sundays. Website: www.bluebonnetcafe.net. $–$$.

BLUE STAR TRADING, 112 S. Pecan Street, Hico, 76457. Call 254-796-2828. Website: www.bluestartrading.com.

BURNET CHAMBER OF COMMERCE, 101 N. Pierce Street, Burnet, 78611. Call 512-756-4297. Website: www.burnetchamber.org.

CANYON OF THE EAGLES RESORT, 16942 RR 2341, Burnet, 78611. Call 512-334-2070. Basic hotel-room style accommodations, cabins, a campground, restaurant, and swimming pool on the shores of Lake Buchanan. Website: www.canyonoftheeagles.com. $–$$.

COUNTRY WOODS INN, 420 Grand Avenue, Glen Rose, 76043. Call 817-279-3002. Family-friendly cabins on wooded acreage with a river running through it. Website: www.countrywoodsinn.com. $$–$$$.

DINOSAUR VALLEY STATE PARK, PO Box 396, Glen Rose, 76043 (about 3 miles west of Glen Rose off FM 205). Call 254-897-4588. Fee. Website: www .tpwd.texas.gov.

DUBLIN DR. PEPPER BOTTLING PLANT AND OLD DOC'S SODA SHOP, 105 E. Elm, Dublin, 76446. Call 1-888-398-1024. Daily 10 AM–5 PM. Website: www.dublindrpepper.com.

DUTCHMAN'S HIDDEN VALLEY COUNTRY STORE, 3408 US 281, Hamilton, 76531. Call 254-386-3018. Closed Wednesdays. Website: www.dutch mans-hiddenvalley.com.

EIS, 220 N. Pecan Street, Hico, 76457. Call 254-796-2231. Closed Sundays and Mondays. Proud purveyors of Texas-made snacks, sandwiches, drinks, and ice cream. Website: www.hicosupstairsinn.com. $–$$.

EVE'S CAFÉ, 521 E. 3rd Street, Lampasas, 76550. Call 512-556-3500. Closed Sundays and Mondays. Folksy German restaurant specializing in schnitzel. Website: www.evesonthesquare.com. $$.

FOSSIL RIM WILDLIFE CENTER, 2299 County Road 2008, Glen Rose, 76043. Seasonal hours; last car admitted 2 hours before close. Fee. Call 254-897-2960. Website: www.fossilrim.org.

GLEN ROSE CONVENTION & VISITOR BUREAU, 1505 N.E. Big Bend Trail, Glen Rose, 76043. Call 254-897-3081. Website: www.glenrose texas.net.

GRANBURY CONVENTION & VISITOR BUREAU, 116 W. Bridge Street, Granbury, 76048. Call 817-573-5548. Website: www.visitgranbury.com.

HAMMOND'S, 1106 N.E. Big Bend Trail, Glen Rose, 76043. Call 254-897-3008. Closed Mondays and Tuesdays; lunch only on Wednesdays and Sundays; lunch and dinner on Thursdays, Fridays, and Saturdays. Local favorite for no-fuss barbecue. Website: www.hammondsbbq.com. $–$$.

HICO CHAMBER OF COMMERCE, 120 W. First Street, Hico, 76457. Call 254-796-4620. Website: www.hico-tx.com.

HILL COUNTRY LAVENDER, 4524 US 281, Blanco, 78606. Call 830-833-2294. Website: www.hillcountrylavender.com.

INN ON LAKE GRANBURY, 205 W. Doyle Street, Granbury, 76048. Call 1-877-573-0046. Luxurious inn, with 2 acres of manicured lawn, a flagstone pool, lake views, and wonderfully appointed rooms. Website: www.innonlakegranbury.com. $$$$.

INN ON THE RIVER, 205 S.W. Barnard Street, Glen Rose, 76043. Call 1-800-575-2101 or 254-897-2929. Restaurant serving dinner Fridays and Saturdays only; reservations required. Serene inn on spacious grounds, with a pool, large oak trees, and Adirondack chairs scattered about. Website: www.innontheriver.com. $$.

KOFFEE KUP FAMILY RESTAURANT, 300 W. Second Street, Hico, 76457. Call 254796-4839. Open daily 6 AM–9:30 PM. Simple menu of country cooking; save room for pie. Website: www.koffeekupfamilyrestaurant.com. Cash only. $–$$.

LONGHORN CAVERN STATE PARK, 6211 Park Road 4 South, Burnet, 78611. Call 1-877-441-2283 or 512-756-4680. Website: www.tpwd.texas.gov.

MAMA'S HOME COOKING, 200 S. West Street, Burnet, 78611. Call 512-234-8030. Serving three square country-style meals a day at this pleasant creekside location in a city park. Website: find them on Facebook. $–$$.

MARBLE FALLS/LAKE LBJ CHAMBER OF COMMERCE, 916 Second Street, Marble Falls, 78654. Call 830-693-1620. Website: www.marblefalls.org.

NUTT HOUSE HOTEL, 119 E. Bridge Street, Granbury, 76048. Call 817-279-8688. Step back in time at this historic hotel on the town square. Website: www.nutthousehotelgranbury.com. $–$$.

PIE PEDDLERS, 102 Walnut Street, Glen Rose, 76043. Call 254-897-9228. Closed Monday through Wednesday. From buttermilk to peach, the pies here are a welcome treat. Website: www.piepeddlers.com. $.

PINK TRACTOR FARMS MARKET, 4524 N. US 281, Blanco, 78606. Call 830-833-4572. Seasonal, call ahead. Website: www.pinktractorfarmsblanco tx.com.

REAL ALE BREWING COMPANY, 231 San Saba Court, Blanco, 78606. Call 830-833-2534. Website: www.realalebrewing.com.

REDBUD CAFÉ, 410 4th Street, Blanco, 78606. Call 830-833-0202. Deli-style lunches and heartier dinners, live music, and local Real Ale Brewing Company beer on tap Friday and Saturday nights. Website: www.redbud cafe.com. $–$$.

ROUGH CREEK LODGE, 5165 County Road 2013, Glen Rose, 76043. Call 254-965-3700. Luxurious lodge rooms in a stunning rural location. Website: www.roughcreek.com. $$$–$$$$.

SPICEWOOD VINEYARDS, 1419 Burnet CR409, Spicewood, 78669. Call 830-693-5328. Website: www.spicewoodvineyards.com.

STUMPY'S LAKESIDE GRILL, 2323 S. Morgan Street, Granbury, 76048. Call 817-279-1000. Closed Mondays. Family-friendly lakeside bar and grill featuring fish and seafood. Website: www.lakegranburymarinainc .com. $–$$.

UPSTAIRS INN, 220 N. Pecan Street, Hico, 76457. Call 254-796-2231. Closed Sundays and Mondays. Gorgeous renovation of the second floor of a stone building, with wood floors, high ceilings, and charm. Website: www .hicosupstairsinn.com. $$.

VANISHING TEXAS RIVER CRUISE, 16942 RR 2341, Burnet, 78611. Call 512-756-6986. Website: www.vtrc.com.

WENZEL LONESTAR MEAT COMPANY, 209 N. Bell Street, Hamilton, 76531. Call 254-386-8242. Closed Sundays. Website: www.wenzellonestar meat.com.

WISEMAN HOUSE CHOCOLATES, 406 W. Grubbs, Hico, 76457. Call 254-459-5865. Website: www.wisemanhousechocolates.com.

4

MAIN STREET, TEXAS

BRENHAM, BURTON, WASHINGTON-ON-THE-BRAZOS,
CHAPPELL HILL, ROUND TOP, LA GRANGE, FLATONIA,
SCHLULENBERG, MOULTON, SHINER, GONZALES

TOTAL DISTANCE: Many of the sites on this route are between Brenham and Flatonia, a distance of 60 miles.

HIGHLIGHTS: Pick up an ice cream cone in **Brenham** or a *kolache* in **La Grange**,
two of the largest towns in this verdant region, and stroll the town squares
and classic Texas main streets. Tiny **Round Top** has must-try dining and
events that draw crowds by the thousands. Start your tour of the painted
churches of Texas, lovely reminders of the area's strong German heritage.
Restaurants in **Schlulenberg**, **Moulton**, **Shiner**, and **Gonzales** offer outstanding steaks, beer, and barbecue, respectively. This route also features a trail
of Texas history, from the first shots of the Texas Revolution fired in **Gonzales**
to the signing of the constitution of the Republic of Texas in **Washington-on-
the Brazos**. Detours to the delightful small towns of **Burton**, **Flatonia**, and
Chappell Hill round out the trip.

GETTING THERE: Brenham is located on US 290, about a 90-minute drive from
either Austin or Houston. The lower portion of this route is bound by I-10, the
interstate between Houston and San Antonio.

To begin the route, from Brenham, take TX 237 12 miles west to Burton and from there an additional 10 miles to Round Top and 16 miles farther to La Grange. From La Grange, you can take either US 77 south 17
miles to Schulenburg or 22 miles on FM 609 to Flatonia. From Flatonia,
it is just another 8 miles south to Moulton on TX 95 and 20 miles west on
FM 532 to Gonzales. Backing up, you can also leave Brenham and head 10
miles east on US 290 to Chappell Hill, then north 18 miles on FM 1155 to
Washington-on-the-Brazos.

INTERSECTIONS: Chapters 2 and 5

LEFT: A NINETEENTH-CENTURY COUNTRY CHURCH STILL STANDS READY TO RECEIVE VISITORS

This route traverses the southern tip of what is technically known as the Prairies and Lakes region of Texas, a swatch of green that stretches from the Oklahoma border to just south of I-10, where the terrain becomes scrubbier as it makes its way toward the Gulf of Mexico.

Travelers have tended to whiz past this region in the past, but these days they're finding time to stop. Since it is fairly compact, folks come for a day trip from Austin, San Antonio, or even Houston, and many have discovered that it makes a wonderful weekend getaway. Less crowded than the Hill Country—the times around antiques fairs and the run of Shakespeare at Winedale in Round Top excepted (page 79)—the area is also less expensive. Even if you are simply passing through, the ease of the region and the proximity of interesting towns to the highway (you can be off the beaten track in minutes) make it a terrific spot to stop for a meal. While it's steeped in history and beautiful as can be, with horses and cattle grazing on the gently rolling hills at every bend, when you get right down to it, this route is really all about the food. Sweet *kolaches,* slices of pie, and ice cream. Steaks, barbecue, and burgers. Maybe it's the country air or the lovely setting, but good food just tastes great out here.

Located almost midway between Austin and Houston on US 290, **Bren-**

ham has long been at the center of the action in Washington County. A magnet for immigrants, by the mid-1800s, Brenham was home to African Americans, Germans, Jews, and various European newcomers, and all have left their mark. One enduring tradition is Maifest (www.maifest.org), a community-wide celebration of German heritage held each year, in early-May. The town is a well-located home base from which to explore the area; the first order of business is finding a spot to spend the night.

Built in the 1920s and renovated and reopened as a bed & breakfast in 2008, **The Brenham House B&B** greets guests with five cozy, well-appointed rooms and freshly baked treats. The three-course breakfast makes getting out of the warm and comfortable beds more than worth the effort. Ask the affable owners Susan and James about the house's German Lutheran roots; they are also a font of knowledge with respect to the area, and lovely people to boot. Really want to get away from it all? Try the **Murski Homestead B&B**. The expansive countryside property is home to cows, donkeys, horses, and other farm animals; many guests choose to spend their stay on the porch swings taking in the view. While the surroundings are decidedly rural, the

OUT TO PASTURE IN WASHINGTON COUNTY

CATTLE ENJOYING THE AFTERNOON SHADE IN A FIELD OF SPRINGTIME WILDFLOWERS

rooms and breakfasts are sophisticated, with obvious attention to quality and detail. Gracious owners are a plus.

Located right in town, the **Ant Street Inn** does have the look and feel of an old-style inn; it's just as cozy as an intimate bed & breakfast. The 14 rooms have different features to recommend them. Try the San Antonio for size, the Mobile for its two queen beds, and the Memphis for the inn's most unusual fixture, a nonworking, century-old freight elevator in the center of the room. Another choice, the historic **Fairview Bed and Breakfast**, also has a variety of rooms to choose from. The prairie-style home was built in 1925, and the solid structure is both utilitarian and graceful. Rooms are simply furnished and decorated in soothing colors, some overlooking the pool and the spacious grounds below. The Carriage House Suite has a small kitchen, and the Pool House Suites are newly constructed, but include old-timey details such as stained glass windows.

Be sure to ask your hosts where they enjoy eating in town, or hit the road again to one of the options in nearby Round Top or Chappell Hill. You'll find **Truth Barbeque** on the side of busy US 290, just on the edge of Brenham, and it's best to just pull over and get in line since some of the state's best barbecue awaits inside. Buttery smooth with a salty, smoky edge, the brisket here comes close to perfect. You can pick up a knife, but you won't need it since the meat separates the moment you poke it with a fork. The well-made traditional sides, such as crisp coleslaw and dense potato salad, round out the meal and you'll find a multi-layer red velvet cake tempting you at the register. If you'd like to dine in Brenham for an easy lunch, try **Must Be Heaven**, a local sandwich franchise with several other shops in towns

Blue Bell

Order a slice of pie or a piece of Texas sheet cake and you'll be asked if you'd like it with **Blue Bell**. Almost everyone says yes, but if you are new to Texas, then Blue Bell might be new to you. This area of Texas—Washington County—is known throughout the state for its milk production, and as you drive the backroads, you'll notice plenty of cows lazing around the fields, munching their way through the thick green grass. Those cows turn out to be very productive when it comes to milk. As early as 1911, local farmers banded together to start the Brenham Creamery Company to produce butter—and later ice cream—with all the leftover cream from their efficient cows. In 1930, they changed their name to **Blue Bell Creameries**.

The ice cream was a huge hit, and generations of Texans have grown up enjoying scoops of Blue Bell. Although the brand is only sold in 20 percent of the nation's supermarkets, primarily in the South and Southwest, it is one of the top-three best-selling ice creams in the nation. That means that folks down here have strong brand allegiance—plus they eat a lot of ice cream. A Texas treat with southern appeal, Blue Bell has become such an icon that people don't order "ice cream," they just order "Blue Bell."

Blue Bell's headquarters are in Brenham; guided tours of their modern production facility are offered on weekdays. The tours are first-come, first-served, approximately 45 minutes long, and conclude with a scoop of ice cream. Check www.bluebell.com for details.

Stop and Smell the Roses

Stop and smell the roses at the **Antique Rose Emporium** in Independence, where the collection of fragrant roses, perennials, herbs, and native plants is just astounding. All the flowers are sure to have your olfactory senses on high alert—the perfect time for a glass of wine! Pull into **Pleasant Hill Winery** for a taste of a Texas vintage.

farther afield. Stop in and order a "chicken diablo" sandwich with creamy jalapeño dressing or the regional classic, pimento cheese, among others, to eat in or take on the road. Save room for a slice of their delicious pie.

Continue your trip by driving 12 miles west of Brenham on US 290 to diminutive **Burton**. The town, established in 1862, is now best known as the site of the **Burton Cotton Gin and Museum**, which makes it the go-to place for all information on cotton processing. If you visit in mid-April, you may have the pleasure of attending the Cotton Gin Festival.

If you're visiting on a weekend, have dinner at the **Brazos Belle**, the pleasant French restaurant in town. From sauces to salad dressings, everything here is made from scratch by Chef Andre and served in an elegant old building that was once the farmers cooperative and general store. The surprise of such a lovely restaurant in such an unexpected place makes the food taste that much better. The Brazos Belle does not accept credit cards, just cash and checks.

From Burton, it's a 35-mile drive along scenic FM 390 (see box on page 79) to the **Washington-on-the-Brazos State Historic Site**. The site, actually several in one, includes the **Star of the Republic Museum**, **Independence Hall**, and **Barrington Living History Farm**. This serene spot was the site of the signing of the Texas Declaration of Independence in 1836, a pivotal event in the history of the state. The site sits on close to 300 acres of rolling green hills and is a lovely park in its own right. The Star of the Republic Museum and the re-created Independence Hall, where the declaration was signed, are highly interesting. The Barrington Living History Farm, at the home of the last president of the Republic of Texas, brings the era to life through interpreters acting as nineteenth-century farmers in period dress and using period tools.

After visiting the park, you can either head back to Brenham on TX 105 or take a 10-minute detour south on FM 1155 that will deposit you in the little hamlet of **Chappell Hill**. It was once a town growing in both size and importance, but the Civil War and a devastating yellow fever epidemic in 1867 left the town with few citizens. These days, tall trees, graceful homes, and well-kept lawns hearken back to a more formal era, giving the town the look and feel of a parlor that has been dusted and cleaned for years while waiting for the lady of the house to return.

If you're here and hungry, have a seat at **Bever's Kitchen**; as one of the only dining spots in town, it's a standout in its own right. Open daily for lunch, with extended hours on Friday and Saturday for dinner, Bever's

The Painted Churches of Texas

n the mid-1800s, Czech and German immigrants moved to Texas in droves, and set about building homes, plowing fields, and establishing churches to guide their communities. As the little towns prospered and they had just a bit of time and money for a few extras, the first priority was to build new churches that more closely matched those they had left behind in Europe.

SOPHISTICATED DETAILS IN ONE OF THE MANY RURAL "PAINTED CHURCHES"

Today, there are just over twenty of these "painted churches" remaining in Texas, many of them clustered around **Schulenburg**. Some are made of stone, some of wood, but all would be quite plain inside were it not for the paint. Itinerant artists traveled from church to church, painting; all were clearly highly skilled, but many of their names are lost to history.

The churches are lovely. Each is unique, yet part of the same tradition. The delicate scrollwork and stenciling seem as bright today as they must have been when the churches were painted. In one church the ceiling might be a clear robin's egg blue; in another, faux gold leaf. In some cases, columns appear to be marble, but are actually simply painted with a deftness of skill that seems astounding today. These buildings are architecturally straightforward from the outside; the painted interiors make them pop.

There are painted churches in the towns of Schulenburg, Dubina, High Hill, Ammannsville, and Praha, to name a few; you can get a complete list in Schulenburg or most visitor centers. If you happen to drive by one on your route, be sure to stop. Or create a detour using two or three. Just driving along the rolling landscape in between and coming upon a steeple that anchors the country road will give you a sense of the companionship and comfort these immigrants must have given each other as they carved community out of the countryside.

Kitchen is like a friend's house—casual and homey. And the food captures that spirit perfectly. Daily Plate Specials take center stage; sandwiches, soups, and burgers playing supporting roles. The dinner menu is much the same as the lunch offering, plus fresh Gulf shrimp, fried catfish, and enchiladas. Specials can include anything from King Ranch Casserole to chicken spaghetti to homemade meatloaf. The folks at Bever's are health-conscious, making almost everything from scratch using natural ingredients, including over a dozen different delicious pies.

Doubling back 22 miles west on US 290 to Burton, the route now turns south on TX 237 and heads toward **Round Top**, once a stop on the old La Bahía Road; people have been settling down in Round Top since 1826, first the people of English descent who arrived from the United States, then Germans, who came straight from Europe. As you will see in the architecture of the town's few buildings, the Germans made a lasting impression. The bucolic countryside around the settlement drew artists to the region, and even today, the minute town captures visitors' imaginations.

Round Top has a bevy of bed & breakfasts. Built in the 1800s, the **Round Top Inn** is a collection of guest rooms, cottages, and a little structure dating back to 1882 that was once used as a cigar factory and now stands in as the dining room. The rooms are updated and fresh, but with a distinct historic feel that comes with wood floors, simple antiques, and iron beds. Old oak trees shade the property, which is a short stroll from town. A two-minute drive into the country will lead you to the **Belle of Round Top**, a grand restored Victorian home with generously sized rooms, high ceilings, and tall windows covered with thick drapes. The surrounding meadow is filled with wildflowers, birds, and butterflies, and makes a lovely view from the wicker chairs on the wraparound porch. The Belle is the sort of place folks come to get away from it all and find they never want to leave. **Wellspring Retreat and Bed & Breakfast** takes your relaxation very seriously. The property, located a few minutes from town, encompasses an eclectic assortment of accommodations, including a restored 1850s Railroad Depot, separated by gardens, walking paths, and a pond. The decor is lovely, with carefully-chosen antiques providing plenty of character throughout. Guests rave about the delicious morning breakfast buffet, served in the communal dining room, the warmth of the hosts, and the peacefulness which seems to settle over Wellspring each evening when the stars come out.

For such a small spot in the road, Round Top has a lot going on. While it is a great place to poke around for antiques year round (check www.round top.org for listings), Round Top has made a name for itself with its **Antiques Fairs**. During the first week in October, it draws thousands upon thousands of eager bargain hunters to the enormous **Fall Antiques Fair**. The scene repeats the first full weekend in April, when the **Spring Antiques Fair** rolls out the red carpet. Renowned for the quality and quantity of their antiques, the fairs have been attracting discerning crowds for over 40 years. If you plan a visit at these times, be sure to make lodging reservations well in advance.

People also flock to the region for Shakespeare. **Shakespeare at Winedale** is a program of the University of Texas English Department, first nurtured by a Professor James "Doc" B. Ayres, who was convinced that the best way to study Shakespeare's plays is to perform them. Doc met Ima Hogg, an extraordinary philanthropist, musician, patron of the arts, governor's daughter, and oil-company heiress, popularly known as the First Lady of Texas, who had just finished a pet project—the restoration and transformation of an old stagecoach inn into the Winedale Historical Center. She then donated the entire 270 acres and its cluster of historic buildings to the University of Texas. Miss Ima, as she was called, suggested to Doc that the old hay barn on the property reminded her of an Elizabethan theater and perhaps he could consider staging some summertime performances there. He agreed and the results were magic; Shakespeare at Winedale has been captivating audiences for almost 40 years now. The program has expanded into a year-long event, engaging groups of all ages, from all around the United States. The summer season generally runs mid-July through mid-August, though there can be additional performances bookending those dates; check the website (www.shakespeare-winedale.org) for details or drive by and take a look around. From Round Top, turn left onto FM 1457, then left onto FM 2714 into the Winedale Historical Center; the Theatre Barn will be on your right after 1 mile.

As the sign greeting you at the city limits asserts, Round Top is home to only 77 people. On a Friday or a Saturday, you would swear they were all down at **Royers Round Top Café**. In 1987, the Royer family quit Houston for Round Top, purchasing the little café. They learned two things quickly.

Scenic Drive

A particularly lovely drive in Washington County is FM 390, a scenic route that arcs for close to 40 miles, skirting Brenham 7 miles to the south and connecting Burton (page 76) to TX 105, near Washington-on-the-Brazos. Known as **La Bahía Road**, the route existed for centuries as a footpath used by Native Americans, explorers, traders, militia, immigrants, and animals, connecting southeastern Texas and Louisiana. Though El Camino Real (page 162) is both longer and better known, La Bahía Road was an important thoroughfare. It ends in Goliad, which was once known as La Bahía (page 101). The road is as beautiful as it is historic; traveling it in the spring, surrounded by wildflowers, is a special treat.

ROYER'S ROUND TOP CAFÉ

One, people will drive as far as they need to for fantastic food, and two, pie is always a hit. The café started with burgers and beer, but ended up with menu items like grilled shrimp BLT and pork tenderloin with peach sauce served with wine. The Royers proved for themselves that location, quality, and service with a smile are still what folks are looking for. The café's signature pie, Bud's Chocolate Chip Pie, is the pie version of the ultimate gooey chocolate chip cookie direct from the oven. Add ice cream and feel the love. The café doesn't accept reservations, but the turnover is brisk. During Antiques Fairs, however, all bets are off. Try your luck in the off hours, perhaps dining earlier than usual, and keep your fingers crossed. If you want to skip the meal and go straight for the pie, head across the street to **Royers Pie Haven**, where they have plenty of fruit, nut, chocolate, and savory pies, baked goods, and coffee to choose from.

From Round Top, it's a quick 16 miles to **La Grange** along TX 237 then TX 159. Located at the intersection of TX 71, TX 159, US 77, and TX 609, the city was a former stop along the old La Bahía Road, and it's been a crossroads ever since. It was once even considered as a possible capital for the new Republic of Texas.

These days, quilters come from all over the world to visit the **Texas Quilt Museum**, where exhibits change every three months to ensure there is always something inspirational on view. The idea for the museum sprang from the success of the enormous annual International Quilt Festival in Houston (www.quilts.com/quilt-festival-houston) and the desire to showcase some of the thousands of outstanding quilts shown there year-round. Opened in 2011, the museum's galleries span two 1890s buildings, where examples of hand-planed planks and pieced together masonry are on display thanks to the building's award-winning restoration. A sweet heirloom garden blooms beside the building.

In the 1840s and 1850s, large numbers of Germans and Czechs immigrated to the area and left a lasting impression here as elsewhere. One great way to experience a little Czech culture is to sink your teeth into a *kolache*, and one of the best places to do that is at **Weikel's Bakery**, on TX 71 in La Grange. The place is actually a gas station; it won't look promising when you pull up, but open the door and you'll become a believer. The shelves are packed with the slightly sweet Danish-like Czech pastries traditionally filled with prunes, cottage cheese, and poppy seeds. Cream cheese, apricot, and other fruit fillings are also popular. A second bakery in Brenham is in the works; check website.

If you are looking for a full meal, one of the nicest places to eat in town is **Bistro 108**, just a door or two off the town square. Entrées such as spinach

KOLACHES AT WEIKEL'S BAKERY IN LA GRANGE

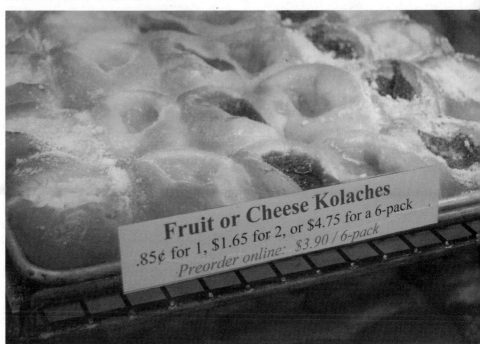

Fruit or Cheese Kolaches
.85¢ for 1, $1.65 for 2, or $4.75 for a 6-pack
Preorder online: $3.90 / 6-pack

and roasted rosemary chicken ravioli with a pesto cream sauce are right at home with pork chops and mashed potatoes, and are sure to please either a traditional or adventurous palate. A nice wine list and homemade desserts complete the meal. Across the street, you can visit two "Texas Treasures." Designated as such by the Texas Historical Commission, the **Lukas Bakery** and **Prause Meat Market** have each contributed to the local economy for at least 50 years, earning them the distinction. Stepping into each is like stepping back in time. The *kolaches*, pecan rolls, and other delicious treat at Lukas are so reasonably priced, you can easily buy several to sample. You'll smell Prause before you enter. Bypass the butcher's counter and follow the line left to the back of the shop where you can order hot meats and sides to go.

Also in La Grange, the Heinrich **Kreische Brewery**, owned by Texas Parks and Wildlife, shares a bluff overlooking the Colorado River with the Kreische family home and **Monument Hill**, where, in 1848, the remains of Texans killed during the War of Independence were interred in a common tomb. A large crowd, which included President Sam Houston, attended the event. In 1849, Heinrich Kreische, a German immigrant and stonemason turned brewer, purchased the land, eventually building a home and a brewery on the site, and cared for the tomb until his death in 1882. While the brewery was once one of the largest in the state, both it and the tomb declined after Kreische's death. Now a state park, the structures are well cared for today.

From La Grange, press southward, this time using pretty FM 609 to travel the 22 miles to **Flatonia**, located on US 90 just south of I-10. Once the tiny hamlets of Flatonia and Oso were neighbors separated by a couple of miles, but when the railroad came through, both towns packed up, moved next to the tracks, and merged to become one. Cattle and cotton fueled the economy, and European immigrants came looking for inexpensive land to farm. When I-10 was completed in the 1970s, travel bypassed the town, but today Flatonia is making a new name for itself. Home to just about 1,500 welcoming, outspoken, and community-minded individuals, the little town has a lot of pluck. If you like small, friendly towns, then you'll like Flatonia. Use it as a comfortable, low-key home base for touring the entire region or just stop in for the Czech heritage festival Czhilispiel during the last full weekend in October (www.czhilispielfestival.com).

Lodging in Flatonia is an easy decision; there is only one place in town, and it's wonderful. In describing the **Olle Hotel**, it's best to begin with its gracious and energetic inn-keeper, Kathryn, who is just as lovely as the inn itself. A rooming house and bed & breakfast in past incarnations, the Olle is over a century old. Lots of elbow grease, lovely colors, and a few well-chosen antiques later, and the Olle is fresh and spirited again, with modern

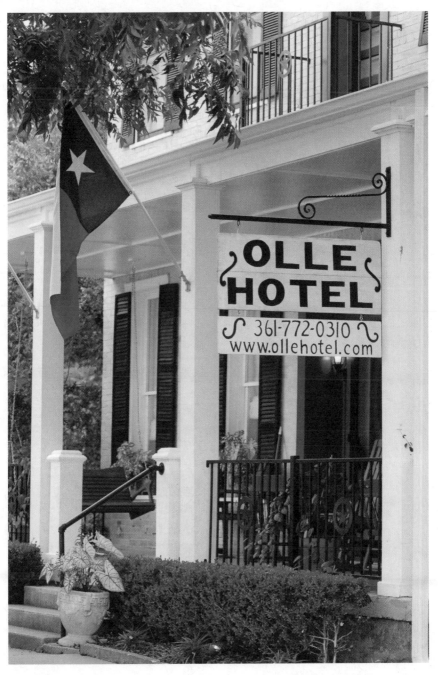

THE OLLE HOTEL IN FLATONIA

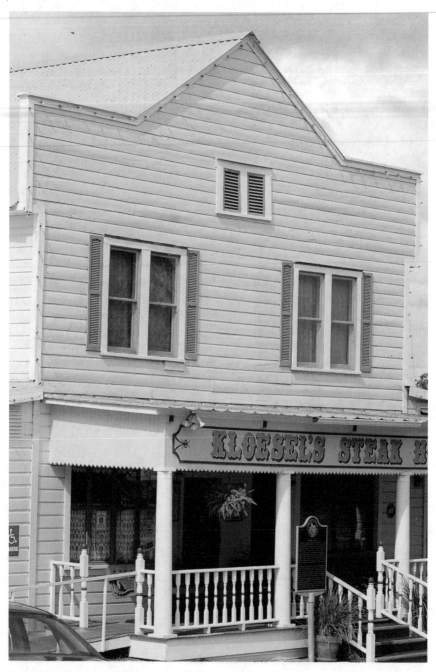

KLOESEL'S STEAK HOUSE IN MOULTON

touches that blend beautifully with its historic charm. Simple, bright, and comfortable rooms, high-speed Internet, and great coffee make it the perfect stay for business travelers. Queen beds, crisp white linens, an open, airy feel, and homemade breakfast treats make it a wonderfully romantic respite. With decor that appeals to everyone, the Olle makes guests always feel comfortable. Kathryn knows everything about the town, so be sure to ask her for recommendations, or just enjoy a small-town tale or two. The Olle Hotel owns several self-service properties in town; check the website for options.

As in most small towns, there aren't many places to eat in Flatonia. **Robert's Steakhouse** is 100 percent pure local and a real treat. The specialty here is steak, served with baked potatoes and several choices of vegetables, and the friendly, efficient folks here will cook yours just the way you like it. Alternatively, take TX 95 south to the small town of **Moulton**, home of some of the biggest steaks in Texas. In a bright yellow storefront just beyond the railroad tracks, you'll find **Kloesel's Steakhouse & Bar.** This building was made of the castaway wood from the demolished Moore Hotel, which was the nineteenth-century hub of social and commercial life in Moulton. The much-loved hotel was razed in the 1940s, but certain details in Kloesel's, such as frosted glass and drawings and photographs of the original hotel, pay homage to its legacy. The steakhouse and its bar are a gathering place, with folks coming in for the homemade salad dressings, pies, breads, and steak sauce as much as the steaks. Just up the street at the center of town is the **Ole Moulton Bank**; instead of doling out cash, it now offers vintage guitars, live music and libations.

The route ends in **Gonzales**, which is where the first shots of the Texas Revolution were fired. In 1835, as tensions mounted between the Anglo settlers in Gonzales and the Mexican government in San Antonio de Béxar, the issue arose of a small cannon in the town. Mexico wanted the cannon, and the settlers were told to relinquish it. Boldly, the Anglos challenged them to "come and take it." Mexican soldiers arriving in Gonzales to retrieve the weapon were met by armed men. The cannon remained in Gonzales. Some of the men who fought to defend it, however, did not: instead they headed north to defend the Alamo. All in all, 32 Gonzales men died at the Alamo. For all the trouble, you may be surprised at the cannon's size (actually an accurate reconstruction). Small, but, it goes without saying, highly symbolic. You can see it at the museum housed in the old town library, where it is surrounded by memorabilia and watched over by a very knowledgeable docent who can give you plenty of history.

Now a peaceful, leafy locale, Gonzales is just like a lot of towns in the region, with plenty of old homes and a few businesses scattered around the square. Should you decide to spend the night, the graceful **Belle Oaks Inn** makes a nice choice. Conveniently located in town, the inn is a Louisiana

SMOKING SAUSAGES AT THE GONZALES FOOD MARKET IN GONZALES

Plantation–style mansion that immediately transports guests to that more gracious time of chandeliers, four-poster beds, antique details, and dressed windows. The grounds here are especially lovely, with huge live oak and pecan trees shielding the gardens, seating, and pathways from the strong sun. Modern amenities such as high-speed Internet and a pool add to the comfort and convenience. The Dilworth Building, built in 1912, has been a bank, offices, department store, church, and finally a bit of an eyesore. After a much-needed renovation, **The Dilworth Inn** opened its doors in 2015 as a 14-room boutique hotel and seems to have found a new lease on life. It may be the charm of the older building or the novelty of a functioning locally-owned hotel on the town square, but guests really enjoy staying at the Dilworth.

If you've just come off the barbecue circuit of Llano, Taylor, Elgin, Lockhart, and Luling (see Chapter 1), you'll have reason to compare them to the **Gonzales Food Market**. The market is an old brick grocery store facing the square, with a meat counter dating back to the 1950s. While the grocery business was brisk, people came from far and wide for the barbecue, and slowly a restaurant began to take shape inside the grocery store. The townsfolk regularly gather here in this true mom-and-pop spot to bask in both the warmth of friendship and the satisfaction of the well-priced lunch special, which features barbecue and a buffet.

Baker Boys BBQ hasn't logged the years yet, but they've added even more tasty barbecue to Gonzales. A father-son team with roots in Luling and experience in barbecue competition, the Bakers know a thing or two about smoking a brisket. The operation is housed is a metal building which doesn't have the same age or charm as others, but the real measure is the taste of the barbecue and by that standard Baker Boys is well worth seeking out.

Leaving Gonzales, you are well-positioned to connect to either the Best BBQ in Texas route (see Chapter 1) or the Texas Coast (see Chapter 5), both of which travel along US 183.

While this route may take a little longer than the interstate, the soothing backroad scenery, great food, and restful bed & breakfasts more than compensate. So, next time you make the trip between Austin, San Antonio, or Houston, be sure to schedule in some time to enjoy the space in between.

IN THE AREA

ANT STREET INN, 107 W. Commerce Street, Brenham, 77833. Call 979-836-7393. Spacious inn with plenty of vintage details, including a large veranda with rocking chairs. Website: www.antstreetinn.com. $$$$.

ANTIQUE ROSE EMPORIUM, 10,000 FM 50, Brenham (Independence), 77833. Call 979-836-5548. Website: www.antiqueroseemporium.com.

BAKER BOYS BBQ, 1404 Sarah DeWitt Drive, Gonzales, 78629. Call 830-519-4400. New barbecue spot with a knack for classic 'cue. Website: www.BakerBoysBBQ.com. $-$$.

BELLE OAKS INN, 222 St. Peter, Gonzales, 78629. Call 830-857-8613. Louisiana Plantation–style mansion turned inn. Website: www.belleoaksinn.com.$-$$.

BELLE OF ROUND TOP, 230 Days End Lane, Round Top, 78954. Call 936-521-9300. Victorian home with generously sized rooms and surrounded by wildflowers. Website: www.belleofroundtop.com. $$-$$$.

BEVER'S KITCHEN, 5162 Main Street, Chappell Hill, 77426. Call 979-836-4178. Casual and homey with specials ranging from King Ranch Casserole to chicken spaghetti to homemade meatloaf, and over a dozen different delicious pies. Website: www.bevers-kitchen.com. $-$$.

BISTRO 108, 108 S. Main Street, La Grange, 78945. Call 979-968-9108. Closed Mondays; Brunch only on Sundays. New American fare in a bistro a block off the square. Website: www.bistro108.com. Reservations recommended. $$.

BLUE BELL CREAMERIES, 1101 S. Blue Bell Road (Loop 577), Brenham, 77833. Call 1-800-327-8135. Tours Monday through Friday. Fee. Website: www.bluebell.com. Reservations sometimes required; call ahead.

BRAZOS BELLE, 600 Main Street, Burton, 77835. Call 979-289-2677. Closed Monday through Thursday. Extended hours on Antiques Fair weekends. French restaurant featuring delicious dining in an elegant building. Website: www.brazosbellerestaurant.com. Cash only. $$-$$$.

Wildflowers

Bluebonnets, Indian paintbrush, and other wildflowers proliferate along the roadsides and in the pastures of Washington County throughout the spring. To find out just where the best viewing is, you can stop in the Brenham Chamber of Commerce, or check the "Maps" section of their website, www.brenhamtexas.com, but FM 1155 between Chappell Hill and Washington-on-the-Brazos is always a good bet.

BRENHAM CHAMBER OF COMMERCE/WASHINGTON COUNTY CONVENTION & VISITOR BUREAU, 115 W. Main Street, Brenham, 77833. Call 979-836-3696. Website: www.visitbrenhamtexas.com.

BRENHAM HOUSE B&B, 705 Clinton Street, Brenham, 77833. Call 979-251-9947. Homey bed & breakfast in town, complete with warm hosts, delicious breakfasts, and plenty of personal touches. Website: www.thebrenhamhouse.com. $$$–$$$$.

BURTON COTTON GIN AND MUSEUM, 307 N. Main Street, Burton, 77835. Call 979-289-3378. Fee. Website: www.cottonginmuseum.org.

CHAPPELL HILL CHAMBER OF COMMERCE, 9000 US 290 E., Chappell Hill, 77426. Call 979-337-9910. Website: www.chappellhilltx.com.

THE DILWORTH INN, 603 N. Saint Joseph Street, Gonzales, 78629. Call 830-519-4109. Modern digs in a renovated building right on the town square. Website: www.thedilworth.com. $.

FAIRVIEW BED AND BREAKFAST, 1804 S. Park Street, Brenham, 77833. Call 1-888-327-8439 or 979-836-1672. Prairie-style home circa 1925, with comfortable rooms and suites. Website: www.fairviewbedandbreakfast.com. $$$.

FLATONIA CHAMBER OF COMMERCE, 208 E. North Main, Flatonia, 78941. Call 361-865-3920. Website: www.flatoniachamber.com.

GONZALES CHAMBER OF COMMERCE, 414 Saint Lawrence Street, Gonzales, 78629. Call 830-672-6532. Website: www.gonzalestexas.com.

GONZALES FOOD MARKET, 311 Saint Lawrence Street, Gonzales, 78629. Call 830-672-3156. Decades-old mom-and-pop spot for barbecue. $–$$.

KLOESEL'S STEAKHOUSE & BAR, 101 E. Moore Street, Moulton, 77975. Call 361-596-7323. Char-broiled steaks and country fixin's served in a homey bright yellow restaurant you can't miss. Website: www.kloesel.com. $$–$$$.

LA GRANGE AREA CHAMBER OF COMMERCE, 220 W. Colorado Street, La Grange, 78945. Call 979-968-5756. Website: www.lagrangetx.org.

LUKAS BAKERY, 135 N. Main Street, La Grange, 78945. Call 979-968-3052. Closed Sundays. Decades-old bakery with sweet treats behind its front screen door. $.

MONUMENT HILL AND KREISCHE BREWERY STATE HISTORIC SITES, 414 TX 92 Spur, La Grange, 78945. Call 979-968-5658. Website: www.tpwd .texas.gov.

MOULTON CHAMBER OF COMMERCE, 405 S. Lavaca Drive, Moulton, 77975. Call 361-596-7205. Website: www.moulton texas.com.

MURSKI HOMESTEAD B&B, 1662 Old Independence Road, Brenham, 77833. Call 979-525-4151. Countryside inn surrounded by farm animals and peace and quiet. Website: www.murskihomesteadbb.com. $$$–$$$$.

MUST BE HEAVEN, 107 W. Alamo Street, Brenham, 77833. Call 979-830-8536. A casual eatery with soup, sandwiches, and plenty of pie. Website: www.mustbeheaven.com. $.

OLE MOULTON BANK, 101 Main Street, Moulton, 77975. Call 361-596-7499. Live music and drinks in the a former bank. Website: www.olemoultonbank .com. $–$$.

OLLE HOTEL, 218 S. Market Avenue, Flatonia, 78941. Call 361-772-0310. Charming inn in tiny Flatonia. Website: www.ollehotel.com. $–$$.

Church Picnics

As you drive around the backroads of this region, be sure to notice any signs announcing **church picnics**. There are many in these parts that have been annual events for over 100 years. With cake walks, desserts, entertainment, and lots and lots of food, these picnics, open to the public, are a great chance to experience small-town life at its very best.

Shiner

Step into a bar, restaurant, or dance hall in Texas and someone is bound to offer you a Shiner. Spoetzl Brewery, located in Shiner a mere 18 miles south of Flatonia and 18 miles east of Gonzales, has been brewing since 1909, making it the oldest brewery in the state. Its beer and the label on the bottle are Texas icons. From the music scene in Austin to the backroads of rural Texas, it seems just about everyone is kicked back with a Shiner. Stop in for a look, and a taste of history. Check www.shiner.com for tour details.

PLEASANT HILL WINERY, 1441 Salem Road, Brenham, 77833. Call 979-830-8463. Weekends only. Website: www.pleasanthillwinery.com.

PRAUSE MEAT MARKET, 253 W. Travis Street, La Grange, 78945. Call 979-968-3259. Closed Sundays. Cash only. Barbecue served in the back of this old-school meat market. $$.

ROBERT'S STEAKHOUSE, 1241 N. TX 95, Flatonia, 78941. Call 361-865-3099. Small town steakhouse with big taste. Website: www.roberts-steakhouse.com. $$–$$$.

ROUND TOP CHAMBER OF COMMERCE, 110 Schumann Lane, Henkel Square Market, Round Top, 78954. Call 979-249-4042. Website: www.roundtop.org.

ROUND TOP INN, 407 South White Street, Round Top, 78954. Call 979-249-5294. A compound of cottages, houses, and lofts, each beautifully configured and appointed, a short walk from the center of Round Top. Website: www.roundtopinn.com. $$$.

ROYERS ROUND TOP CAFE, 105 Main Street, Round Top, 78954. Call 979-249-3611. Closed Monday through Wednesday. All kinds of country cooking and a go-to spot for pie. Website: www.royersroundtopcafe.com. $–$$.

ROYERS PIE HAVEN, 190 Henkel Circle, Round Top, 78954. Call 979-249-5282. Plenty of pies—sweet and savory—baked goods, and coffee. Website: www.royerspiehaven.com. $.

SCHULENBURG CHAMBER OF COMMERCE, 618 N. Main Street, Schulenburg, 78956. Call 979-743-4514. Website: www.schulenburgchamber.org.

SHAKESPEARE AT WINEDALE, Winedale Historical Center, 3738 FM 2714 Road, Burton, 77835. Call 979-278-3530. For more information, call 512-471-4726 or write James Loehlin, Director, Shakespeare at Winedale, University of Texas at Austin, 208 W. 21st Street, Stop B5000, Austin, 78712. Website: www.shakespeare-winedale.org.

SPOETZL BREWERY, 603 E. Brewery Street, Shiner, 77984. Call 361-594-3383. Tours weekdays only. Website: www.shiner.com.

TEXAS QUILT MUSEUM, 140 W. Colorado Street, La Grange, 78945. Call 979-968-3104. Fee. Website: www.texasquiltmuseum.org.

TRUTH BARBEQUE, 2990 US 290, Brenham, 77833. Call 979-830-0392. This little place works some magic turning out superb barbecue; a must-stop. Open Friday through Sunday. Website: www.truthbbq.com. $$.

WASHINGTON-ON-THE-BRAZOS STATE HISTORIC SITE, 23400 Park Rd 12, Washington, 77880. Call 936-878-2214. Free and Fee. Website: www. tpwd.texas.gov.

WEIKEL'S BAKERY, 2247 W. TX 71, La Grange, 78945. Call 979-968-9413. Roadside *kolache* emporium. Website: www.weikels.com. $.

WELLSPRING RETREAT AND BED & BREAKFAST, 580 N. Washington Street, Round Top, 78954. Call 979-256-2619. Gorgeous compound of relaxing accommodations outside of town, with a fantastic communal breakfast buffet. Website: www.wellspringretreat.net. $$$.

5

THE TEXAS COAST

FULTON, ROCKPORT, PORT ARANSAS

TOTAL DISTANCE: 25 miles from Fulton to Port Aransas

HIGHLIGHTS: This route captures the free-spirited Texas Gulf lifestyle. Brush up on your local history in the seaside hamlet of **Rockport**, home to the **Texas Maritime Museum**, or take a tour of the **Fulton Mansion** located in the casual small town of **Fulton**. Get out the binoculars or camera and spend some time birdwatching in the **Aransas National Wildlife Refuge** or one of the other parks and preserves designated by the **Great Texas Coastal Birding Trail**. Take the ferry to the laid-back beach town of Port Aransas and then a short drive to **Padre Island National Seashore**. **Detours:** Coming from Dallas or Austin, some travelers like to take the less-traveled **TX 183/US 77** to the coast and through Goliad (see box on page 101), home of **Presidio La Bahía** and the **Mission Espíritu Santo**, remnants of South Texas' Spanish heritage. The drive south on TX 77 to the Rio Grande Valley, the route outlined in Chapter 6, will take you through the legendary **King Ranch**.

GETTING THERE: Take TX 35 from Fulton, through Rockport, and south to Aransas Pass. In Aransas Pass, follow TX 361 southeast to the free 24-hour ferry landing. Take the ferry to Port Aransas and from there it's just a short drive to the Padre Island National Seashore.

INTERSECTIONS: Chapter 6

The Texas shoreline of the Gulf of Mexico is over 600 miles long, with seven barrier islands, including Galveston (see Chapter 7), Matagorda, Mustang, and Padre Island (see Chapter 6), the longest barrier island in the world, stretched beside it. A utilitarian coast, it supports fishing boats, oil and gas rigs, several dozen cities, state parks, and recreational beaches. Of

LEFT: THE ROCKY SHORE NEAR FULTON

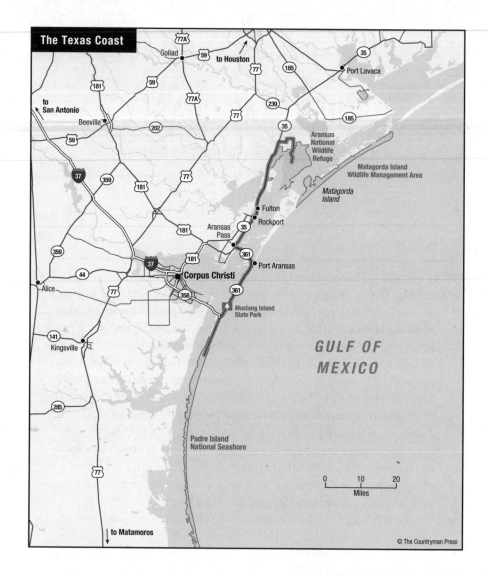

The Texas Coast

Goliad
to Houston
Port Lavaca
to San Antonio
Beeville
Aransas National Wildlife Refuge
Matagorda Island Wildlife Management Area
Matagorda Island
Fulton
Rockport
Aransas Pass
Port Aransas
Corpus Christi
Alice
Mustang Island State Park
Kingsville
GULF OF MEXICO
Padre Island National Seashore
0   10   20
Miles
to Matamoros
© The Countryman Press

course the landscape you see today looks very different than what explorers encountered centuries ago.

As with the rest of Texas, humans have lived in this coastal region for millennia; scientists believe they first arrived 6,000 to 8,000 years ago. Evidence suggests that the nomadic Aransas Indians left the area around A.D. 1200 to 1300; then a century later, the Karankawas moved in. The Karankawas were joined by various other groups of Native Americans who hunted and gathered while on the move along the barrier islands from what is now Galveston to Aransas Pass. Though the Gulf had been sighted previously by several other European explorers, it was Alonso Álvarez de Pineda who put "the hidden sea" on the map in the early 1500s. As the Spanish gained a foothold in the region, native peoples retreated inland or to Mexico. By the 1800s, the Spanish had established a port on Copano Bay with which to serve their settlements in Goliad (page 101), Refugio, and San Antonio de Béxar (now known as San Antonio). At the time of the Texas Revolution, in 1836, the Texas coast was sparsely settled, largely wild, and vulnerable to raids by invading Native Americans and Mexicans.

The Civil War brought its ruin to the Texas coast, too, destroying and damaging existing towns. It wasn't until the fighting stopped that the towns of **Rockport** and **Fulton** were founded, in 1867 and 1866, respectively, as centers for processing and shipping cattle. During this boom time, cattle

Hurricanes

The 2017 hurricane season quickly established itself as one for the record books. In September of that year, Hurricane Harvey took aim for the Texas Gulf Coast, raking over Mustang Island and destroying the popular beach town of Port Aransas before slamming into pretty, low-key Rockport. Corpus Christi was largely spared, but the hurricane settled over Houston, some 215 miles to the east, depositing over 40 inches of rain almost immediately, followed by a deluge lasting for days. Texas was not alone as the season delivered hurricane after hurricane to weary Gulf, Caribbean, and Atlantic coast communities. While rescue and recovery dominated the news at the time, larger issues of rebuilding loomed.

For example, the town of Port Aransas, once a tiny fishing village, is still quite small. Before Hurricane Harvey, approximately 3,500 people lived in the 12 square miles—8.8 square miles of land and 3.3 square miles of water—which made up this little town on the northeastern end of the barrier island. The 1916 Texas Hurricane obliterated Port Aransas and the town was quick to rebuild. But in the early 1900s, rebuilding meant getting docks, wharfs, warehouses, and basic housing up and running so that the fishing could start and the economy around it could take root. These days, Port Aransas relies heavily on tourism, and with condos, restaurants, and surf shops damaged, it is hard to woo visitors.

So while Mother Nature may have struck with force, she is also quickest to recover. As Port Aransas and Rockport work to adjust their economic and city-planning sails, the beaches and birds still beckon. Follow these towns on social media, check their websites, and, once they're ready to welcome visitors again, please enjoy all they have to offer. The hurricane did a lot of damage in the region, but it didn't put a dent in the community's resourcefulness, resilience, and friendliness.

SNOWY EGRET ON THE ROCKPORT WATERFRONT

were prized for their hides and tallow; the raw meat was either fed to pigs or thrown into the bay. The advent of refrigeration changed that, but the rise in beef-packing plants in Chicago and Kansas City provided competition. Still, until the 1880s, the Rockport-Fulton area processed over 90 percent of all Texas beef. Commerce faltered when the shipping lines the beef industry relied upon withdrew from the area, leaving the boat-building and fishing businesses to fill the gap. A hurricane flattened Rockport in 1919, but by the 1940s it had rebounded again, this time aided by shrimping and tourism. In 2017, Hurricane Harvey plowed directly into the Rockport-Fulton area, once again leaving a path of utter destruction. The rebuilding efforts are underway, but will likely take years as coastal communities continue to grapple with the realities of living so close to the edge along the Gulf.

Though Rockport and Fulton are two distinct towns, they are separated by only 3 miles and are often referred to as **Rockport-Fulton**, a blurring of boundaries that represents their neighborliness. Let's start the journey in relaxed, artsy **Rockport**.

The **Texas Maritime Museum** is a modest installation right on the Rockport waterfront. Slip inside and have a look at their fine collection of scale model ships, art, and artifacts, and walk out with a new appreciation for hardworking sailors. Next door, the **Rockport Center for the Arts** has several art galleries featuring local, regional, and sometimes farther-flung artists and is the organizational force behind the summertime **Rockport Art Festival** (page 109).

Walk out toward the water and you'll quickly come upon **Rockport Beach**, the mile-long sandy beach on Aransas Bay. A well-groomed stretch, with restroom facilities, picnic cabanas and grills, and a bird-observation deck, the beach is popular for its clear, shallow water and gentle lapping waves.

While the **Bay Education Center** in Rockport was damaged in Hurricane

Harvey and plans to reopen, they remain an important resource for all the details of the ecology of South Texas and the Gulf of Mexico. Check their website for details and engaging videos about concepts such as weather patterns, the dynamics of hurricanes, and ocean temperatures.

If being so close to the water has piqued your interest in estuaries, island habitats, and marine life, then make a side trip to the **Texas State Aquarium** in Corpus Christi to find out more about marine life. The aquarium features rescued and rehabilitated animals, many from the Gulf of Mexico, giant sea turtles, and dolphin shows. Head to Corpus early and have a big breakfast at **Andy's Country Kitchen**, a local favorite since 1958. Pancakes, omelets, Mexican *migas*, and standard breakfast fare are served all day, joined by chili, enchiladas, tilapia, catfish, and daily specials starting at lunchtime. Regardless of when you visit, this friendly country-style cafe will have a complimentary basket of blueberry muffins on your table in a flash.

Up early and looking for a java jolt? **Rockport Daily Grind** fills the morning food gap nicely; pop in for a cup of coffee and a scone, or try a slice of their savory homemade quiche or a sandwich for lunch. You're in luck for later repasts as well. In the right hands, Texas seafood shines, and **Glow** uses only the freshest fish on the local market for their menu. The restaurant is lovely—slightly upscale, but still very homey—and the food is exceptional. The Rockport Stew consists of locally caught drum, Gulf shrimp, oysters, and crabmeat simmered in a ginger, tomato, lemongrass broth and served with a garlic aioli crostini. Foodies rejoice. Or consider having dinner at **Latitude 28°02' Restaurant and Art Gallery**. Feast your eyes on the menu, then just feast. Choices include the zippy Latitude Oyster appetizer of fresh oysters with a margarita and jalapeño sorbet, and the rich and creamy oysters Rockefeller with spinach Florentine and Hollandaise sauce. The catch of

Palacios

Approximately 75 miles east of Fulton, the sleepy close-knit town of **Palacios** is a great spot to spend the night seaside. The sprawling **Luther Hotel** (www.lutherhotelpalacios.com), built in the early 1900s has weathered over 100 years of hurricanes and decades of guests. Rooms are well-worn and one of the best seats in the house is a rocker on the front porch overlooking the water. The Luther is the sort of spot folks return to year after year for its casual come-as-you-are friendliness. The elegant **Peaceful Pelican B&B** (www.thepeacefulpelican.com), circa 1910, hosts guests in five well-appointed rooms. Take time to notice the details—door hinges engraved with what look like herons and egrets. Dinner served Friday and Saturday nights, reservations required.

Island Time

The little towns along the coast rely heavily on the ebb and flow of seasonal tourism. As you make your way from one to the next, consider resetting your internal clock to "island time" and prepare to be flexible. Service may be a little slower and hours of operation a little relaxed, especially off-season. The very same establishment can be empty one day and swamped with customers the next; it just depends on the day. Make like a local and go with the flow.

the day comes broiled with crab meat and asparagus, or steamed in a brown paper bag with white wine, or encrusted in a garlic butter crust, among other preparations. Latitude 28°02' is only open for dinner, when, predictably, reservations are strongly encouraged.

Leaving Rockport, heading to Fulton along Aransas Bay, S. Austin Street will become N. Austin Street. Follow the fork in the road slightly to the east, and N. Austin Street funnels into Broadway, which in turn becomes S. Fulton Beach Road, then N. Fulton Beach Road, before finally merging into TX 35 at the northern tip of the peninsula.

From Rockport, it's just a quick trip north on N. Fulton Beach Road to the **Fulton Mansion**, which is set back from the road, grand and dignified. One can only imagine what the neighbors thought in 1874 when the Fulton family started building this overstated French Second Empire home by the sea, complete with newfangled amenities such as plumbing, heat, and gas lights. Easterner George Fulton came to Matagorda Bay as a fighter in the Texas Revolution and stayed to marry Harriet, a woman who inherited thousands of acres of Texas land from her father, the Secretary of the Treasury of the Republic of Texas. The Fultons founded the Coleman-Fulton Pasture Company, becoming cattle barons in the midst of a cattle boom, and the mansion stands as a testament to both their wealth and ingenuity. In 2017, Hurricane Harvey damaged the roof of the home, adding yet another chapter to the mansion's long story. Texas Parks and Wildlife Department manages the site and offers an engaging introduction to the Fultons, their mansion and its history.

While it was damaged in Hurricane Harvey, everyone is rooting for the **The Lighthouse Inn** to reopen. The inn offered typical rooms and larger suites, the latter with kitchens; those overlooking the bay tend to be the guests' favorites. The outdoor pool was a plus, and the rocking chairs on the porches overlooking the harbor and the lighted fishing pier were a big draw. The towering white lighthouse in front, toppled in the storm, made the inn easy to spot. Folks are hopeful that they'll see it in place again.

FULTON MANSION IN FULTON

Across the street, **The Boiling Pot** restaurant steams up pots of Cajun-style seafood—shrimp, crab legs, and crawfish with sausage, corn, and potatoes—every night, dumping it straight onto the butcher-paper-covered tables for guests to dig into with their bare hands. The place is almost always crowded and stays open till the food's gone. Since you cannot make reservations, be sure to get there early. Enjoy dishes such as shrimp in a lime cream sauce over orzo or coconut curried shrimp served alongside fantastic views of the Gulf courtesy of **Cheryl's**. The eclectic decor pairs well with the eclectic menu. **Moondog Seaside Eatery** is a very casual seaside spot at which to while away the afternoon nursing a beer and snacking on fish tacos.

Jump on TX 35 and take it a bit north to the **Pelican Bay Resort**, a throwback to the family-style camps of yesteryear. Individual, closely spaced cottages are painted in tropical pastels, their tiny front porches shaded by dozens of leafy oak trees. That is, they were before Hurricane Harvey visited. Heavy winds knocked trees down, damaging the cottages, but efforts to restore them are well underway. Once the welcome mat goes out again, families will flock back to make more memories at Pelican Bay.

THE MASSIVE TRUNK OF THE BIG TREE OF LAMAR IN LAMAR

The Missions of Goliad

Goliad dates back to 1749, making it one of the oldest Spanish colonial settlements in Texas. Home to the Nuestra Señora del Espíritu Santo de Zúñiga Mission (**Mission Espíritu Santo**) and its protective fort, **Nuestra Señora de Loreto de La Bahía del Espíritu Santo Presidio (Presidio La Bahía)**, the town makes for an interesting historical detour en route to the Texas coast. Amazingly, you can spend the night in the fort. Thick stone walls, a comfy bed, and the chance to wander the courtyard all alone in the evening when the doors are locked, make for a memorable stay. Find out more at www.presidiolabahia.org or call 361-645-3752 to make reservations.

Mission Espíritu Santo, located in the **Goliad State Park and Historic Site**, is a reconstruction of a Franciscan mission—the original was decimated by a hurricane in 1886—that was home to one of the most expansive ranching operations in its day. Across the river, the Presidio La Bahía figured prominently in the Texas Revolution. Colonel Fannin and his men were executed here by the infamous Santa Ana; the nearby **Fannin Memorial Monument** marks the burial spot of the war heroes. Beside the presidio, the **Zaragoza Birthplace State Historic Site** is the reconstructed birthplace of Mexican general Ignacio Zaragoza, who defeated the French at the Battle of Puebla on May 5, 1862. Cinco de Mayo (May 5) celebrates the victory with festivities throughout Texas and Mexico.

Oak trees are common here, and there's a famous one nearby. The **Big Tree of Lamar**, located approximately 10 miles north of Rockport, is more than 35 feet in diameter and 44 feet tall, with branches spreading 89 feet across, some supported by cables and iron braces. Estimated to be over 1,000 years old, the tree is thought to have been a council meeting place for the Carancahua Indians. The Big Tree has seen a lot in its time. It's survived dozens of hurricanes, floods, wildfires, droughts, and even the Civil War. To reach it, take I-35 north from Rockport, crossing the Copano Causeway; you will see signs approximately half a mile over the bridge on the right, directing you through the oaks on Park Road 13. Nearby, **Goose Island State Park** is a peaceful place for camping.

Even farther north on TX 35, you'll find the **Aransas National Wildlife Refuge**, established in 1937 to protect the habitat of the endangered whooping crane and now managed by the US Fish and Wildlife Service. The refuge takes in a large swath of land on the Blackjack Peninsula (named for the prevalent blackjack oak trees) north of Lamar and northwest of Matagorda Island. The refuge's many sand dunes, tidal marshes, small ponds, and vegetation make it attractive to almost 400 separate species of birds, among them the large flocks of magnificent whooping cranes that swoop in around

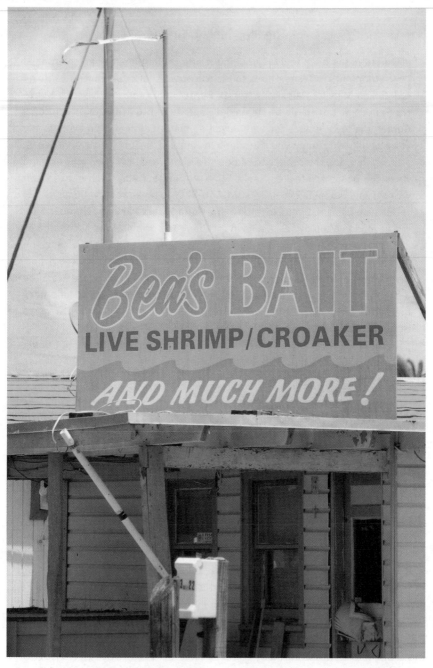

ONE OF THE MANY BAIT SHOPS ALONG THE GULF COAST

November and stay through March. From Rockport-Fulton, take TX 35 to FM 774, turn right and follow to FM 2040, turn right again and proceed to the entrance.

While you can hike the trails, watch from the observation tower, or cruise the paved tour road, one of the best places to see the cranes is on a boat. **Rockport Birding and Kayak Adventures** routinely takes passengers from Rockport to the refuge aboard the *Skimmer* and is particularly known for its Whooping Crane Tours. (In Port Aransas, stop in at Fisherman's Wharf for more information on fishing trips and boat tours to both the Aransas National Wildlife Refuge and St. José's Island; see page 104) The truly dedicated might be able to catch a glimpse of the cranes from the fishing pier at Goose Island State Park in Lamar.

Back in Rockport and heading south, it is a 17.5-mile drive to **Port Aransas**, including the ferry trip over the Port Aransas Causeway. This trip can take anywhere from one hour to two, depending on the time of day, week, and year. From Rockport, take TX 35 south to TX 361, following signs to the ferry.

Port Aransas, or "Port A" as it is known, anchors the northern end of Mustang Island, so named for the wild horses found running free here in the 1800s. While it is now a fishing community and consummate beach town, Port Aransas got its start when Englishman Robert Mercer used it as a grazing station for sheep and cattle. In time a small community grew, acquiring the name Port Aransas in 1910. Today, commercial fishing boats lumber in and out of the port, a reminder of the local economy's dependence on the Gulf waters.

The biggest draw here is the beach. Port A is laden with shops hawking swimsuits and sunscreen to retirees, college students on spring break, and families down for a week at the shore. Just to set the record straight before you go, at the beaches here, like at all beaches in Texas, you won't find soft, white sand; instead it's dark gray and hard-packed with plenty of washed-up

Port Aransas on the Web

Like many of the towns featured in this book, Port Aransas has an informative website (www.portaransas.org) that can come in quite handy as you plan your trip. The sections on birds and nature will be of particular interest to nature enthusiasts, who will find detailed directions to the town's somewhat hard-to-find birding sites and nature preserves. The fishing and boating sections outline fishing regulations and permits, provide photographs to help with fish identification, and spell out details of the Seagrass Law, which places depth restrictions on outboard motors.

GULLS HITCH A RIDE ON THE FERRY TO PORT ARANSAS

kelp, shells, and shark teeth. They are perfect for long walks and sand-castle building, and the relatively low waves are fun for novice boogie boarders.

Nearby the ferry, **Fisherman's Wharf** offers fishing trips, and boat tours to Aransas National Wildlife Refuge and St. José Island, known around here as simply "St. Jo." The island, 28 miles long and less than 2 miles wide, is located just north of Port Aransas. Privately owned, but open to the public for gentle recreational use, St. Jo is a great place to fish, bird-watch, or roam the beach. There are no facilities or shelters on the island, and the only access is by boat, making it a wind-swept paradise for those who want to commune with nature.

While today most of the lodging in Port Aransas consists of condominium rentals, the **Tarpon Inn**, on E. Cotter Avenue across from Fisherman's Wharf, has been renting out rooms since 1886. The Tarpon has recently had a much-needed facelift, but considering that this simple, two-story wooden inn is continuously exposed to the harsh elements, it must be hard just to keep a coat of paint on it. Hurricane Harvey didn't make life any easier, but the inn is rallying in its wake to restore its time-tested relaxed, coastal ambiance.

For a memorable gourmet meal, from Cotter Avenue, head southwest on Alister Street to Beach Avenue, where you will find the **Venetian Hot Plate**, one of the more enjoyable restaurants on the island. The menu features Italian dishes skillfully made by the restaurant's Italian owners, including wonderful fresh pastas, some with vegetables and some with seafood, and homemade lasagnas. Keep your eye on the specials board, where you'll find the chef's daily creation and some of the most expertly cooked seafood around. While you can probably squeeze in for lunch, reservations at dinner are essential.

Port Aransas is a good spot to eat your fill of seafood; there are a number of places that will bake, sear, grill, or fry the catch of the day—theirs or yours. Tucked into the coastal development known as Cinnamon Shores,

Lisabella's Bistro is known for its fresh fish and inventive menu, with Latin, Mediterranean, and Asian influences, Lisabella's wows diners with items such as lobster enchiladas, grilled salmon topped with mango habanero, and beef tenderloin with a roasted tomato, garlic, and feta salsa. The dining room is more chic than most in Port Aransas, making Lisabella's a terrific choice for a special night out. **Irie's Island Food** is a super casual spot to grab some tacos, but don't let the ambiance fool you. Homemade tortillas, a wide-ranging menu of perfectly-spiced seafood, and outstanding sauces make this a flavorful favorite. **Coffee Waves** coffeehouse offers an alternative to the seafood-shack vibe. Coffee, couches, grilled panini sandwiches, and gelato make this a good place to take a break from the sun, sand, and surf.

While there are miles of public beach to enjoy in Port Aransas itself, a short drive south will take you even closer to nature. Heading out of town now on Padre Island Drive/TX 361, you'll find **Mustang Island State Park** approximately 13 miles south of Port Aransas. Located right on the beach and away from the crowds, the park is a popular spot for camping. The policy is first come, first served. Be sure to call in advance to make sure there aren't any closures due to high tides or other weather conditions.

ROCKING CHAIRS ON THE PORCH OF THE TARPON INN

When you're this close to the shore, seafood makes perfect sense. Though it began as a burger and bait shop in 1980, laid-back **Snoopy's Pier** now offers seafood straight from the Gulf. Reasonable prices, quick service, and a lively atmosphere make this family restaurant an easy choice for eating out. Choose from fried shrimp, boiled shrimp, fried oysters, and fresh fish, served with fries, onion rings, rice, hushpuppies, or fried okra. Outdoor seating means plenty of uninterrupted views of the intracoastal waters and evening sunsets. Overall a good mix of casual and tasty. Corpus Christi address, but located just over the bridge here on Mustang Island.

Continue on Padre Island Drive/TX 361 to the end of this route, **Padre Island National Seashore**. The park, dedicated in 1968 by Lady Bird Johnson, is the longest seashore in the National Parks

Great Texas Coastal Birding Trail

Amazingly, three-fourths of all American birds are represented in the diverse avian habitats of Texas. While some are year-round residents, others are migratory. Texas, the center of the Central Flyway between Canada and Central and South America, hosts an abundance of migratory birds in the spring and fall of each year. Though many migratory birds were hunted to near extinction by European settlers in the nineteenth century, laws are now on the books to protect them, as most of these birds are insect-eaters and play a crucial role in keeping regional bug populations in check. Now seen as both beautiful and useful, the birds fascinate enthusiasts who flock to the coast to observe the phenomenon of migration up close.

In October, birds share the Central Flyway with the monarch butterfly, Texas' State Insect. Monarchs are unique among butterflies in their ability to migrate instead of hibernate; those that make the trip through Texas tend to originate in the upper Midwest, funneling through the state on their way to Mexico. Plan your trip just right and you may be treated to the sight of millions

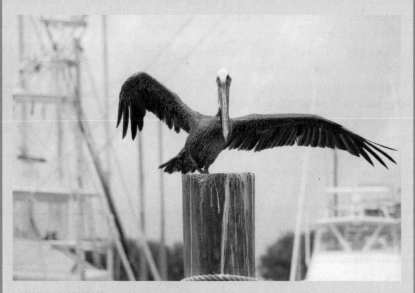

A PELICAN STRETCHES ITS WINGS

of orange and black butterflies flitting and floating along on the breezes, with miles to go, but taking the trip one day at a time.

Given that Texas is one of the top birding destinations in the world, it made sense to map out the best viewing locations to help birders know where to go. Texas Parks and Wildlife established the **Great Texas Coastal Bird-**

ing Trail to guide bird-watchers as well as protect these valuable natural resources.

The trail is divided into three regions. The **Upper Coast** covers the area from the Louisiana border to the region west of Houston. The **Central Coast** takes in Matagorda Bay, the area surrounding Victoria and Corpus Christi, and south past Kingsville. The **Lower Coast** picks up here, encompassing the south Texas towns of Brownsville, Harlingen, and McAllen, and South Padre Island. (The Rio Grande Valley area is also served by the World Birding Center, described in Chapter 6, page 121) The Great Texas Coastal Birding Trail exemplifies continuing efforts in the Lone Star State to highlight native wildlife, foliage, and ecosystems. These efforts have spurred economic development, preserved habitats, and created recreational opportunities. They provide an education now that one hopes will lead to conservation later.

Brown and white signs featuring a bird flying over the coast at sunset mark the Great Texas Coastal Birding Trail. Maps are available online at www.tpwd .texas.gov/huntwild/wildlife/wildlife-trails/coastal. As you migrate along the trail, you'll notice that some of the designated sites along it are in rural areas, and others are hidden in the bustle of cities; some are on the thoroughfares and others are on the backroads. In all cases, if you pause and really look, you'll see something special—a bird, a butterfly, perhaps a plant or insect— that you definitely wouldn't have noticed from the highway.

System and a magnet for nature lovers. What makes this stretch of beach special is the lack of development around it. There's nothing here but a visitor center with an observation deck, snack bar, and showers. Intact dunes, migratory birds, and miles of beach to comb make this park a must. There is not necessarily very much to do or see—wildlife, waves, and the sunsets over the Gulf excepted—and the folks here wouldn't have it any other way.

IN THE AREA

ANDY'S COUNTRY KITCHEN, 5802 S. Staples Street, Corpus Christi, 78413. Call 361-993-0251. South Texas country cooking, with homemade blueberry muffins, for breakfast and lunch. Website: www.andyskitchen .com. $–$$.

ARANSAS NATIONAL WILDLIFE REFUGE, 1 Wild Life Circle, Austwell, 77950. Located on FM 2040. Call 361-286-3559. Daily sunrise to sunset; visitor center daily 8:30 AM–4:30 PM. Website: www.fws.gov/refuge/aransas.

BAY EDUCATION CENTER, 121 Seabreeze Drive, Rockport, 78382. Call 361-729-2213. Free. Website: www.utmsi.utexas.edu.

THE BOILING POT, 201 S. Fulton Beach Road, Rockport, 78382. Call 361-729-6972. Cajun-spiced seafood boil dumped right onto butcher-paper-covered tables. $$.

CHERYL'S, 212 S. Fulton Beach Road, Rockport, 78382. Call 361-790-9626. Imaginative menu and a relaxed, yet refined, ambiance. Website: www.cherylsbythebay.com. $$–$$$.

COFFEE WAVES, 1007 TX 361, Port Aransas, 78373. Call 361-749-0825. Easy-going spot for sandwiches, ice cream, and, of course, coffee. Website: www.coffeewaves.com. $.

FISHERMAN'S WHARF, 900 Tarpon Street, Port Aransas, 78373 and 320 Navigation Circle, Rockport, 78382. Call 1-800-605-5448. Website: www.texaswhoopers.com.

FULTON MANSION, 317 Fulton Beach Road, Fulton, 78358. Call 361-729-0386. Fee. Website: www.visitfultonmansion.com.

GLOW, 1815 Broadway Street, Rockport, 78382. Call 361-727-2644. Cute as a button Gulf-to-table seafood restaurant. Website: www.glowrockport.com. $$.

GOLIAD STATE PARK & HISTORIC SITE, 108 Park Road 6, Goliad, 77963. Call 361-645-3405. Website: www.tpwd.texas.gov.

GOOSE ISLAND STATE PARK, 202 S. Palmetto Street, Rockport, 78382. Call 361-729-2858. Website: www.tpwd.texas.gov.

GREAT TEXAS COASTAL BIRDING TRAIL. Website: www.tpwd.texas.gov.

IRIE'S ISLAND FOOD, 503 N. Alister Street, Port Aransas, 78373. Call 844-200-7830. Closed Sundays and Mondays. Well-seasoned seafood tacos with homemade tortillas. Website: www.iriesislandfood.com. $–$$.

LATITUDE 28°02' RESTAURANT AND ART GALLERY, 105 N. Austin Street, Rockport, 78382. Call 361-727-9009. Art gallery paired with a bistro specializing in well-prepared seafood. Website: www.latituderockport.com. Reservations recommended. $$–$$$.

Festivals

The Rockport-Fulton area hosts Oyster Fest (www.fultontexas.org) in March; the **Rockport Art Festival** (www.rockport-fulton.org), a juried fine arts fair, on the first weekend in July; and Seafair (www.rockport-seafair.com), an October celebration, complete with a carnival, parade, and gumbo cook-off, that reels in over 20,000 visitors. In Port Aransas, **SandFest** (www.texassandfest.com) in April is the largest master sandcastle competition in the United States, with participants coming from all over the world to line the beach with amazingly detailed sand sculptures. Catch a big one at the Deep Sea Roundup (www.deepsearoundup.com) in July, one of the coast's largest and oldest fishing contests.

THE LIGHTHOUSE INN, 200 S. Fulton Beach Road, Rockport, 78382. Call 1866-790-8439. Hotel-style rooms and pool with lovely views. Website: www.lighthousetexas.com. $$–$$$.

LISABELLA'S BISTRO, 5009 TX 361, Port Aransas, 78373. Call 361-749-4222. Closed Sundays. Coastal cuisine in a refined casual dining room. Website: www.lisabellasbistro.com. $$–$$$.

MATAGORDA ISLAND STATE PARK, Call: 979-323-9553. Website: www.tpwd.texas.gov.

MOONDOG SEASIDE EATERY, 100 Casterline Drive, Fulton, 78358. Call 361-729-6200. Seaside spot for a fish taco washed down with a beer. $–$$.

MUSTANG ISLAND STATE PARK, 17047 TX 361, Port Aransas, 78373. Call 361-749-5246. Website: www.tpwd.texas.gov.

PADRE ISLAND NATIONAL SEASHORE, 20420 Park Road 22, Corpus Christi, 78418. Call 361-949-8068. Fee. Website: www.nps.gov.

PELICAN BAY RESORT, 4206 N. I-35 at Pelican Bay Lane, Rockport, 78382. Call 361-729-7177. Family-friendly memory-maker resort by the bay. Website: www.pelicanbayresort.com. $–$$.

PORT ARANSAS CHAMBER OF COMMERCE TOURIST & CONVENTION BUREAU, 403 W. Cotter, Port Aransas, 78373. Call 1-800-45-COAST or 361-749-5919. Website: www.portaransas.org.

Matagorda Island State Park

While the huge green island to the north marked **Matagorda Island State Park** might catch your eye if you're scanning the map, this state park and wildlife refuge is accessible only by private or chartered boat through its northernmost point of entry, Port O'Connor. While there are campsites for the adventurous, you'll need to bring all your own supplies, including drinking water, and there are no motorized vehicles allowed on the island. Your efforts will be rewarded with pristine nature, utter seclusion, and silence, except for the sounds of the wind and the waves. Visit www.tpwd .texas.gov for details.

ROCKPORT BIRDING AND KAYAK ADVENTURES, 202 N. Fulton Beach Road, Fulton, 78382. Call 877-892-4737. Website: www.whoopingcrane tours.com.

ROCKPORT CENTER FOR THE ARTS, 902 Navigation Circle, Rockport, 78382. Call 361-729-5519. Open Tuesday through Saturday 10 AM–4 PM, Sunday 1 PM–4 PM. Website: www.rockportartcenter.com.

ROCKPORT DAILY GRIND, 302 S. Austin Street, Rockport, 78382. Call 361-790-8745. Coffee and breakfast treats, served with enthusiasm. Website: www.rockportdailygrind.com. $.

ROCKPORT-FULTON CHAMBER OF COMMERCE, 319 Broadway, Rockport, 78382. Call 1-800-729-7661. Website: www.rockport-fulton.org.

SNOOPY'S PIER, 13313 S. Padre Island Drive, Corpus Christi, 78418. Call 361-949-8815. Cash only. Longtime seafood restaurant with views of the bay. Website: www.snoopyspier.com. $$.

TARPON INN, 200 E. Cotter Avenue, Port Aransas, 78373. Call 361-749-5555. Time-tested relaxed, coastal ambiance in this weathered nineteenth-century inn. Website: www.thetarponinn.com. $$–$$$.

TEXAS MARITIME MUSEUM, 1202 Navigation Circle, Rockport, 78382. Call 361-729-1271. Tuesday through Saturday 10 AM–4 PM, Sunday 1 PM–4 PM. Fee. Website: www.texasmaritimemuseum.org.

TEXAS STATE AQUARIUM, 2710 North Shoreline Boulevard, Corpus Christi, 78402. Call 361-881-1200. Fee. Website: www.texasstate aquarium.org.

VENETIAN HOT PLATE, 232 Beach Avenue, Port Aransas, 78373. Call 361-749-7617. Closed Sundays and Mondays. Authentic Italian cuisine in an intimate setting. Website: www.venetianhotplate.com. Reservations recommended. $$–$$$.

6

THE RIO GRANDE VALLEY

EDINBURG, McALLEN, ALAMO, THE WORLD BIRDING
CENTER, SANTA ANA NATIONAL WILDLIFE REFUGE,
WESLACO, LOS FRESNOS, SOUTH PADRE ISLAND

TOTAL DISTANCE: 80 miles from McAllen to South Padre Island

HIGHLIGHTS: Folks who grew up here say that you used to be able to smell the
sweet scent of orange blossoms wafting in on the breezes. Needless to say,
times have since changed. The Rio Grande Valley, or simply "the valley" to
most Texans, abuts the Rio Grande and neighboring Mexico, and has been
drawing people and wildlife for centuries. This route begins at the **Museum
of South Texas History**—winding its way through the region's many parks
and preserves that have been set aside for the millions of migratory birds
in the area, including the popular **Santa Ana National Wildlife Refuge** and
those designated as part of the network of the World Birding Center—and
ends on the shores of **South Padre Island**. You'll spend much of the route on
Business 83, considered a slow and scenic byway and not to be confused with
the longer and busier US 83, with detours south to sights along the border.

GETTING THERE: To reach the region from San Antonio, it is approximately 140
miles south to McAllen on I-37 and US 281. From Corpus Christi it is approximately 160 miles to Brownsville on US 77, passing through King Ranch (see
box on page 116) en route.

From McAllen, travel 12 miles north on US 281 to Edinburg or 8 miles east
on Business 83 to Alamo. Directly south of Alamo, approximately 7 miles on
FM 907, is the Santa Ana National Wildlife Refuge. Retrace your steps north
and continue along Business 83 to Weslaco, then hop on US 83, taking it east
to McAllen, then south to TX 100, and finally to Los Fresnos for a total of 37
miles. From Los Fresnos, continue along TX 100 23 miles to South Padre
Island. Details for touring the sites in the World Birding Center are found
on page 121.

INTERSECTIONS: Chapter 5

LEFT: ITEMS FOR SALE AT THE MARKETS ALONG THE BORDER

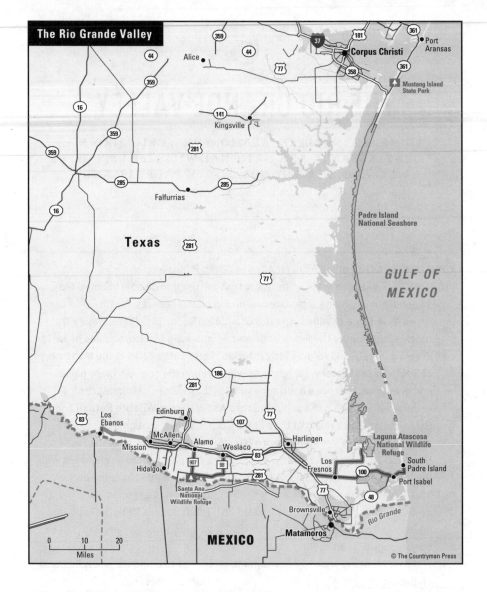

The Rio Grande Valley

Alice
Corpus Christi
Port Aransas
Mustang Island State Park
Kingsville
Falfurrias
Texas
Padre Island National Seashore
GULF OF MEXICO
Los Ebanos
Edinburg
McAllen
Mission
Alamo
Weslaco
Hidalgo
Santa Ana National Wildlife Refuge
Harlingen
Laguna Atascosa National Wildlife Refuge
Los Fresnos
South Padre Island
Port Isabel
Brownsville
Matamoros
Rio Grande
MEXICO

0   10   20
Miles

© The Countryman Press

The Rio Grande Valley is relatively small, approximately 40 miles by 140 miles. It is diverse, growing, fascinating, and vulnerable. I recommend taking at least five days to see it, more if you are a serious birder or nature lover. This corner of Texas has a culture all its own, so leave plenty of time for chatting with locals. You can either pick one place to stay for the duration of your tour, and make day trips, or move every other night or so just to experience a new perspective. I have laid out a basic route that includes the essentials of a sojourn into the valley, suggesting detours to help you customize or extend your trip, according to your schedule or interests.

The history of this region is complex, and most likely unknown to the first-time visitor, which is why the **Museum of South Texas History** in Edinburg is the perfect place to start any journey into the Rio Grande Valley. The museum began in 1967 as a county museum housed in the 1910 Hidalgo County jail. A massive $5.5 million expansion yielded the present building in 2003. An impressive space, the museum has plenty of catching details, from the grand lobby with its fantastic iron and stonework to the well-presented interpretative exhibits tracing regional history from prehistoric days to the twentieth century. With even more improvements and additions already in the works, this museum is on the rise, and set to join the ranks of other extremely well-done regional museums such as the Panhandle-Plains Historical Museum in Canyon (page 179). Walking through, visitors will grow to appreciate the borderland heritage of South Texas and northeastern Mexico, and the old and enduring relationship between the two countries. In fact, many of the exhibits overlook national boundaries, treating the region as a unified whole, highlighting its shared ecology, geology, and prehistory, and speaking to the shared cultural influences of both native peoples and European colonization. Be sure to spend some time in this pleasant and informative museum. You'll leave with a much better idea of the depth of this region's history, history not readily apparent on its twenty-first-century surface.

ENTRANCE TO THE MUSEUM OF SOUTH TEXAS HISTORY IN EDINBURG

The next stop is **McAllen**, 12 miles to the south. The land that McAllen currently occupies was once the Santa Anita Ranch, established in 1797 and known for raising cattle, sheep, goats, and horses. Eventually, through marriage and inheritance, it became the McAllen Ranch. To give you an idea of the size of the enterprise, consider the fact that McAllen, a city of over 100,000, now sits within the former boundaries of the McAllen Ranch. As with many other regions of Texas, the arrival of the railroad in the 1900s ushered in new patterns of commerce and transportation. Here the effect of the railroads was compounded by the establishment of large-scale irrigation, a combination that set the stage for changes that would alter the way of life in South Texas forever.

South Texas was put to work growing many of the nation's staples. Cotton, corn, alfalfa, citrus fruit, grapes, and figs grew fast in the hot Texas sun; by 1920, McAllen was booming. Over time, this transformation from a ranching to a farming economy heightened cultural tensions as Hispanics, who historically had exercised a certain amount of self-determination, were overpowered by largely Anglo business interests. To this day, the region continues to grow, stretching the limits of its ecology, cultures, and borders.

The busy, modern city of McAllen is home to one of the lodging options on this route, the Colonial-style **Renaissance Casa de Palmas Hotel**. While the hotel is part of the Marriott chain, like all of their Renaissance establishments it retains much of its original charm. Painted brick, exposed beams, and a lush courtyard with a gurgling fountain complete the Old South Texas ambiance. The Casa de Palmas is a good bet for visitors who like such practicalities as a convenient urban location paired with such amenities as a swimming pool.

The Patio on Guerra is pricey enough to be on the "special occasion" list, but the combination of food and ambiance really does make it a standout. Located in the 17th Street Arts and Entertainment District, the building features exposed brick, well-worn wooden doors, wrought ironwork, and a lovely cobbled patio dotted with palms. The restaurant is known for its succulent steaks, serving some of the best in the valley. Serious tamale lov-

King Ranch

King Ranch is legendary. One of the world's largest ranches, it spreads over 825,000 acres of pure South Texas between Corpus Christi and Brownsville. Founded by Captain Richard King and Mifflin Kenedy, former steamboat owners, in 1853 the ranch encompassed a rugged region known as the Wild Horse Desert, with the cool Santa Gertrudis Creek running through it. When Captain King started stocking the ranch with cattle, as the story goes, he traveled to the tiny northern Mexican town of Cruillas in the state of Tamaulipas to purchase herds that were advertised for sale. Upon his arrival, King was so taken with the townspeople, who were suffering a persistent drought and selling their livestock as a last resort, that he offered jobs on his ranch to anyone who might like to follow him back north to Texas. The promise of food, shelter, and work was too much to resist and much of the town's already skilled cattle workers took him up on the offer. They became known as **Los Kineños**—King's people. Expert horsemen and cattlemen, Los Kineños soon became legends themselves, a revered and essential part of the ranch's success.

Bzzz

South Texas is subtropical, which means that the sun is hot, the air is humid, and mosquitoes are abundant. Before venturing out into the region's various parks and nature preserves, be sure to bring along some extra sunscreen, insect repellent, and water. Despite the heat, consider wearing closed footwear (not sandals or flip-flops) and long pants for protection.

ers won't mind the effort it takes to seek out **Delia's**, a no-frills Rio Grande Valley institution, with various locations including a nondescript stretch of South 23rd Street. Folks say the ones with jalapeño and cream cheese are genius.

Another option is the **Alamo Inn** in the little town of **Alamo**, just 8 miles east of McAllen along Business 83/TX 347. Gracious owner Keith very much embodies the spirit of the valley and is someone any birder would love to meet. A native Australian who in the 1960s spent a year as an exchange student in a Progreso-area high school, Keith returned in the 1990s to marry his high school sweetheart and settle down in South Texas. A walking encyclopedia of birding knowledge and an all-around nice guy, Keith shares handy maps with guests, patiently gives directions, and is happy to make recommendations of nearby restaurants.

THE ALAMO INN IN ALAMO

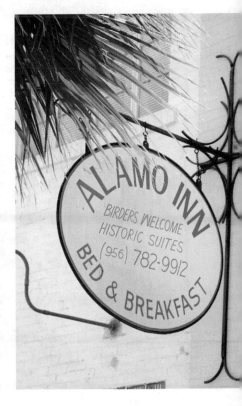

Originally built as an office building, the inn was remodeled as apartments in the 1940s; consequently all of the rooms are actually roomy suites, containing a bedroom (sometimes two), bathroom, and living room. The charming period tile work remains in the bath, and the high ceilings, wooden floors, and comfortable furniture create an open, airy feel. Breakfast is served each morning. Should you need birding books or insect repellent, Keith has them for sale in his bird-centric boutique. Alamo's small-town personality combined with the innkeeper's personal, yet unobtrusive manner make the Alamo Inn a terrific experience.

More Texas hospitality awaits at

El Dorado. This Mexican restaurant located just across the street from the Alamo Inn is a local stand-by, and buzzes with diners from breakfast through dinner. Comfortable and casual, El Dorado serves seafood fresh from the Gulf, Mexican staples such as enchiladas and slow-cooked *carne guisada* (beef tips in gravy), and American burgers, more than enough to keep the locals happy and coming back.

In many ways, the Rio Grande Valley is a region of contrasts. The loca-

La Virgen de san Juan de los Lagos

Leaving McAllen and heading southeast on Business 83 you will soon pass the town of **San Juan**, home of the shrine of **La Virgen de San Juan de los Lagos**. Built in 1954, the shrine quickly became a popular destination for tourists and pilgrims until the building was destroyed by a small wayward airplane in 1970. The crash turned out to be intentional; the person responsible radioed 20 minutes before the strike that all Methodist and Catholic churches in the region should be evacuated. These malicious motives weren't enough to destroy the statue of the virgin, which was pulled from the wreckage unscathed. Though the crash caused $1.5 million in damages, the community of San Juan rallied, raising funds to rebuild the shrine, which was rededicated in 1980. If you are passing by, it is worth pausing for a look—not only at the statue of the virgin and the grounds of the shrine, but at the diverse crowds that come in droves daily to pay their respects.

ON THE GROUNDS OF THE SHRINE OF LA VIRGEN DE SAN JUAN DE LOS LAGOS

ALOE VERA PLANT GROWING ON A BLUFF OVERLOOKING THE GULF OF MEXICO

tion of some of the nation's richest farmland, it is also home to the nation's poorest county. The region has an astounding amount of diversity, from ecosystems to cultures, but the diverse parts don't necessarily coexist in harmony. The natural environment in South Texas is as endangered as the species that rely on it for life. In Texas, 97 percent of the land is privately owned, and so its fate is directly linked to the ethics and interests of its owners. With so much development in the region, economic interests tend to be put before any other. But, by that very token, tourism is becoming a larger part of the South Texas economy, and **ecotourism** and **birding** top the list of sights to see.

More and more, people are coming to South Texas to see the birds. There are 11 separate and distinct biotic communities in the Lower Rio Grande Valley. From temperate to tropical, desert to forest, saltwater to freshwater, the variety of landscape and the wildlife it supports is truly remarkable. Whether birds are migrating between North and South America or wintering in Texas, you can count on seeing hundreds of species right here in the valley. Migratory travel tends to be from mid-March to May and again from September to December, though there is an enormous variety on view all year long, including rare species unlikely to be seen elsewhere.

While McAllen and its environs do constitute a metropolitan area, as far as the birds are concerned it's just a place to fly over on their way to a respite.

Mama's Cookin'

While you'd think that great Mexican food would be easy to find on the border, the fact is, pickings are a bit slim. Everywhere I went, I asked folks where their favorite place to eat was, and the answers fell into one of two categories, either "my mother's house" or "my grandmother's house." As this tight-knit, family-centered culture knows, the best meals in the world are almost always prepared at home.

Several wildlife refuges are within easy reach of the city, and birders flock here as frequently as the birds themselves.

A mini-backroads route on its own, the journey to the **World Birding Center** is fascinating for the serious bird-watcher. From McAllen, it is about 8 miles west on US 83 to Mission and an additional 48 miles to Roma. Within

WATERFOWL ENJOYING A PERCH
BESIDE A *RESACAS*

more immediate proximity to McAllen, it is 13 miles north on US 281 to Edinburg or 9 miles south on TX 336. Heading east, it is 18 miles to Weslaco and an additional 20 miles to Harlingen, all driven on US 83. You can then continue on US 83/US 77 27 miles south to Brownsville and then an additional 28 miles east along the Brownsville/Port Isabel Highway before ending on South Padre Island. The sites included in the World Birding Center are organized here from west to east:

Roma Bluffs is a small preserve in Roma that sits on what was, in the days when the Rio Grande was allowed to run its natural course, a steamboat port. Wooded and right beside the river, this unique habitat is home to birds so specialized they are not seen even a few miles farther downstream.

The **Edinburg Scenic Wetlands** is located in the city of Edinburg, just north of McAllen, and has pathways and observation platforms spread out over 40 acres. Back in McAllen, the

Quinta Mazatlan ("country estate," in Spanish) is a lovely 1930s Spanish Revival adobe hacienda built in what was then a rapidly developing McAllen. Today the facility, used as an events and conference center, is surrounded by the city, but its grounds are a study in conservation. Lush native foliage and more formal gardens are an oasis for birds and visitors, both of whom come seeking peace and quiet. One visit and you'll want to go home and start planting.

The **Estero Llano Grande State Park** is made up of 200 acres of wetlands

The World Birding Center

The **World Birding Center** is a network of parks and preserves in the Rio Grande Valley dedicated entirely to birding and the preservation of the native habitat of South Texas. Illustrating the truism that "birds of a feather flock together," the center represents the extraordinary vision, cooperation, and shared interests of various valley organizations that have pooled resources and expertise to give visitors the best opportunity to see the Rio Grande Valley for the ecological treasure that it is.

A series of nine sites, strung along 120 miles of the Rio Grande from Roma to South Padre, the center is an intense concentration of birding opportunities. It's a paradise for birders and hikers, nature lovers, and photographers alike who also enjoy the parks and preserves year-round. All visitors can appreciate the beauty of the native South Texas landscape, especially after driving through the growing sprawl of the McAllen/Harlingen/Brownsville metro area. The center ultimately hopes to preserve 10,000 acres of native habitat, with paths and bird-watching stations for the public.

The headquarters of the center is the **Bentsen–Rio Grande Valley State Park** in Mission. What makes this spot particularly distinctive are its many "valley specialties," birds so unique they are found only in the park, and "Mexican vagrants," birds that occasionally cross over from northern Mexico to visit the region. It is no accident that this area along the Rio Grande is so attractive to birds. The river has a natural cycle of trickling and flooding, and this ebb and flow of water has made the earth on its banks very rich and fertile, able to support the cedar elm, sugar hackberry, Rio Grande ash, Texas ebony, and anaqua trees the birds favor. In the 1950s, Falcon Dam was constructed across the Rio Grande, restricting and controlling its flow for purposes of irrigation, water storage, and flood management. What was good for people wasn't especially good for the ecosystem, and the birds' habitat suffered. These days, the center, like the Santa Ana National Wildlife Refuge (page 122), simulates the original conditions of the river, re-creating the natural habitat of the birds, who can't resist returning.

in Weslaco. Abundant water in late summer makes this park a magnet for migrating waterfowl.

In Hidalgo, the **Old Hidalgo Pumphouse**, a leftover reminder of the area's agricultural history, is now a museum. The museum's grounds, along with the neighboring 600 acres of US Fish and Wildlife land, are home to dozens of kinds of birds, especially hummingbirds. The land is being restored, with native grasses and trees, in the hopes that the preserve's popularity will grow.

The **Harlingen Arroyo Colorado** has peaceful wooded paths amid a tangle of highways in Harlingen.

The **Resaca de la Palma State Park** is the largest piece of land in the World Birding Center. This park, located in Brownsville, features the region's characteristic *resacas*, the shallow ponds that remain when a swollen river retreats, and the wildlife they support.

Finally, the **South Padre Island Birding and Nature Center** is a wonderful spot of natural land on an island bursting at the seams with development.

Approximately 7 miles directly south of Alamo, on FM 907, is the **Santa Ana National Wildlife Refuge**, considered one of the top 10 birding destinations in the country. The 2,000-acre refuge runs along the banks of the Rio Grande in an area where the subtropics, Gulf Coast, Great Plains, and Chihuahuan desert merge. Surrounded by cities and fields, this pocket of subtropical forest is an oasis for 400 different types of birds, not to mention half the nation's butterfly species. When the Rio Grande flowed in its natural state, flooding across the delta formed distinctive *resacas,* which supported both plants and animals. Dams have altered this pattern, threatening the river ecosystem, but the Santa Ana Wildlife Refuge has taken steps to recreate the normal flooding cycle of the river to sustain the region's native foliage, trees, birds, animals, and insects.

Visiting Santa Ana is not only a chance to spot birds and other wildlife,

Cabezas de vaca, a tasty South Texan tradition

Vera's Backyard BBQ is one of the last—perhaps the last—of a breed of endangered eateries. The name is a bit misleading since most readers will think of ribs, brisket, and sauces when they think barbecue and while Vera's adds these to their menu on occasion, their specialty is *cabezas de vaca*, traditional South Texas barbacoa, cow's heads slow-cooked in underground mesquite-fired pits. Obviously, this practice is against current health code, but Vera's has been grandfathered in for years. Open since 1955, Vera's barbacoa plate, served with flour tortillas and salsa, is on the bucket list of many barbecue aficionados.

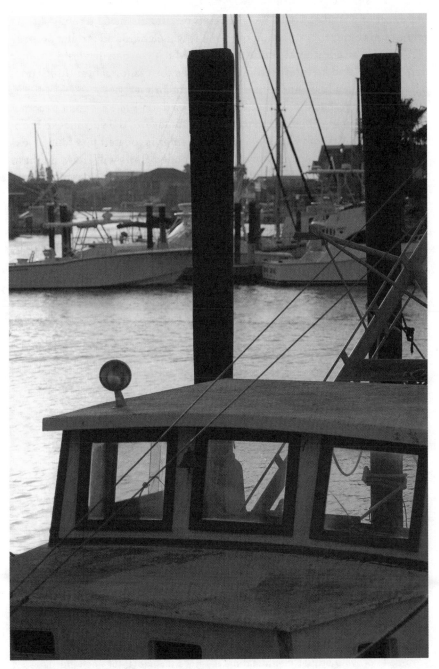

BOATS DOCKED NEAR SOUTH PADRE ISLAND AT SUNSET

but to see the land of South Texas as nature intended it. The refuge has 12 miles of hiking trails, a portion of which is wheelchair and stroller accessible. There is an additional 7-mile tour road, which you can drive at your own convenience, and an interpretive tram leaves the visitor center three times a day to make an hour-and-a-half circuit of the property.

Continue southeast on US 281, turning north on FM 88, which becomes S. Texas Boulevard. Head north to S. Texas Boulevard, the entrance to **Frontera Audubon Preserve** in **Weslaco**. The center is located just four blocks south of downtown, but, as a stroll on its wooded trails will show, might as well be miles away. The preserve contains many citrus trees, reminders of its former role as an orchard. Several man-made waterways and plenty of native vegetation draw wildlife like a magnet. The paths are flat, easy to navigate, and while they aren't entirely paved, in dry weather the dirt is packed hard enough to make stroller and wheelchair use a possibility. The center has undergone many changes over the years, with more to come. As

The Border

The Texas-Mexico border has a culture all its own. Far from displaying the rich cultural heritage of Mexico's interior, the border towns can seem crass markets desperate for dollar-spenders from north of the border. Factories just over the border, *maquiladoras*, supply US companies with products at what many consider great environmental and social cost. Many Americans, harboring no great curiosity about Mexican culture, come to border towns to buy trinkets, name-brand knockoffs, and cheap medications, venturing just a few hundred feet into the country before returning stateside.

Should you decide to make a trip into Mexico, the most manageable town in the region is Progreso. Be prepared for a dramatic culture shift; while south Texas may not be prosperous, the Mexican side of the Rio Grande is even less so. While haggling over prices might be the way business is transacted here, be sure to be respectful. Be especially mindful of your surroundings and personal safety, and careful to abide by the country's laws. As with any culture, a smile goes a long way.

You can drive to the border, park your car in an unsecured though relatively safe lot for a few dollars and simply walk across. Most car insurers' policies do not extend into Mexico, so confirm the extent of your policy. It will cost you 25 cents to walk the bridge to Mexico and 30 cents to walk back, and you will need to provide proper identification, ideally a passport, for each individual crossing.

As economic, political, and social tensions fluctuate, please refer to the U.S. State Department's most recent travel alerts and warnings at www.travel.state.gov before planning any sojourns to Mexico.

Colonias

Though McAllen is a modern city, it is bordered, as are most of the cities and towns in South Texas, by *colonias*. These unregulated settlements are the homes of immigrants from both Mexico and Central America, both legal and illegal, who are employed as agricultural workers but are unable to pay for proper housing in the United States. In Texas many of the *colonias* are tiny plots of former farmland that cotton farmers sold to workers for very little money after the cotton market collapsed in the 1960s. While the land was unregulated with minimum building requirements, a plus for workers looking to build their own modest homes, there were also little or no public utilities. Though promises were made about future services, the utilities rarely followed; many have lived in these *colonias* without running water or sewers for decades. Not surprisingly, these conditions have been the breeding ground for illness; dysentery, hepatitis, tuberculosis, and skin rashes can be common. This complex problem serves to illustrate the political and social complexities of life on a border, especially a border between two countries at such different stages of development.

you approach the center, you'll find an older home gracing the front of the property (drive around to the left to find parking in the back). An outstanding example of local architecture and rife with charm and detail, the home had fallen into disrepair by the time it was donated to the center. The dream is to see this gem restored and used for social functions and events. Also in Weslaco, the **Valley Nature Center** is a modest community-center-style building tucked into a shaded public park. A good resource for nature lovers, the center can offer helpful suggestions and tips.

If you are looking for a meal, **The Smoking Oak** is located just a few blocks from US 83, and worth the several minute detour. The backstory is that South Texas native Mario Dominguez Jr. went off to college and developed a taste for Central Texas barbecue. Returning to the Rio Grande Valley, he built a brick pit, tinkered with recipes, found the perfect oak to burn, and his persistence paid off. Opened in 2015, the Smoking Oak has already kudos for its outstanding 'cue and it a great addition to South Texas' offerings.

From Weslaco, take the larger US 83 20 miles east to Harlingen, and follow US 83/US 77 south 18 miles to TX 100 and cruise into the small town of **Los Fresnos**. Here you'll find the **Inn at Chachalaca Bend**, one of the most relaxing and luxurious places to stay in the valley. The place is so lovely they are booked every weekend for weddings and private functions every weekend a year in advance. However, there is usually room at the inn Monday through Thursdays, making it the perfect midweek respite. The gated prop-

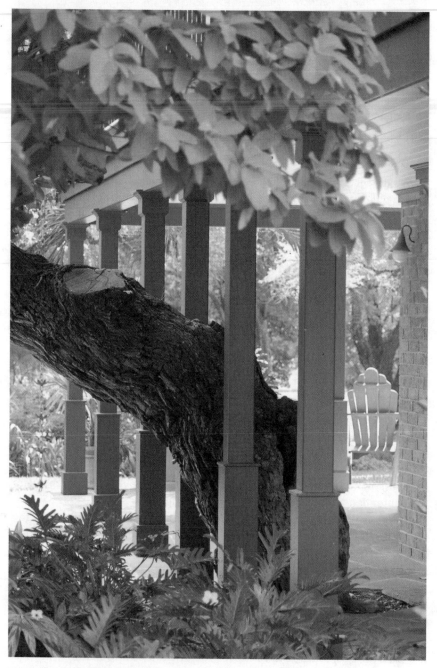

LUSH GROUNDS OF THE INN AT CHACHALACA BEND

erty is on the edge of Los Fresnos and thick with native foliage and spectacular trees teeming with buzzing, cawing, and chirping wildlife. Stone paths wind their way throughout and the porches, balconies, and waterside seating are inviting. Each room has a king-size bed, Jacuzzi, and outdoor access for relaxing. The free-standing Lodge offers plenty of room to spread out, with a great room, fireplace, and loft bedroom. Complimentary refreshments are available in the comfortable common room throughout the day, and the morning buffet breakfast of fresh fruit, eggs, and pancakes is superb. Once you arrive at the Inn at Chachalaca Bend, you may not want to leave. It isn't a place to spend the night so much as it is a retreat, and just the sort for travelers who like solitude.

Many people find Los Fresnos to be a good jumping-off point into either the **Laguna Atascosa National Wildlife Refuge** or **South Padre Island**, as it is equidistant to both. The Laguna Atascosa National Wildlife Refuge is the largest surviving swatch of natural habitat in the Rio Grande Valley. The 45,000-acre refuge is located on the mainland, protected from the Gulf of Mexico by South Padre Island. The refuge has many *resacas* that become low-level ponds and tidal mud flats (*atascosa* means "muddy" in Spanish). In addition to hundreds of species of birds, the refuge is also home to the endangered ocelot and other mammals, and native brush has been planted in former agricultural fields in an attempt to regain habitat for this wildlife. To get there from Los Fresnos, take Paredes Line Road north, then east on San Jose Ranch Road to the refuge.

Going south, South Padre Island is a breezy half-hour drive from Los Fresnos, just 23 miles along TX 100. South Padre is Texas' vacation hot spot. From "spring breaks" to summer vacations, thousands upon thousands of tourists descend on South Padre for sun, sand, and surf. TX 100 takes you from Port Isabel, on the mainland, to the southern tip of South Padre, where it is a short drive north along Padre Drive to the start of the **Laguna Madre Nature Trail**, the southern anchor of the World Birding Center. Located beside the convention center and whaling wall no. 53, the Laguna Madre Nature trail is the antidote to the high-rise condos, hotels, and restaurants that weigh down the island. The 1,500-foot boardwalk allows visitors to gingerly cross 4 acres of wetlands for an up-close look at the many birds, butterflies, and other wildlife that live in the natural dunes of the Laguna Madre.

Since South Padre Island is the first strip of land birds encounter on their migration north across the Gulf, many stop to rest and refuel, gracing the region with their presence. The island's diverse habitat of dunes, salt marshes, and intertidal flats attracts a huge variety. Spring rains attract warblers, orioles, and thrushes to the thick native foliage, and the wetlands host the endangered brown pelican and peregrine falcon. For photographers, it's ideal.

While you may have had your eye in the sky looking for birds, when you're this close to the Gulf, it's a great time to take a look in the water. On South Padre, there are several organizations dedicated to the survival of marine creatures. **Sea Turtle, Inc.,** began in 1977, when the "Turtle Lady of South Padre Island," the spirited Ila Loetscher, championed the cause of the at-risk Kemp's Ridley sea turtle. Together with the US Fish and Wildlife Service, Sea Turtle scouts local beaches for nests; they maintain a facility for rescued and recovering turtles. The public is welcome to attend the "Meet the Turtles" demonstrations, led by volunteers, which focus on education, conservation, and interesting turtle tips and facts. Sea Turtle, Inc., is a home-grown, seaside learning experience with a big heart. Another local organization with an admirable mission is the **South Padre Island Dolphin Research and Sea Life Nature Center**. Visitors can spend some time in the low-tech, high-interest Sea Life Nature Center checking out all the photos and display about the different dolphins the center has been researching. Get out on the water with **Breakaway Cruises** and see the dolphins up close in their natural habitat of the Gulf.

Pay a visit to the spectacular Rio Grande Valley and make an investment in the future of Texas. Spend some time—and money—supporting some of the great organizations that are contributing to the survival of this complex and fragile region and working to preserve it for generations to come.

IN THE AREA

ALAMO CHAMBER OF COMMERCE, 803 Main Street, Alamo, 78516. Call 956-787-2117. Website: www.alamochamber.com.

ALAMO INN, 801-B Main Street, Alamo, 78516. Call 956-782-9912. Clean and comfortable rooms and a feeling of camaraderie among the birders who flock here. Website: www.alamoinnbnb.com. $.

BENTSEN–RIO GRANDE VALLEY STATE PARK, 2800 S. Bentsen Palm Drive (FM 2062), Mission, 78572. Located several miles southwest of Mission, at the end of FM 2062, and can be reached from several marked exits off Loop 373 and/or US 83. Fee. Call 956-584-9156. Website: www.tpwd.texas.gov or www.theworldbirdingcenter.com.

BREAKAWAY CRUISES, 33384 State Park Road 100, South Padre Island, 78597. Call 956-761-2212. Fee. Website: www.breakawaycruises.com.

DELIA'S, 4800 S. 23rd Street, McAllen, 78503. Call 956-630-3502. Delicious handmade tamales at various locations throughout the Rio Grande Valley. Website: www.deliastamales.com. $.

EL DORADO, 755 Main Street, Alamo, 78516. Call 956-787-8822. Large portions of Tex-Mex classics served behind an unassuming storefront. $$.

FRONTERA AUDUBON PRESERVE, 1101 S. Texas Boulevard, Weslaco, 78596. Call 956-968-3275. Fee. Website: www.fronteraaudubon.org.

INN AT CHACHALACA BEND, 36298 Chachalaca Bend Drive, Los Fresnos, 78566. Call 956-233-1180. Gated inn with luxurious rooms and lush surroundings. Website: www.chachalaca.com. $$$–$$$$.

KING RANCH VISITOR CENTER, 2205 TX 141 W., Kingsville, 78364. Call 361-592-8055. Website: www.king-ranch.com.

LAGUNA ATASCOSA NATIONAL WILDLIFE REFUGE, 22688 Buena Vista Boulevard, Los Fresnos, 78566. Call 956-748-3607. Fee. Website: www.fws .gov/refuges.

LAGUNA MADRE NATURE TRAIL, 7355 Padre Boulevard, South Padre Island, 78597. Call 956-761-3000. Website: www.sopadre.com.

McALLEN CHAMBER OF COMMERCE, 1200 Ash Avenue, McAllen, 78501. Call 956-682-2871. Website: www.mcallenchamber.com.

MUSEUM OF SOUTH TEXAS HISTORY, 200 North Closner Boulevard, Edinburg, 78541. Call 956-383-6911. Closed Mondays. Fee. Website: www .mosthistory.org.

THE PATIO ON GUERRA, 116 S. 17th Street, McAllen, 78501. Call 956-661-9100. Closed Sundays. Atmospheric restaurant specializing in seafood and steaks; a local favorite for a special night out. Website: www.patioon guerra.com. $$$.

Festivals

Experience South Texas hospitality by visiting during a festival. Mission kicks off the festivities in January with the **Texas Citrus Fiesta** (www. texascitrusfiesta.org), followed in March by the wildly popular **Border-Fest** (www.hidalgoborderfest.com) in Hidalgo. **The Texas Tropics Nature Festival** (www.mcallen.org) in April and the Fourth of July Fajita Cookoff in July are both in McAllen. And Harlingen hosts the **Rio Grande Valley Birding Festival** (www.rgvbf.org) in November.

QUINTA MAZATLAN, 600 Sunset Avenue, McAllen, 78503. Call 956-681-3370. Closed Sundays and Mondays. Fee. Website: www.quintamazatlan.com.

RENAISSANCE CASA DE PALMAS HOTEL, 101 N. Main Street, McAllen, 78501. Call 956-631-1101. Historic property with restful rooms and lush landscaping. Website: www.renaissancehotels.com. $–$$.

SANTA ANA NATIONAL WILDLIFE REFUGE, 3325 Green Jay Road, Alamo, 78516. Call 956-784-7500. Fee. Website: www.fws.gov/refuges.

SEA TURTLE, INC., 6617 Padre Boulevard, South Padre Island, 78597. Call 956-761-4511. Open Tuesday through Sunday, 10 AM–4 PM. Fee. Website: www.seaturtleinc.org.

THE SMOKING OAK, 544 Hidalgo St, Mercedes, 78570. Call 956-565-2246. This newcomer has earned praise as one of the spots to sample barbecue in the Rio Grande Valley. Website: www.thesmokingoak.com. $$.

Los Ebanos Ferry

In the Rio Grande, 18 miles northwest of Mission is the little border town of **Los Ebanos**, the site of the last international ferry crossing on the border. This fact is made all the more remarkable by the ferry's source of power: several men pulling a rope. This little boat hauls people, cars, and any number of other items across this shallow 25-foot span of the Rio Grande each day as they've done without fail for years. There's been talk of building a bridge, but no one seems in a rush to get it done. After all, this hands-on method has worked for over two generations with enormous efficiency, punctuality, and friendliness. Due to its size, the ferry can only transport several dozen cars a day, and it stops running in bad weather. On a good day, however, the crossing takes about 8 minutes, and the charge is a reasonable 50 cents per person or $2.50 per automobile. A quick, easy, and low-cost—not to mention lowtech—alternative to driving the half hour to the nearest bridge in nearby Rio Grande City.

There isn't much to the town of Los Ebanos except a little collection of homes and a border patrol outpost hugging the river. On the Mexican side of the crossing you'll be greeted by an open field, a taxi willing to take you the mile and a half south to Diaz Ordaz, and a shaved ice truck. While there's nothing scenic about it, Los Ebanos serves to illustrate that while the Rio Grande may be an international border to some, to others it is still just the local river that needs crossing.

SOUTH PADRE ISLAND CHAMBER OF COMMERCE, 600 Padre Boulevard, #B, South Padre Island, 78597. Call 956-761-4412. Website: www.spichamber.com.

SOUTH PADRE ISLAND DOLPHIN RESEARCH AND SEA LIFE NATURE CENTER, Lighthouse Square, 110 N. Garcia, Port Isabel, 78578. Call 956-299-1957. Fee. Website: www.spinaturecenter.com.

VALLEY NATURE CENTER, 301 S. Border Avenue, Weslaco, 78596. Call 956-969-2475. Closed Mondays. Fee. Website: www.valleynaturecenter.org.

VERA'S BACKYARD BBQ, 2404 Southmost Road, Brownsville, 78521. Call 956-546-4159. Open Friday through Sunday, early morning through 2 PM. Traditional South Texas barbacoa, cow's heads slow-cooked in mesquite-fired pits. $–$$.

WORLD BIRDING CENTER. Website: www.theworldbirdingcenter.com.

7

GALVESTON ISLAND

TOTAL DISTANCE: Galveston Island is 27 miles long and less than 3 miles wide at its widest point. The city of Galveston anchors the northern end of the island. This entire chapter is devoted to the island, much of it within the city itself.

HIGHLIGHTS: From the historic old business district, the **Strand**, to the architectural charm of the lovely homes on the tree-lined blocks of the **East End**, to the sun and sand along the **Seawall**, Galveston offers multilayered insights into Texas history. Nature lovers will enjoy a trip to **Moody Gardens**, and bird-watchers will relish the opportunities to comb the beach, particularly at **Galveston Island State Park**.

GETTING THERE: From Houston, take I-45 50 miles south to Galveston.

Graceful and gritty, storied and stately, Galveston Island is a backroad to another time. Its own history is as old as any in Texas. One of the sandy barrier islands strung across the length of Texas, Galveston first appears in the historical record as home to the Karankawa Indians. It is thought to be the site of the 1528 shipwreck of explorer Alvar Núñez Cabeza de Vaca, the first European to set foot on Texas soil. In 1785, José de Evia, an explorer mapping the Texas coast, named these waters Galveston Bay, after Bernardo de Gálvez, the viceroy of Mexico. The name was soon shortened to Galveston and applied to the island. The first European inhabitants began living here in 1816 when Louis Michel Aury, an opportunistic privateer, established a port and began running ships to Mexico to aid in the Mexican Revolution. In 1817, Jean Lafitte grabbed control of the island and used it for smuggling and pirate activities until 1820, when the United States government ran him off the island.

LEFT: FISHING FROM A ROCK JETTY

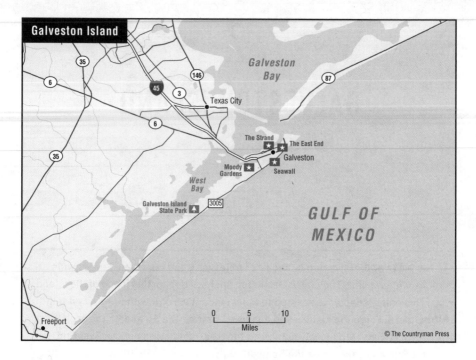

Under the Texas flag, Galveston got organized. A group of investors purchased over 4,500 acres of harborside land, laid out a grid, and started building a city. Its port grew by leaps and bounds, shipping cotton, monitoring oceangoing traffic and the steamers moving along the coast, and welcoming immigrants. A new bridge brought the railroad, linking the island to the mainland, to Houston and East Texas.

Then came the Civil War, spelling disaster for Galveston, as for much of the south. The city struggled under Union troops' occupation. After the war, beginning in 1867, an outbreak of yellow fever killed 20 people a day for years. Despite this rough spell, Galveston quickly regained its prominence. The largest city in Texas by 1870, it would be the first to have electricity, telephones, newspapers, and even baseball games. The Galveston you see today, with its layered and intricate architecture, arts, and cultural organizations, is very much a legacy of this period. At the twilight of the nineteenth century, genteel Galveston was thriving, paving the way to the twentieth century. Then disaster struck. In 1900, the Great Storm (see box on page 136) hit Galveston head-on, taking thousands of lives and crippling its infrastructure.

No matter how wounded the city was, it still had the waterfront; in just a few years, Galveston had remade itself as a seaside resort. Grand hotels such as the Galvez (see page 137) opened; the Balinese Room (see box on page 144) and numerous other nightclubs kept visitors and locals entertained through the 1950s. Big names in showbiz—Frank Sinatra, Bob Hope, Jack Benny—all came to perform. Gambling was commonplace: roulette, blackjack, craps tables, and slot machines fed the frenzy. In addition, Galveston became known for drinking, carousing, and prostitution. While this debauchery was frowned on by some, it was embraced by others who saw the rogue city as "the free state of Galveston." Illegality was rampant until 1957, when Attorney General Will Wilson rode in with a pack of Texas Rangers to restore the city's dignity.

THE BEACH BESIDE THE SEAWALL

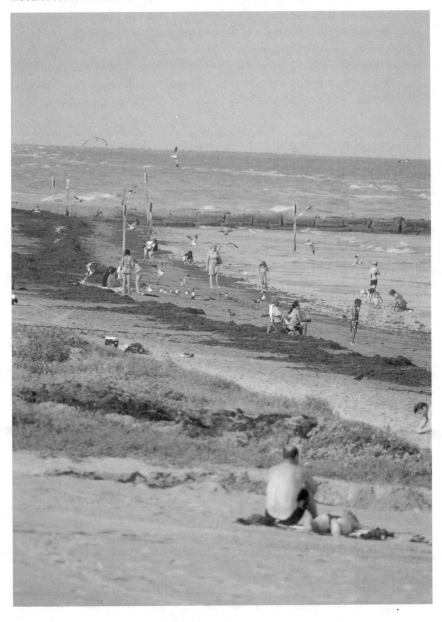

The Great Storm

On September 8, 1900, a hurricane roared into Galveston, killing 6,000 people within the city limits and between 4,000 and 6,000 others nearby. Winds of 135 miles an hour, rain, and sea surges meant flooding and the near destruction of the city. The storm is often referred to as the Galveston Hurricane of 1900 or the Great Galveston Hurricane, but locals call it simply the Great Storm or the 1900 Storm.

In many ways the disaster was unavoidable, but it was not without warning. Throughout the 1800s, the citizens of Galveston watched nearby towns succumb to powerful and unpredictable hurricanes. Though there was talk of building a seawall to protect the island, Galveston had handily survived all previous storms; people believed their luck would continue into the future. Instead of building a seawall, the city went right on building, expanding the municipality, increasing its vulnerability.

While the United States Weather Bureau had reports of hurricane conditions in the Gulf, in those days their skill at predicting a storm's path was rudimentary, as was their ability to communicate with residents. In the hours preceding the storm, though a hurricane warning had been issued, the weather was still pleasant and residents didn't grasp its urgency.

Conditions quickly changed. Soon rising winds and water cut off all roads, bridges, evacuation routes, and telegraph communication; as darkness fell, the city began to crumble. When the 15-foot storm surge washed over the city, it mowed down over 3,600 homes; those that survived often have a plaque reading "1900 Storm" on display. Daybreak revealed cloudless skies and mass devastation.

Without telegraph service, residents sent several messengers to the mainland to get help and waited for a ship to come. It took several days for aid to arrive. Rescues were attempted, the dead moved, and damage assessed. In the final count, it was found that 20 percent of the island's population had lost their lives. The Great Storm remains the deadliest natural disaster in American history.

In order to prevent such devastation in the future, Galveston reconsidered the idea of a seawall; by 1902 construction was under way. The 17-foot-tall, 7-mile-long Seawall was completed 8 years later. It protects the city to this day.

Coupled with the Seawall, there were efforts to raise the city itself above the danger of the sea. Workers moved massive amounts of sand to the island, placing it underneath buildings and filling in low-lying areas. Over time, thousands of buildings were elevated in this manner, a feat so remarkable that the entire project has been dubbed a National Historic Civil Engineering Landmark by the American Society of Civil Engineers.

In 2008, Hurricane Ike—classified as a high Category 2 hurricane—roared ashore following much the same route as the Great Storm and cresting the seawall. While the compromised wall provided some protection, many homes and businesses and much of the city's infrastructure were damaged or destroyed. Strongly worded evacuation warnings encouraged residents to leave the island in advance of the storm, minimizing injury and loss of life. When all was said and done, while Ike dealt the island a blow, thanks to lessons learned in the Great Storm it wasn't fatal.

The future fate of Galveston Island, though all possible precautions have been taken, is ultimately Mother Nature's decision.

These days, Galveston is still a popular destination. Visitors come to stroll its three distinct neighborhoods—the Seawall, the Strand, and the East End—and the leafy blocks in between. Each of Galveston's districts offers great places to spend the night; each is atmospheric with plenty of individual detail, each a little piece of the city's history.

Wyndham Historic Hotels has done a lovely job with three hotels that are consistently recommended by fellow travelers. The **Hotel Galvez**, which opened in 1911, has always been known as the Queen of the Gulf for its seaside location.

SCULPTURE ON PIER 21

The hotel is very elegant and makes quite a first impression. A grand entrance with rich fabrics, lush Victorian-era elements, and striking architectural detail make the hotel a standout. By modern standards, the rooms may seem small, but they are cozy and charming, and there are plenty of common spaces in which to stretch out and relax. The pool is private, nestled in below sidewalk level and surrounded by trees and foliage; it's particularly enjoyable in the evening, when the entire area is softly lit and the warm Gulf breezes blow by.

In the historic Strand District, and therefore not within walking distance to the ocean, the **Tremont House** is another renovated beauty. Once a warehouse, this hotel has an urban, European feel, with a four-story atrium lobby complete with airy birdcage-style elevators, and full-grown palm trees. Period furnish-

RIDING A SURREY BIKE ALONG THE SEAWALL

ings, high ceilings, wood floors, and marble bathrooms give the rooms an understated elegance; details like towel warmers provide luxury, while the rooftop deck is all fun.

Nearby, the **Harbor House** is altogether different. Located in another renovated warehouse at Pier 21, behind the Strand and along Galveston Bay, the Harbor House is more casual and more nautical in its details. The rooms feel large, with tall ceilings and windows, exposed beams, and plenty of light. The decor and bathrooms are updated, and the price includes a morning coffee bar and fresh-baked locally made muffins. Regardless of which Wyndham you stay in, you are welcome to use the pool at the Galvez free of charge. Each of these hotels has different policies regarding parking and breakfast options, so be sure to inquire when you make your reservations.

For a more personal stay, **The Lasker Inn Bed & Breakfast** offers is a two-storied galleried Greek revival gem and warm hospitality in the heart of the historic district. After the Great Storm of 1900, the house served as a home for homeless children, a role it filled for decades. The current owners have meticulously renovated the inn and the results are lovely. Some rooms have balconies and others clawfoot tubs, but all have distinguished period furnishings and as strong sense of the breezy elegance of the home's era. Exquisite breakfasts; guests have fallen in love with biscuits and dewberry jelly.

Eating out is a pleasure in Galveston; if you visit the places listed below, you are sure to leave happy.

The Strand is home to a variety of eateries, from cafés to sandwich shops to date-night restaurants. Many diners just enjoy a leisurely walk up and down, checking out the options. One of the favorites is the **Saltwater Grill**, which features imaginative cuisine, served in an upscale yet casual setting on Post Office Street. The menu has steaks, salads, and seafood, some with an Asian flair; diners rave about the almond-coconut-entrusted shrimp served with peanut sauce. From grilled snapper to gumbo loaded with shrimp, the food is all excellent—a little pricey—and service is consistently top-notch. Folks like to go to **Rudy and Paco** for birthdays, anniversaries, and special occasions. The mixture of romantic, old world ambiance, and the flavors of Latin American cuisine make events feel extra festive. The baked Gulf red snapper with sautéed lump crab meat, pico de gallo, and avocado slices is a favorite. Be sure to leave room for one of their decadent desserts. Reservations recommended and no shorts allowed. Nearby, **The Gumbo Bar** proves that New Orleans–style seafood fits right in all along the Gulf Coast. The soft shell crab po'boys have a Tabasco-laced mayo that gives 'em a little kick, and the Mumbo Gumbo includes shrimp, crab, oyster, chicken, sausage, and, in case you forgot you are in Texas, prime rib. The restaurant has a buzzing, bistro vibe, with a smallish, cozy dining room and shaded seating on the sidewalk patio.

If you are looking for a treat, stop by **La King's Confectionery** for some homemade ice cream, peanut brittle, or fudge. La King's dates back to the 1920s; they've been doing business on the Strand since the 1970s. Another easy choice is **Star Drug Store**. The store traces its roots back to 1886, but the current building you see, a brick replica of the original wooden structure, was built in 1909. Though the store has changed hands several times since, the milkshakes still taste just the way they should. Stop in at lunchtime for the nice selection of burgers, sandwiches, and salads served at the horseshoe-shaped soda fountain.

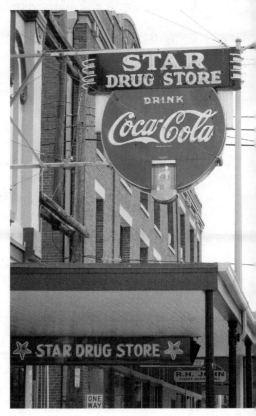

STAR DRUG STORE ON THE STRAND

Many of Galveston's more off-beat and down-home eateries cluster in an area known as the East End, particularly along 14th Street. If you don't plan wisely around their operating hours, you just might miss dinner at the **Mosquito Café**, though lunch or breakfast is always a safe bet. Best described as "understated upscale," the Mosquito Café uses such ingredients as goat cheese, homemade fruit chutney, oven-roasted tomatoes, basil herb mayonnaise, and tamari sesame vinaigrette to enliven burgers, roasted chicken, grilled portobello mushrooms, and yellowfin tuna. The super-fresh meals run the gamut from Mediterranean to

Asian, with lots of solid American standbys too. Before you order, be sure to take a peek at the daily specials on the chalkboard. Farther down the block you'll find the **Sunflower Bakery and Café**, where cinnamon rolls and a wonderfully moist blueberry coffee cake are the stars of the morning. The Texas Gulf crab cakes topped with poached eggs and hollandaise sauce are a brunch hit, and the over-stuffed sandwiches made with homemade bread are perfect to take along for picnicking at the beach. The dessert case will undoubtedly catch your eye, as it's difficult to walk by such an enormous concentration of chocolate and whipped cream and not notice.

This close to the ocean, you'll want to sample some seafood. Folks come from all over the city, and beyond, to the Seawall for a meal at **Gaido's**. Universally praised for both service and food, Gaido's has been making a name for itself since it opened in 1911. The consensus is that the grilled shrimp and the shrimp bisque are wonderful, as is the snapper, cooked any way you like it. This is not a seaside clam shack, it's old-school dining, complete with fresh bread on the table and a dessert cart at the end. Not only does Gaido's shuck their own oysters and peel shrimp by hand, but they make all their own sauces and salad dressings as well. This dedication to real food, along with white table cloths and an efficient waitstaff, has people coming back year after year. Dining is first come, first served, so go early.

The Spot is also laid back, with a distinctive beach-town ambiance. Burgers, some seafood, and plenty of fried appetizers are all available, as are drinks in the Tiki Bar, but mostly people come for the view. When it comes to watching the waves, the Spot really is the spot. The folks behind it have become mini-moguls of shoreside dining. They also own the festive **Rum Shack**, chill **Sideyard**, and funky **Squeeze**, featuring 'ritas and tequilas. Each has a similar menu and fantastic Gulf views.

For another great vantage point, visit **Murdoch's Bathhouse**, just down the street on the beach side. You can purchase all sorts of souvenirs here, from T-shirts to seashells, but the best things about this store are the dozen or so white rocking chairs on the deck out back, offered free to customers for their enjoyment. Murdoch's has been doing business here for over 100 years, but not always in the same building. The original bathhouse was destroyed by the 1900 Storm (page 136) and rebuilt, only to be battered by the storms of 1909 and 1915. Hurricane Carla washed Murdoch's out to sea in 1961 and it was rebuilt again, this time on piers. In 2008, Mother Nature struck yet again and Hurricane Ike took Murdoch's out to sea. Amazingly, the beloved souvenir shop was rebuilt in 2009 and has carried on selling seashells by the seashore ever since.

Leaving the Gulf shore, head across the island to the **Strand**, one of Galveston's oldest neighborhoods. Located along Avenue B, between 20th and 25th Streets, the area was known for handling the commerce that floated in and out of Galveston Harbor; it was nicknamed the Wall Street of the Southwest. Part of the original settlement of the city in the 1830s, the district was occupied by Confederate troops during the Civil War. It thrived throughout the nineteenth century with merchants, bankers, attorneys, and seamen sharing the bustling streets. The Great Storm damaged many of the buildings; restoration efforts have saved those you see today. That the area is so atmospheric is as much a testament to the tremendous community revitalization efforts as to nineteenth-century architecture. At the annual Mardi Gras celebration and a holiday-season production of "Dickens

SHELLS FOR SALE AT MURDOCH'S

ARCHITECTURAL BEAUTY IN THE EAST END

on the Strand," the district is especially vibrant.

Despite the loss of buildings in the 1900 Storm, Galveston still represents one of the largest concentrations of Victorian architecture in the United States. A stroll down Broadway will take you past some of the highlights, all managed by the **Galveston Historical Foundation**.

At 2328 Broadway sits **Ashton Villa**, built in 1859 by one of the richest men in Texas at the time, James Brown. The brick Italianate mansion is an antebellum masterpiece—an architectural treasure. Though the home represents the apex of design for its time, it was almost demolished in 1970 due to lack of interest and money. The **Galveston Historical Foundation** was formed to save it, and has since gone on to save other local buildings; it now offers tours of each. At number 1402 Broadway, **Bishop's Palace** is a fantastic study in Victorian turrets, stained glass, carvings, and sculpture. The stone building was designed by local architect Nicholas Clayton and built by Colonel Walter Gresham, a lawyer, in 1888. Grand, yet delicate, rife with detail, the building proudly occupies a spot on the American Institute of Architects' list of the 100 most important buildings in America. Farther along, at number 2618, **Moody Mansion** was the home of one of Galveston's most powerful families, and one home that the hurricanes just don't seem to miss. As the story goes, W. L. Moody purchased the home less than a week after it was damaged in the 1900 hurricane. He raised his family in its 28,000 square feet, parceled out into 32 lavishly decorated rooms. The home was also hit by hurricane Alicia in 1983, but has since been restored. Visitors can tour these properties individually or purchase a ticket to see all three of the "Broadway Beauties."

Make time to catch two short films—*The Great Storm* and *The Pirate Island of Jean Lafitte*—shown at the **Pier 21 Theater**. Each under a half hour, the films will give you a great overview of the formative events in Galveston's history. Hop next door to the **Texas Seaport Museum**, also on Pier 21, home to the tall ship *Elissa*. This three-masted beauty was constructed in

Scotland in 1877 and moved to Galveston in 1982. The *Elissa* spent the intervening 90 years roaming the seas, her rigging trimmed again and again as she was bought and sold. She finally ended up as a smuggling ship in the Greek Isles. There she caught the eye of a curator for the National Maritime Historical Society in Britain, who appreciated her as one of the last surviving square-riggers in the world. He purchased her and solicited requests from cities who would like to own her.

San Francisco and Vancouver both made bids for the ship, but in the end she came to Galveston. Years of renovation brought her back to her original splendor. The *Elissa* now stays docked in Galveston, though she did travel north in 1986 to join other famous ships in New York Harbor as part of the Statue of Liberty's 100th birthday celebration. A throwback to the romance of sailing the open sea, the *Elissa* is a thrill for young and old.

If you've had enough of the shore, then hop aboard the **Seagull II** at the Texas Seaport Museum and take a tour of the harbor and shipyard. The red and white engine-powered catamaran, operated by the Galveston His-

GALVESTON ISLAND PIER

torical Foundation, was built for comfort, with restrooms, a roof for protection from sun and rain, and plenty of views from all angles. The captain narrates the tour, pointing out tidbits of the history, ecology, and marine biology of the fourth-largest seaport in America.

Baywatch Dolphin Tours tools around the channel offering fun and educational tours with plenty of dolphin action. Tour guides are knowledgeable, presenting marine facts and answering questions with ease, and the dolphins seem to show up on schedule. Dolphins also perform for riders of the

The Balinese Room

The Balinese Room, built on a pier at 21st Street and Seawall Boulevard across from the Hotel Galvez, was a local institution with a very colorful past.

When the Balinese Room opened in 1929, the club immediately attracted big names. Bob Hope, Frank Sinatra, and George Burns all worked the club, while Howard Hughes and other celebrities rubbed elbows with Texas oil barons in the audience. In 1932, the establishment became a Chinese restaurant; after WWII, the Balinese Room.

Advertisements of the day encouraged folks to "Come Down and Play on Galveston Island." By "play," of course, they meant gamble. High rollers rolled in, attracting the Mob like bees to honey, and the whole operation flourished in spite of its illegality. Corruption ruled, and payoffs and favors were traded regularly. According to the record, when the sheriff of Galveston was asked in front of the Texas Legislature why he had not put a stop to the gambling at the Balinese Room, he stated that since he wasn't a member of the private club, he'd never been in. It was answers like this that got the attention of the attorney general, who rode into town with the Texas Rangers in 1956 to put an end to the shenanigans. The Balinese Room did not go down easily. Each time the Rangers raided the nightclub, the band would play "The Eyes of Texas"; it was a signal to warn employees and patrons farther down the 600-foot pier that the law had arrived and they had better hide the evidence. Eventually, the Rangers adopted a siege strategy. They simply sat in the club all day long, making it the last place in the world anyone would want to "come and play."

The club was finally shut down in 1957, and it sat vacant for years. It was purchased in 2001 and brought back to life—minus the gambling—by a respectable local attorney. Things were pretty quiet for a while as the Balinese Room slipped into a respectable retirement as a quiet place folks would come for a drink or two. Hurricane Ike destroyed the club in 2008, and a piece of Galveston's colorful history was reclaimed by the sea.

Buried Treasure

Jean Laffite, the French pirate, was an accomplished mariner; his exploits on the sea were legendary. One story goes so far as to claim he rode a massive storm surge up and over Galveston Island, guiding his ship to the safety of the inner coastal harbor. The most enduring of the tales about Lafitte involve buried treasure.

Since the pirate was known to have plundered many ships in his time spent trolling the Gulf—none American, he insisted—he was thought to possess a trove of treasures. Lafitte took his secret with him to the grave. His death was never documented, and speculation as to the whereabouts of his booty abounds to this day. Some believe that the man and his loot went down with his ship, *The Pride*. Others suspect it is buried in the marshes, swamps, and bayous of the Louisiana coast. The most common assumption is that it is buried on Galveston Island. So when you are out making sand castles on the beach, be sure to dig deep. You just might get lucky.

free **Galveston–Port Bolivar Ferry**, which can feel like a high seas adventure with them swimming alongside. Back on land, there are two more points of interest in the Strand neighborhood. **The Grand 1894 Opera House** showcases the grand style that Victorian Galveston was famous for. Built in 1894, the opera house has been restored several times, once after the Great Storm and again in the 1970s and '80s. It has been declared "The Official Opera House of Texas," and hosts a wide variety of performances. Along different lines, the **Railroad Museum**, housed in an art deco former train depot, tells the story of the railroads in Texas, so important to the state's history. It has one of the largest collections of railroad memorabilia in the country, as well as three steam and three diesel engines.

With the historical portion of the visit under your belt, consider a trip to **Moody Gardens**. The organization that runs this educational attraction began as a therapeutic horseback-riding program for people with various disabilities and neurological issues. It has grown into a multifaceted facility that draws two million visitors a year. Moody Gardens' grounds are organized under three glass pyramids, each with a theme. The hot, humid, and lush **Rainforest Pyramid** has reptiles, lots of green foliage, and Technicolor-like birds. The **Discovery Pyramid** is best described as a science museum. You enter the **Aquarium** through an aboveground pyramid, but quickly move underground, past enormous tanks of tropical fish, sharks, penguins, and other aquatic animals. Moody Gardens allows guests to customize their visit by purchasing individual tickets to the different pyramids. The Aquar-

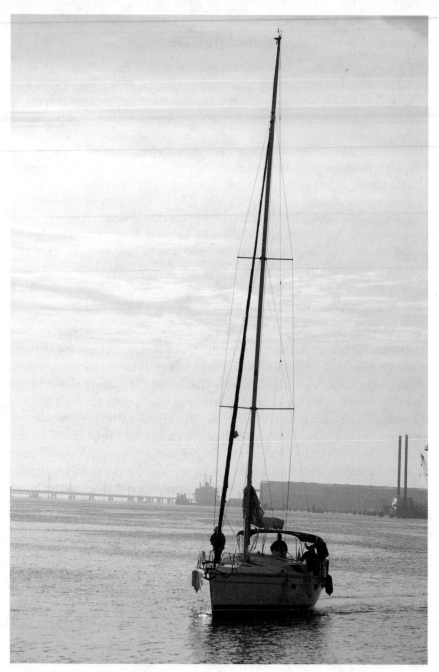

SAILBOAT ENTERING GALVESTON HARBOR

Galveston on Foot

One of the most enjoyable things to do in Galveston is just wander around on foot. Considering that you have most likely paid for parking, get your money's worth; leave your car in the lot and walk the seawall, the shady neighborhoods, or the piers. Rent a bicycle or hop on and off the **trolley** (see box on page 144) as you make your way from neighborhood to neighborhood.

One particularly nice urban neighborhood to stroll is the historic **East End**. Bound by Broadway to the south, 10th Street to the east, Mechanic Avenue to the north, and 19th Street to the west, the entire district is a National Historic Landmark.

The amount of architectural detail concentrated in this area is impressive. From stained glass and turrets to.wrought iron fences and side porches with swings, there are many different styles represented and something interesting to look at around every corner. Some of the homes are grand mansions and some modest cottages, but they co-exist easily, just as they have, through good times and bad, for over a century.

The East End Historical District Association has a downloadable walking tour. Visit www.eastendhistoricdistrict.org.

---

ium is always on everyone's list. Wet and wild family fun awaits next door at **Schlitterbahn**, a popular Texas-based water park with three locations throughout the state, consistently voted "best water park in America."

For a less-crowded, natural setting, leave Galveston and drive southwest along the Seawall. As development thins, the road becomes FM 3005; and approximately 12 miles from the city, you'll come to **Galveston Island State Park**, which extends from the Gulf to the bay. This park has seen a lot of use, but people looking for that quintessential low-cost, family-style beachside experience will find it quite serviceable. There is camping right on the beach, but many just come to enjoy a walk on the sand and the unobstructed views. The bayside is best for bird-watching.

IN THE AREA

1859 ASHTON VILLA, 2328 Broadway, Galveston, 77550. Call 409-762-3933. Website: www.galvestonhistory.org.

1892 BISHOP'S PALACE, 1402 Broadway, Galveston, 77550. Call 409-762-2475. Fee. Website: www.galvestonhistory.org.

BAYWATCH DOLPHIN TOURS, 2100 Harborside Drive, Galveston, 77550. Call 832-859-4557. Fee. Website: www.baywatchdolphintours.com.

GAIDO'S, 3802 Seawall Boulevard, Galveston, 77550. Call 409-761-5500. Old-school seafood restaurant, offering stemware, seafood, and Gulf views since 1911. Website: www.gaidos.com. $$.

GALVESTON HISTORICAL FOUNDATION, 2228 Broadway, Galveston, 77550. Call 409-765-7834. Website: www.galvestonhistory.org.

GALVESTON ISLAND STATE PARK, 14901 FM 3005, Galveston, 77554. Call 409-737-1222. Fee. Website: www.tpwd.texas.gov.

GALVESTON ISLAND TROLLEY. Call 409-797-3900. Fee. Website: www.galvestontx.gov.

GALVESTON ISLAND VISITOR INFORMATION CENTER, 2328 Broadway, Galveston, 77550. Call 1-888-425-4753. Website: www.galveston.com.

GALVESTON–PORT BOLIVAR FERRY, 1000 Ferry Road N., Galveston, 77550. Call 409-795-2230. Daily. Free. Website: www.txdot.gov.

THE GRAND 1894 OPERA HOUSE, 2020 Postoffice Street, Galveston, 77550. Call 1-800-821-1894 or 409-765-1894. See website for schedule. Website: www.thegrand.com.

HARBOR HOUSE, Pier 21, Galveston, 77550. Call 409-763-3321. Simple, casual rooms in a renovated warehouse on the Harbor. Website: www.harborhousepier21.com. $$.

The Great Texas Coastal Birding Trail

Organized by the Texas Parks and Wildlife Department, the Great Texas Coastal Birding Trail comprises several recommended sites for bird-watching up and down the Texas coast. The trail is divided into three segments. Galveston Island, falling into the region known as the Upper Texas Coast, has birding sites both in the city and along the shores of its state park. Some sites are all-season, and others are active during migrations, but all are lovely little natural spots. The route is marked with roadside signs featuring a white bird, sunset, and coastline on a brown background. You can print or purchase a map at www.tpwd.texas.gov.

Getting Around Galveston

Horse-drawn carriages circulate the Strand and the East End, giving elegant tours of the historic neighborhoods; try Island Carriages or Seahorse Carriages. On the seawall, the Island Bicycle Company, among others, rents bicycles and multi-seat surrey bikes for exploring the island at a leisurely pace. They also let fishing poles, boogie boards, binoculars, and everything you'll need to recreate on the beach. The Trolley is a great way to see Galveston. Designed to resemble the trolleys that lumbered around the city between the late 1800s and the late 1930s, the Galveston Island Trolley circulates between the Strand Landmark Historic District, Pier 21, the seawall, and the University of Texas Medical Branch. Check www.galvestontx .gov for route specifics.

HOTEL GALVEZ, 2024 Seawall Boulevard, Galveston, 77550. Call 409-765-7721. A grand historic hotel with fantastic architectural features and Gulf views. Website: www.hotelgalvez.com. $$–$$$.

ISLAND BICYCLE COMPANY, 1808 Seawall Boulevard, Galveston, 77550. Call 409-762-2453. Website: www.islandbicyclecompany.com.

ISLAND CARRIAGES, 2528 Postoffice Street, Galveston, 77550. Call 409-765-6951 for hours and reservations. Cash only.

LA KING'S CONFECTIONERY, 2323 Strand, Galveston, 77550. Call 409-762-6100. A must for malts, saltwater taffy, and chocolate covered anything. Website: www.lakingsconfectionery.com. $.

LASKER INN BED & BREAKFAST AND EVENT VENUE, 1019 16th Street, Galveston, 77550. Call 409-497-4318. Elegant inn in the heart of the historic district. Website: www.laskerinn.com. $$$$.

LITTLE DADDY'S GUMBO BAR, 2107 Postoffice Street, Galveston, 77550. Call 409-744-8626. Gumbo, po'boys, and New Orleans favorites at this funky eatery. Website: www.littledaddysgumbobar.com. $–$$.

MOODY GARDENS, One Hope Boulevard, Galveston, 77554. Call 1-800-582-4673. Fee. Website: www.moodygardens.com.

MOODY MANSION MUSEUM, 2618 Broadway, Galveston, 77550. Call: 409-762-7668. Fee. Website: www.moodymansion.org.

MOSQUITO CAFÉ, 628 14th Street, Galveston, 77550. Call 409-763-1010. Closed Mondays. Inventive bistro fare made with fresh, high-quality ingredients. Website: www.mosquitocafe.com. $–$$

MURDOCH'S BATHHOUSE, 2215 Seawall Boulevard, Galveston, 77550. Call 409-762-7478. Website: www.galveston.com/murdochsbathhouse.

PIER 21 THEATER, Pier 21 at Harborside Drive, Galveston, 77550. Call 409-763-8808. Website: www.galvestonhistory.org.

RAILROAD MUSEUM, 2602 Santa Fe Place, Galveston, 77550. Call: 409-765-5700. Website: www.galvestonrrmuseum.com.

RUDY AND PACO, 2028 Postoffice Street, Galveston, 77550. Call 409-762-3696. Closed Sundays. Upscale dining featuring a refined Latin American menu of steaks and seafood. Inquire about reservations and dress code. Website: www.rudyandpaco.com. $$$–$$$$.

SALTWATER GRILL, 2017 Postoffice Street, Galveston, 77553. Call 409-762-3474. Steamed seafood and succulent steaks in the heart of the Strand. Website: www.saltwatergrill.com. Reservations strongly recommended. $$–$$$.

SCHLITTERBAHN, 2109 Lockheed Road, Galveston, 77554. Call 409-770-9283. Call or check online for seasonal schedule. Fee. Website: www.schlitterbahn.com.

SEAGULL II, Texas Seaport Museum, Pier 21 (Harborside Drive at 21st Street), Galveston, 77550. Call 409-763-1877. Fee. Website: www.galvestonhistory.org.

SEAHORSE & CLASSIC CARRIAGE COMPANIES, departing from downtown Galveston, 77550. Call 409-925-3312. Cash only.

THE SPOT RESTAURANT AND TIKI BAR, 3204 Seawall Boulevard, Galveston, 77550. Call 409-621-5237. Overgrown beach bar atmosphere with outsize views. Website: www.islandfamous.com, which also covers **Rum Shack, Sideyard, The Spot Tiki Bar and Squeeze.** $–$$.

STAR DRUG STORE, 510 23rd Street, Galveston, 77550. Call 409-766-7719. Sit at the counter and enjoy a treat or a meal at this vintage soda fountain. Website: www.galvestonstardrug.com. $–$$.

SUNFLOWER BAKERY & CAFÉ, 512 14th Street, Galveston, 77550. Call 409-763-5500. Cheerful bakery known for fantastic brunches and a huge lunch menu with everything from cinnamon rolls to crab cakes. Website: www.thesunflowerbakeryandcafe.com. $–$$.

TEXAS SEAPORT MUSEUM, Pier 21, Galveston, 77550. Call 409-763-1877. Fee. Website: www.galvestonhistory.org.

TREMONT HOUSE, 2300 Ship's Mechanic Row, Galveston, 77550. Call 409-763-0300. Urban style in the heart of the Strand. Website: www.thetremont house.com. $$–$$$.

8

THE PINEYWOODS

JEFFERSON, CADDO LAKE, SAN AUGUSTINE,
NACOGDOCHES, CROCKETT, DAVY CROCKETT
NATIONAL FOREST

TOTAL DISTANCE: 150 miles from Jefferson to Crockett, via San Augustine.

HIGHLIGHTS: Follow TX 59 from the former port town of **Jefferson** to **Nacogdoches**, a small college town tucked in among the pine trees. Nacogdoches, **San Augustine**, and **Crockett** were all once points along the historic **El Camino Real**, the legendary trade route that passed through the region on its way from Louisiana to San Antonio, and are still pleasant places to stop today. Nature lovers will enjoy the stillness and solitude of both **Caddo Lake** and the **Davy Crockett National Forest**. Overall, the route captures the unhurried pace of the road less traveled.

GETTING THERE: From Dallas, take I-20 east to Marshall and TX 59 north to Jefferson for a total of 170 miles. From Jefferson, it is approximately 19 miles east to Uncertain along FM 134 and FM 2198. Double back to TX 59 and take it 34 miles south to Carthage and an additional 49 miles south to San Augustine. From San Augustine, take TX 21 west to Nacogdoches, where you can take either TX 21 or TX 7 west approximately 60 miles to Crockett.

This route leads through the towns that the steamboats and the railroads built, towns that first linked commercial Texas to the rest of the new, post–Civil War United States. In time, however, major interstate highways and airports passed the region by, depressing its economy and leaving it a bit stuck in the past. This corner of the state has shouldered on, however, and now, as it turns out, is reviving its economy by trading on its past. Country lanes, flowering dogwood trees, and old-time eateries are just what frazzled city folks crave.

The pace in East Texas is decidedly slower. The towns feel a bit dated

LEFT: THE PINEYWOODS OF EAST TEXAS

in decor, but the region's old-fashioned friendliness is heartwarming. And, thankfully, hospitality never went out of style here; there's butter in the pie crusts, homemade rolls on the table, and the hot coffee's always on. This route is best traveled with an eye toward detail. Slow down and you'll hear folks greeting each other by name or catch a glimpse of the light glistening off the dew of the still-damp forest floor.

Though **Jefferson** is approximately 2½ hours east of Dallas, it is only 40 minutes from Shreveport, just over the Louisiana border, so it isn't surprising that this little pocket of Texas feels a bit like the Old South. Over the years, Jefferson has shrunk from a bustling port to the little East Texas town you see today, known mostly now for its history, concentration of detailed Victorian architecture, and old-fashioned small-town atmosphere.

Built on a bluff overlooking the Red River, Jefferson was perfectly positioned to become a port. In the 1840s, Jefferson was shipping cotton and produce to Shreveport and New Orleans, and quickly establishing itself as a wealthy city. In fact, by 1870, only the Gulf port of Galveston was doing more commerce than Jefferson.

In 1873, two unfortunate events conspired to end the era of prosperity for Jefferson. First, a naturally occurring dam, called the Red River Raft, was removed, lowering the water levels in Caddo Lake and the surrounding waterways, making riverboat passage difficult and, at times, impossible. Second, a newly completed railroad line bypassed Jefferson on its way to Marshall, diverting trade away from the port city. While a second rail route

Diamond Bessie

In the late 1870s, Jefferson became the unwitting location of one of the region's more gruesome and sensational murders. In January 1877, Bessie Moore, a New York girl and sometime prostitute, pulled into town with Abraham Rothschild, son of a wealthy jeweler. Just a few days later her body was found in the woods.

Diamond Bessie, so known for the many diamonds she'd been given as gifts from admirers, was certainly living a rough life with Rothschild, and their relationship was tumultuous, but no one predicted that murder would be the result. One day the couple (who were staying at the Brooks House in Jefferson) went out for a picnic, but several hours later only Mr. Rothschild returned, wearing some of Bessie's diamonds. Several weeks later, a woman collecting firewood stumbled upon the remnants of a picnic and a body. Since Bessie died from a bullet wound, the case was declared a homicide and Mr. Rothschild was charged with the crime.

The prominence of Mr. Rothschild's family pushed the story into the headlines, and they quickly secured 10 high-powered attorneys to defend him. Since the Jefferson jury was considered tainted by all the publicity, the case was moved to Marshall, where he was convicted and then sprung on appeal. The case was retried in Jefferson, where the defense was so overpowering that Rothschild was acquitted.

While the case was sensational, involving a handsome and wealthy man and a woman known to live by her wits, the shocking outcome of the trials shook many folks' faith in the justice system. Now, while Rothschild's notoriety has come and gone, Diamond Bessie is something of a cult figure. Tourists visit her grave and the city performs a play telling the tale each year during the annual Pilgrimage Festival.

completed the following year did pass through the town, Marshall and Dallas had gotten a head start and quickly surpassed Jefferson in importance. As the water level sank and the dominance of the railroads rose, Jefferson became just a charming East Texas town filled with history and ghosts of the past (see box on page 155).

As you may have noticed by now, most towns in Texas are laid out around a town square with a courthouse in the center. Jefferson is different. The town is organized in a neat grid pattern along Big Cypress Creek, with an addition tacked on to the east at a jaunty 45-degree angle. Tall shade trees shelter the homes and hang over the streets, covering all with a dappled light. Squint your eyes and you can practically see the horse and buggies and hear the whistle of the steamboats pulling into the docks.

Want to delve a little deeper into local history? Stop by the **Jefferson Historical Society Museum** and get a clearer picture of what living here was like years ago. The museum, housed in a stately brick building built in the late 1800s, has four floors of collections on display ranging from Caddo Indian artifacts and early Texas quilts to Civil War–era items and Victorian

HORSE-DRAWN CARRIAGE IN FRONT OF THE JEFFERSON HOTEL IN JEFFERSON

EXCELSIOR HOUSE IN JEFFERSON

china. When it comes to lodging, while most of East Texas might be lacking, Jefferson has a surplus. Known as the Bed and Breakfast Capital of Texas, Jefferson has so many choices that it can be hard to sort through them all. On one end of the spectrum are the historic hotels; the best examples of these are the **Jefferson Hotel** and its neighbor just up the street, the **Excelsior House**. Both are steeped in lore. A peek into the lobby of each gives you a pretty good idea of what to expect throughout. The Jefferson and Excelsior are perfect for guests who love the low-lit and slightly musty ambiance of living history. The older rooms will feel small to some and cozy to others, the bathrooms either charming or worn; it all depends on how you look at it and what you enjoy. The Jefferson, though, is thought to be haunted, and guests report hearing voices, capturing unexpected images on their cameras, and getting the heebie-jeebies all night long. It's a must for folks who like to vacation with the spirits.

Head down S. Alley Street and behold the promise of a porch. It's like an invitation to drop everything, have a seat, and just watch the world go by. If numbers of porches corresponds to degrees of relaxation, suffice it to say that the **Claiborne House** will be tranquil. The home was built in 1872 by Captain Claiborne; it's a modified Greek Revival gem that's neat as a pin, painted a crisp white with black trim and surrounded by greenery. Communal breakfasts are served in the dining room, and guests tend to be a friendly bunch, chatting as they eat. Hospitality takes center stage at the **Old Mulberry Inn Bed & Breakfast**, where innkeepers Lana and Glen warmly welcome all guests. The rooms are crisp, clean, and painted in soothing, con-

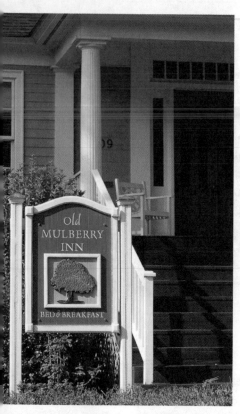
OLD MULBERRY INN BED & BREAKFAST
IN JEFFERSON

temporary colors. Polished wood floors, immaculate linens, and modern bathrooms make this inn an unfussy counterpart to some of its more extensively decorated peers and the three course breakfasts are a treat.

Built in the 1920s, the **Delta Street Inn** is a lovely example of prairie-style architecture, with generously sized, sun-filled rooms, each with tall windows and beautiful wood floors, and a wide front porch overlooking the peaceful property. The gracious owners have stylishly updated the home, while preserving its historic look and feel, making it a soughtafter place to spend the night. The **Carriage House B&B** exudes a welcoming feeling that has guests returning again and again. A white picket fence greets visitors and homemade quilts adorn the beds at this charming and cheerful bed & breakfast. Details such as a fire pit with s'mores, napping hammock, and the fact that they always serve dessert first at breakfast are obvious pluses.

The high-water mark for barbecue in the area, **Joseph's Riverport Barbecue** has also started to pop up on statewide "Best of" lists. The brisket, described as "moist and perfect," is a must-try. While the meats are classics, the sides veer off into uncharted waters. The beans taste a bit more like tangy traditional baked beans rather than savory ranch-style beans served elsewhere. The sweet potato fries are an unusual choice, but consensus seems to be that they pair really well with the smoked meats. Hushpuppy lovers will enjoy the hot water cornbread, small disks of cornbread with crunchy outsides masking light and fluffy interiors. Expect a line at the counter, but expect the wait to be worth it.

Stop in the **Hamburger Store** for a more casual meal. From jalapeño chili cheddar burgers to chicken-fried steaks, the Hamburger Store churns out a steady stream of comfort foods behind its weathered exterior. Be sure to leave room for the pies. From chocolate pecan to strawberry to chocolate cream and lemon, topped with a dome of meringue, these pies are tasty. Very popular, the Hamburger Store is frequently crowded, so stop in midafternoon for a late lunch, an early dinner, or just a piece of pie. Another casual option is **The Bayou Bakery**, on the same block as the Excelsior House, where you'll have plenty of treats to choose from along with lunch staples such as Cajun-inspired soups and sandwiches made with freshly baked breads.

For a memorable dinner, locals and out-of-towners enjoy **Stillwater Inn**, an 1890s Victorian home where fine dining prevails; the grilled duck with either blackberry or rosemary red wine sauce comes highly recommended, as do the rack of lamb and pecan-encrusted fresh trout.

Afternoon or weekend evenings are a good time to pop in to the **Jefferson General Store** on E. Austin Street. This old-fashioned soda fountain, in business since the 1870s, is great for a milkshake, Coke float, or a five-cent cup of coffee. The Store makes its own pralines fresh every day, as well as jellies and hot sauces. They sell retro toys, knickknacks, and all sorts of things you didn't know you wanted. Have a look around and take home a little bit of Texas.

Leaving Jefferson, it is a 14-mile ride to **Caddo Lake**. Surprisingly, Caddo Lake is the only natural freshwater lake in Texas. The lake was formed by a naturally occurring logjam so thick that it was known as the Great Raft of the Red River. In 1874, the dam was broken apart to make way for riverboats, but so much water drained away, only a swamp remained, defeating the purpose. A man-made dam was constructed to replace the old logs, and the lake has filled again.

THE HAMBURGER STORE IN JEFFERSON

Jefferson Ghost Walk

Jefferson bills itself as the most haunted city in Texas. If you want to find out for yourself just how haunted it is, consider taking the **Jefferson Ghost Walk**. The walk begins in front of the Jefferson Historical Society, at night, naturally, and will take you wandering the streets of Jefferson, lamp in hand and your wits about you, to hear of the various oddities, sightings, and unexplained phenomena that the city has embraced with pride and pragmatism.

Over the years, the stories have added up. The Jefferson Hotel has countless ghost stories to tell. The way they figure it, if you hear it directly from them, then the creaky floors, dancing shadows, and other logic-defying peculiarities might seem a bit less intrusive. Room 19 is said to be one of the more "visited" rooms, so if you enjoy a good haunting, be sure to request it. You don't have to be a believer to enjoy Jefferson; just come with an open mind and consider yourself warned!

Stop by the chamber of commerce for detailed information or visit www .jeffersonghostwalk.com.

Its unique history makes Caddo Lake much different than any other lake in Texas. It has a very distinct primeval quality and is even a bit surreal. A thick forest of bald cypress trees, draped with Spanish moss, grows throughout the lake. The aquatic growth is so dense that 42 miles of channels, or "boat roads," have been created just to make navigation possible. Its age means it is a mature lake, with an astounding diversity of species and ecosystems. Alligators, turtles, frogs, and snakes all live in the lake, and raccoons, minks, and beavers are popular on its shore. Anglers come to Caddo Lake for the 71 species of fish including bass, crappie, blue gills, and catfish.

One of the best ways to see the lake is to visit **Caddo Lake State Park**. Dense and shady forest trails are popular for hiking, and you can stroll to the end of the observation deck jutting out into Saw Mill Pond. Almost immediately, you'll be struck by the sound of squawking birds, buzzing insects, and squirrels jumping among the trees. The place is just teeming with life and growth. While the lake is pretty year-round, blooming dogwoods during the last part of March and the first part of April make it something really special. Overnight guests love the little log **cabins** in Caddo Lake State Park; built by the Civilian Conservation Corps in the 1930s, they are still popular for their simple, rustic charm. If you want to get out on the water, sign up for one of **Captain Ron's Swamp Tours**, featuring a lively and informative narrated tour of the Caddo Lake ecosystem while adrift in a 28-foot pontoon boat.

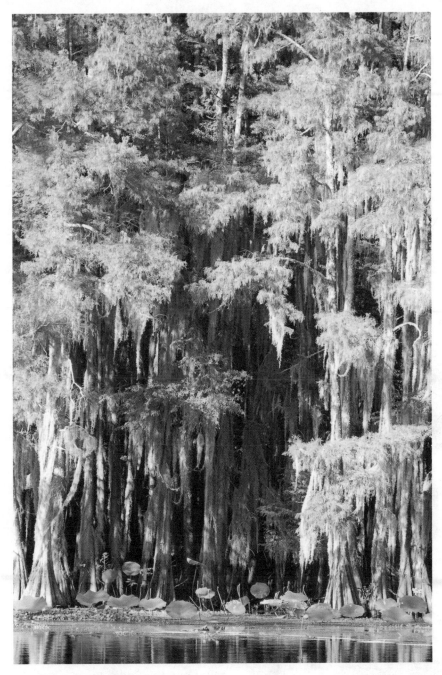

SPANISH MOSS IN THE TREES BESIDE CADDO LAKE

From Jefferson, it's an easy 52-odd miles along US 59 to **Carthage**, home of the **Texas Country Music Hall of Fame and the Tex Ritter Museum**— a must stop for country-music lovers who will appreciate the chance to snap their photo with the statue of Tex out front. From Carthage, it's about another 49 miles south on US 59 to sleepy little **San Augustine**, the start of the Texas portion of **El Camino Real**, the eighteenth-century route that ran between the Spanish missions. While *camino real* is a rather generic term, also used to describe routes in California and New Mexico, El Camino Real in Texas is also known as the King's Highway, or the much more descriptive San Antonio–Nacogdoches Road. It makes the most sense to think of El Camino Real not as one road, but as a series of interconnected trails, almost like a braid, that fell in and out of use depending on their purpose, travelers, and weather. While many of these trails already existed as footpaths used by Native Americans, the missions established by the Spanish increased their traffic. The route was used for trade, protection, cattle drives, and immigration, delivering products, goods, animals, and people to the interior of Texas, a role it filled for centuries. Many Texas roads and highways lie over the footpaths carved by the El Camino Real. Rising public awareness and interest in these historic trails have spawned renewed efforts to preserve them. Visit www.elcaminorealdelostejas.org to learn more.

DOWNTOWN SAN AUGUSTINE

The **Mission Dolores Visitor Center** welcomes the curious who would like more information about the historic route. Located on the site of the Mission Nuestra Senora de los Ais, established in 1717 but no longer in existence, the new visitor center evokes the mission's spirit with interesting exhibits and an informative film depicting the lives and times of the Spanish missionaries and the Ais Indians who once lived here, and the relationship between them.

Mention you need a sip of something cold and the friendly folks in San Augustine will send you right down to the **San Augustine Drug**

A Texas Christmas

The Victorian charm of Jefferson is the perfect backdrop for Christmas, and every year the town pulls all the lights, ribbons, wreaths, garlands, and ornaments out of storage and decks the halls. Residents wear period clothing and a horse-drawn carriage makes its way through the streets. Throughout the month of December, there are candlelight tours of various historic homes. The only thing missing is the snow. For Candlelight Tour information call 903-665-7064 or visit their website at www.jeffersoncandle light.com.

Company with instructions to order the signature drink, the Grapefruit Highball. After establishing the drug store in 1904, the adventurous owner began experimenting with mixing drinks. By 1928, everyone in the region was swooning for the Grapefruit Highball, a nonalcoholic mix of grapefruit and orange juice, sugar, and a secret ingredient. Though the drug store burned to the ground, the soda fountain was rebuilt in 1988, thanks in large part to locals' dedication to the highball. Stop in and taste a little bit of history; be sure to tell them it is your first time—they may serve you the drink in a frosty glass cowboy boot, on the house.

Ask anyone in San Augustine where the best place to grab lunch is and they'll tell you **Mary Kay's**. Located just north of the intersection of Highway 21 and 96, Mary Kay's is a simple building with a distinctive black awning surrounded by a parking lot jammed with cars. While the burgers and sandwiches are great, the daily lunch plates, and "all you can eat" fried fish special can't be beat for both value and taste. Eat your fill of country diner favorites, wash it down with a cold sweet tea, and save room for dessert. Comfort food at a comfortable price.

Press on, traveling TX 21 west to **Nacogdoches**, that small East Texas town with the lived-in feel of a place that's been around awhile, but with the youthful atmosphere of the college town that it is. Folks here say it's the oldest town in Texas, and the fact is it's been here an awfully long time. Nacogdoches (pronounced nack-a-DOEchiz) is often confused with Natchitoches (pronounced NACK-a-tish), the Louisiana town to its east. According to Caddo legend, an elderly Caddo chief sent his grown twin sons, Nacogdoches and Natchitoches, in two different directions to settle and prosper. Nacogdoches was sent 3 days' journey toward the setting sun, and Natchitoches was sent to travel 3 days toward the rising sun. The men became leaders of their own communities, but remained in contact, with the road between them friendly, safe, and well traveled. Nacogdoches was a Caddo settlement until 1716, when the Spanish established a mission and staked their claim in East Texas. By the later quarter of the century, the French were a formidable challenge and the settlers in the area picked up and moved to San Antonio, far from the arm of France. But, in 1779, some settlers moved back to the region and asked the government of Mexico, whose flag was flying over Texas at the time, to declare them a pueblo. Despite politics and changing influences, the town remained in close contact with its twin, Natchitoches, and together they compose the eastern section of the historic El Camino Real.

Of the few places to stay in Nacogdoches, the one with the most character is the **Hotel Fredonia and Conference Center**. Decades ago, in an effort to welcome more visitors to their city, 75 citizens of the town decided to pool resources and build a hotel to be owned by the community. By the end of 1952, the little town of 13,000 had raised a half a million dollars, and won over many naysayers. In fact, over 1,000 residents bought stock in the fledgling project. Work started in 1954 and the doors were opened in 1955 to a crowd of 6,000 optimistic well-wishers. The hotel has since had its ups and downs, several different owners, and a facelift or two, but a fantastic recent top-to-bottom renovation has restored to what it was in the beginning, "the city's living room." These days, the Fredonia's swanky midcentury style shines through and it's fun to see visitors chatting in the common rooms, having a drink by the pool, or enjoying a meal in the on-site café, steakhouse, or bar and grill. In keeping with the hotel's vintage, rooms are on the small side, but their simple, uncluttered design helps them feel spacious. The hotel is very well located, just blocks from the center of town, and is an admirable addition to city's offerings.

Though the choices are somewhat limited, eating is easy in Nacogdoches. The **Clear Springs Café** has several locations in Texas, including a bustling one in Nacogdoches. One reason people keep coming back is the fish, espe-

Detour to Jonesville

Pulling into sleepy little Jonesville, you might drive right past T. C. Lindsey & Co. if you weren't sure what to look for. The big white clapboard building has a squeaky screen door and several long wooden benches out front, but it's what's inside that has people pulling over to park. The old general store is so old and so chock-full of curios of a bygone era that Disney has used it as a setting in several movies. The place has been in continuous operation since 1847, and is a wonder to behold and a treat to poke around in. T. C. Lindsey & Co., FM 124 where it intersects I-20, just 2 miles shy of Louisiana.

cially the fried catfish, which is consistently cited as outstanding. The popular pan-seared tilapia with Dijon peppercorn crawfish sauce is usually served with a scoop of garlic mashed potatoes and steamed vegetables. The "small" Texas onion rings are enormous, as are the portions of just about everything else. Clear Springs Café sits next to a rail yard in what was once a refrigerated warehouse, the history of which is displayed on the walls inside. The turn onto Old Tyler Road is just west of the TX 21 and US 59 intersection. Also located here, and under the same ownership, is **Auntie Pasta's**, where generous portions of familiar Italian dishes are served up every night. Locals pile in for lasagna, homemade meatballs, and huge plates of pasta.

For some local history, follow TX 21 from Nacogdoches west to Grapeland and the **Mission Tejas State Historical Park**. Though built in the 1930s, the structure is meant to resemble the Mission San Francisco de los Tejas,

CUTTING A SLICE OF EAST TEXAS PIE

the very first Spanish mission in Texas, which was established in 1690, and once stood on these very grounds. When the Spanish first began missions in Texas, they started here to remind the French, building just over the border in Louisiana, of their presence in Texas. The peaceful Indians who lived in the area were friendly to the missionaries. As the story goes, the tribe's word for welcome, *tejas*, became the region's name, Texas.

After hopeful beginnings, however, the missionaries were blamed for the sickness and death that befell the tribe after their arrival; they had little choice but to burn the mission and return to Spain. In the early 1700s, a second attempt was made to establish a mission here, but the project was eventually relocated to San Antonio, where it began a new life as Mission San Francisco de la Espada.

Also nestled in the park is the **Rice Family Log Home**, which is thought to have been built in the early 1800s. A fine example of an early Texas dwelling, the home was a well-used way station for travelers along El Camino

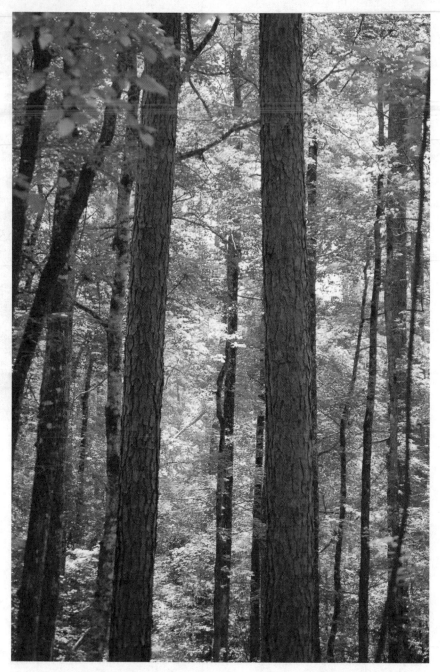

DAVY CROCKETT NATIONAL FOREST

Real (page 162). Farther along TX 21, you will come to the **Caddoan Mounds State Historic Site**, located about 6 miles southwest of Alto. Archaeologists estimate that the Caddoan people started living in the region in approximately A.D. 800 and stayed for 500 years. Though the term is now used in a general sense, prior to the mid-1800s, Caddo referred to only one of 25 separate groups living in sections of Texas, Louisiana, Arkansas, and Oklahoma. The site has three large mounds of earth, one of which served as a burial site, and several re-created structures, with a distinctive beehive shape. The site is an interpretive experience; there are some archaeological artifacts on display, along with artists' renderings of what life might have been like for the Caddoans and plenty of natural scenery, which remains relatively unchanged.

Continuing along toward Crockett, you'll pass through the **Davy Crockett National Forest**. While the thick, primarily pine forest is scenic to drive through, hiking is another popular way to explore the area; many people enjoy the **Four C National Recreation Trail**, which stretches 20 miles from **Ratcliff Lake Recreation Area to Neches Bluff Overlook**. The trail follows old roads once used by the lumber companies that logged the virgin forests, taking the freshly harvested trees to a sawmill on Ratcliff Lake. As you walk the trail, look around; many of the trees you see were planted after the company stopped logging in the 1920s. The trail passes through **Big Slough Wilderness Area**, a parcel of primitive land untouched by modernity, and ends at an overlook atop the Neches River. Since there are hardwoods in the forest, spring and fall are particularly pretty times of year to hike. Outdoor enthusiasts may want to explore the two other national forests in the region, Sabine National Forest, just east of San Augustine, and Angelina National Forest, south of Nacogdoches and east of Lufkin; the Davy Crockett National Forest website will provide the details.

Just west of the Davy Crockett National Forest on TX 21 is the little town of **Crockett**. Monday is fried chicken day at **The Moosehead Café**, and once it's gone, it's gone. Console yourself with your choice of any number of meringue-topped pies or perhaps a slice of warm apple pie with a scoop of Blue Bell. With red checkered tablecloths, counter seating, and ridiculously low prices, The Moosehead keeps it simple, and delicious.

The **Camp Street Café and Store** keeps feet tapping in Crockett with live concerts in its rustic 1930s-era tin storefront. Though the building has been many things over the years, it's now one of the best live-music venues in East Texas, with everything from blues to western to bluegrass on the lineup. There are two ways to catch a concert. One is to stop in Saturday evenings at 8 PM (sometimes Fridays) for a live show. The other is to tune in to the Camp Street Café and Store Music Hour Saturday mornings at 8 AM on the radio. Try 1290 AM or 92.7 FM.

APPLE PIE AT THE MOOSEHEAD CAFÉ IN CROCKETT

Stay the night in Crockett at the comfortable **Warfield House** and you'll wake up feeling refreshed. This is an old-fashioned bed & breakfast, right down to the quilts, many of which were made by the very talented owner. Cozy beds, hearty breakfasts, and a backyard pool make the Warfield House a terrific base from which to explore the Davy Crockett Forest, or just hole up for the weekend. From Crockett it is a 35-mile drive north to **Palestine** on TX 19/US 287 or a 46-mile drive northeast on TX 21/US 69 to **Rusk,** where you can hitch a ride on the **Texas State Railroad** and enjoy a view of the East Texas countryside from a moving steam train. The railroad has been around since the turn of the twentieth century, when the line was built to provide freight and passenger service. In 1921, when it was no longer economically feasible to operate the line, it was sold to a company that used it to transport lumber. In 1972, the railroad was brought under the auspices of the Texas Parks and Wildlife Department, which refurbished the trains, built Victorian-style train depots at either end of the line, and kept the operation on track. The railroad changed hands again in September 2007, when the American Heritage Railroad Company took over operations. Today the railroad really shines. Seasonal theme rides, such as A Day with Thomas or The Polar Express, keep things fresh, yet the thrill of the whistle and the first lurch of the train as it gathers steam on the track just never grow old.

The railroad runs several steam and diesel engines, built between 1901 and 1956, along the 50-mile round-trip route between Palestine and Rust. You can get on in either town. The trip takes approximately four hours, one and a half hours each way with a layover in the middle. Time flies as you watch the East Texas scenery slip by, the flowering dogwoods in late March and early April and the red and gold leaves of autumn in November. From Palestine, it's a 112-mile drive back to Dallas and 130 miles from Rusk. A short way to drive for a trip back in time.

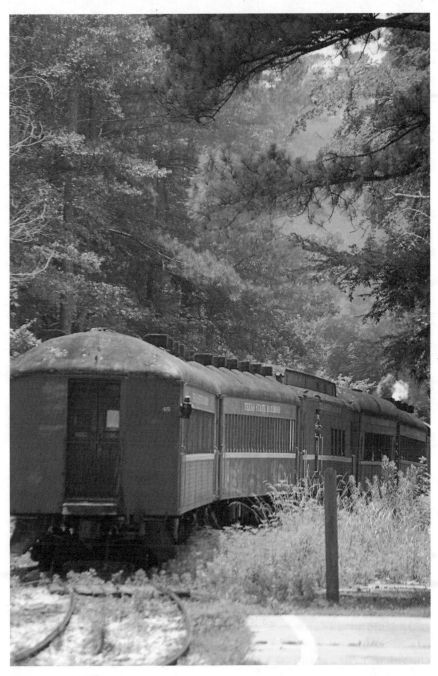

THE TEXAS STATE RAILROAD

IN THE AREA

AUNTIE PASTA'S, 211 Old Tyler Road, Nacogdoches, 75964. Call 936-569-2171. Generous portions of pasta dishes served in the casual setting of a repurposed warehouse. Website: www.auntiepastas.com. $$.

THE BAYOU BAKERY, 201 W. Austin Street, Jefferson, 75657. Call 903-665-2253. Hearty breakfasts and deli-style lunches with a Cajun kick. Website: www.bayoubakerycafe.com. $.

CADDOAN MOUNDS STATE HISTORIC SITE, 1649 TX 21, Alto, 75925. Call 936-858-3218. Closed Mondays. Fee. Website: www.thc.texas.gov or www.visitcaddomounds.com.

CADDO LAKE STATE PARK, 245 Park Road 2, Karnack, 75661. Call 903-679-3351. Fee. Website: www.tpwd.texas.gov.

CAMP STREET CAFÉ AND STORE, 215 S. Third Street, Crockett, 75835. Call 936-544-8656. Fee. Great live music venue. Website: www.campstreetcafe.com.

CAPTAIN RON'S SWAMP TOURS, Call 903-679-3020. Fee. Website: www.captronswamptours.com

CARRIAGE HOUSE B&B, 401 N. Polk Street, Jefferson, 75657. Call 903-665-9511. Relaxed atmosphere coupled with attention to detail. Website: www.carriagehousejefferson.com. $$–$$$.

CLAIBORNE HOUSE, 312 South Alley, Jefferson, 75657. Call 903-665-8800. A modified Greek Revival gem. Website: www.claibornehousebnb.com. $$–$$$.

CLEAR SPRINGS CAFÉ, 211 Old Tyler Road, Nacogdoches, 75964. Call 936-569-0489. Plenty of seafood to choose from at this local favorite found tucked into an old dance hall. Website: www.clearspringscafe.com. $$.

CROCKETT CHAMBER OF COMMERCE, 1100 Edmiston Drive, Crockett, 75835. Call 936-544-2359. Website: www.crockettareachamber.org.

DAVY CROCKETT NATIONAL FOREST, 18551 TX 7 E., Kennard, 75847. Call 936-655-2299. Fee. Website: www.fs.usda.gov.

DELTA STREET INN, 206 E. Delta Street, Jefferson, 75657. Call 903-665-2929. Prairie-style home with gracious hosts. Website: www.deltastreetinn.com. $$–$$$.

EXCELSIOR HOUSE, 211 W. Austin, Jefferson, 75657. Call 903-665-2513. Historic hotel with details of yesteryear. Website: www.theexcelsiorhouse.com. $–$$.

HAMBURGER STORE, 101 N. Market Street, Jefferson, 75657. Consistent go-to place for burgers. Call 903-665-8302. $–$$.

HOTEL FREDONIA AND CONVENTION CENTER, 200 N. Fredonia Street, Nacogdoches, 75961. Call 936-564-1234. Midcentury style shines at this renovated boutique hotel. Website: www.thefredonia.com. $$.

JEFFERSON GENERAL STORE, 113 E. Austin St., Jefferson, 75657. Call 903-665-8481. Website: www.jeffersongeneralstore.com.

JEFFERSON HISTORICAL SOCIETY MUSEUM, 223 W. Austin Street, Jefferson, 75657. Call 903-665-2775. Fee. Website: www.jeffersonmuseum.com.

JEFFERSON HOTEL, 124 W. Austin Street, Jefferson, 75657. Call 903-665-2631. Historic hotel, with good-natured rumors of hauntings. Website: www.historicjeffersonhotel.com. $–$$.

Uncertain

Not sure where to start exploring Caddo Lake? Try Uncertain. This little town, with a population of around 150, welcomes Caddo Lake visitors with a laid-back nonchalance that characterizes the area. Just how the town got its name is . . . uncertain. Sometimes called Uncertain Landing, the town may have been named this due to the difficulty steamboat captains had mooring their boats along its irregular shoreline. Another popular explanation is that residents, unable to discern if they were part of the United States or the Republic of Texas, simply resigned themselves to the confusion. Nearby, and beside Caddo Lake Park, is the hamlet of Karnack, birthplace of Lady Bird Johnson, though it is not open to the public. The town was once anchored by an army ammunitions plant, but that has since been transformed into the much more peaceful Caddo Lake National Wildlife Refuge. Visit www.cityofuncertain.com for details.

JOSEPH'S RIVERPORT BARBECUE, 201 N. Polk Street, Jefferson, 75657. Call 903-665-2341. High-water mark for barbecue in East Texas. Find them on Facebook. $–$$.

MARION COUNTY CHAMBER OF COMMERCE, 115 N. Polk Street, Jefferson, 75657. Call 903-665-2672. Website: www.jefferson-texas.com.

MARY KAY'S COUNTRY DINER, 806 Highway 96 North, San Augustine, 75972. Bustling country diner with great food at great prices. Call 936-275-0121. Find them on Facebook. $–$$.

MISSION DOLORES VISITOR CENTER, 701 S. Broadway, San Augustine, 75972. Call 936-275-3815. Free, but donations appreciated. Website: www.sanaugustinetx.com.

MISSION TEJAS STATE HISTORICAL PARK, 120 Park Road 44, Grapeland, 75844. Call 936-687-2394. Fee. Website: www.tpwd.texas.gov.

THE MOOSEHEAD CAFÉ, 412 E. Houston Avenue, Crockett, 75835. Call 936-544-5278. Closed Sundays. Red checkered tablecloths, counter seating, country cooking, and low prices. Website: www.the mooseheadcafe.com. $.

NACOGDOCHES COUNTY CHAMBER OF COMMERCE, 2516 N. Street, Nacogdoches, 75965. Call 936-560-5533. Website: www.nacogdoches.org.

OLD MULBERRY INN BED & BREAKFAST, 209 E. Jefferson Street, Jefferson, 75657. Call 903-665-1945. Crisp and uncluttered, with delicious three-course breakfasts. Website: www.old mulberryinn.com. $–$$.

PALESTINE TEXAS CONVENTION AND VISITOR BUREAU, 825 Spring Street, Palestine, 75801. Call 903-723-3014. Website: www.visitpalestine.com.

RUSK CHAMBER OF COMMERCE, 184 S. Main Street, Rusk, 75785. Call 903-683-4242. Website: www.ruskchamber.com.

SAN AUGUSTINE DRUG COMPANY, 104 E. Columbia Street, San Augustine, 75972. Vintage drug store with sweet treats and gifts. Call 936-275-3401. $.

STILLWATER INN, 203 E. Broadway, Jefferson, 75657. Call 903-665-8415. Closed Sundays and Mondays. Dinner only. Fine dining in an atmospheric Victorian inn. Website: www.stillwaterinn.com. $$.

T. C. LINDSEY & CO., 2293 FM 134, Waskom, 75659. Call 903-687-3382. Find them on Facebook.

TEXAS COUNTRY MUSIC HALL OF FAME AND THE TEX RITTER MUSEUM, 310 W. Panola Street, Carthage, 75633. Call 903-694-9561. Closed Sundays. Website: www.tcmhof.com.

TEXAS STATE RAILROAD PALESTINE DEPOT, 789 Park Road 70, Palestine, 75801. Call 855-632-7729. Fee. Reservations by phone or online. Website: www.texasstaterailroad.net.

UNCERTAIN, 199 Cypress Drive, Uncertain, 75661. Call 903-789-3443. Website: www.cityofuncertain.com.

WARFIELD HOUSE BED & BREAKFAST, 712 E. Houston Avenue (Highway 21), Crockett, 75835. Call 936-544-4037. Cozy, old-fashioned bed & breakfast, right down to the homemade quilts. Website: www.warfield-house.com. $.

9

THE PANHANDLE PLAINS AND CANYONS

CANYON, AMARILLO, PALO DURO CANYON STATE PARK, ADRIAN, TURKEY, CAPROCK CANYON STATE PARK

TOTAL DISTANCE: From Canyon, most attractions are within 60 miles.

HIGHLIGHTS: A long way from the triangle of traffic created by Dallas, Houston, and San Antonio, the laid-back **Panhandle Plains** are one of the best-kept secrets in the state. The region features miles and miles of classic western tableaux, punctuated by deep canyons and lovely backroads. The story of the Texas Panhandle very much revolves around the relationship between Native Americans, pioneers, ranchers, and the railroad, and this history is beautifully told at the **Panhandle-Plains Historical Museum** in **Canyon**. You can get a kick or two—or at least a burger and a piece of pie—on historic **Route 66**, spray-paint a half-buried car at **Cadillac Ranch**, and test the limits of your digestive tract with the 72-ounce steak challenge offered by the **Big Texan Steak Ranch** in **Amarillo**. Stunning views, native plants, cowboy cooking, and the musical **Texas** are all part of the **Palo Duro Canyon** experience. If you really want to get off the beaten path, consider exploring **Caprock Canyon** and the nearby tiny town of **Turkey**, birthplace of music legend Bob Wills.

GETTING THERE: Amarillo is the largest city in the Panhandle Plains, located at the intersection of I-40 and US 87. It is approximately 365 miles northwest of Dallas via US 287 or directly 240 miles north of Midland and 120 miles north of Lubbock on US 87.

    This route uses the small town of Canyon as a center point. From Canyon it is a 10-mile drive along TX 217 to Palo Duro Canyon; to return, simply retrace your steps. It is an 18-mile drive along I-27 from Canyon to the intersection with I-40 in Amarillo, and from that point you'll need to travel 50 miles west on I-40 to reach Adrian. Again, retrace your steps to return. To reach Turkey and Caprock Canyons, take I-27 south from Canyon for 30 miles, then TX 86 east 54 miles to Turkey, passing signs to Caprock Canyons along the way, and retrace your steps to return.

LEFT: PALO DURO CANYON VISTAS CONTINUE FOR MILES

The northern section of the Panhandle, the high plains of Texas, is divided from the southern section, the rolling plains, by a dramatic escarpment known as the Caprock, which you will see if you approach the region from I-20 and US 84. The region has several natural resources, the largest of which are the Ogallala Aquifer located beneath the high plains, the grasses that have supported herds of buffalo and cattle, and the canyons that sheltered humans for millennia.

The herds of buffalo that roamed the area attracted Native Americans from several tribes. The Apache rose to dominance here in the 1700s; the Comanche, on horseback, overtook them by the 1800s. Though the peoples of the region traded, communicated, and interacted with other groups throughout what we now consider the Southwest, political events conspired to shift the region's focus from westward to eastward toward the growing United States.

The Mexican War of Independence in 1821 led to new trade relations throughout the region, thus altering trade routes. Soon after, Pacific Railroad surveyors and United States Army officers started exploring the Panhandle, and the various groups of the Plains Indians started to chafe at so many intruders in the land they had enjoyed with little disruption for centuries. Then the Civil War began and distracted all interested parties. It wasn't until the early 1870s, when professional buffalo hunters encroached on the Panhandle, violating the Medicine Lodge Treaties of 1867, which guaranteed exclusive hunting rights to the Native Americans, that tensions finally boiled over and the battle over the West began.

Native Americans, led by the legendary Quanah Parker and Isa-Tai, mounted an attack on the intruders, an attack that would spark the Red River War of 1874–1875, a US military campaign to drive the Native Americans from the region. Many skirmishes, battles, and deaths later, in September of 1874, the Fourth United States Cavalry, led by Col. Mackenzie, encircled the Native Americans camped in the Palo Duro Canyon and took their horses to nearby Caprock Canyon for slaughter. Unable to defend themselves, hunt, or leave of their own will without their horses, the Native Americans were taken to reservations. Over the course of these years of conflict, the buffalo were hunted to near extinction, and with the Native Americans gone, the Panhandle lay empty. In 1876, Charles Goodnight moved his cattle from Colorado into the Palo Duro Canyon, eventually partnering with James Adair to create the JA Ranch. Suddenly ranches were organizing, towns and businesses springing up around them. The ranches themselves may have started as small enterprises with a hundred cattle or so, but soon corporations moved in, creating huge ranches and financing the large-scale projects that brought barbed wire, deep-drilled wells, and windmills. Some of this progress added worth, efficiency, and value, while some inflated the market, spawning poor management and many a personal disaster. A century later, however, modern ranching survives as an essential component of the Panhandle's economy and culture.

REMINDERS OF THE OLD WEST

Everything changed again in 1888, when the railroad rolled into town. In its efforts to bypass the steep, rocky caprock between the high plains and the rolling plains, the Fort Worth and Denver line ran straight through Amarillo, ensuring the town's future as a regional cultural, social, and commercial center. Similarly, the path the railroad took determined where towns

Route 66

One of the country's first highways, Route 66 was built to link Chicago and Los Angeles. Unlike many routes that cut a straight shot across the landscape between cities, Route 66 zigzagged its way along, linking the main streets of big cities and small towns. By the late 1920s, the route connected urban and rural America, allowing for the produce of the heartland to make its way to the densely populated cities.

In the midst of the Great Depression, tens of thousands of desperate people traveled Route 66 as they made their way from the Dust Bowl to the promise of California. In *The Grapes of Wrath*, John Steinbeck details this migration, christening Route 66 "the Mother Route."

Thousands of otherwise unemployed men paved the road between 1933 and 1938, and the military used it extensively during WWII. The thriving postwar economy made cars more accessible to the general public, and Americans itching to test their new wheels set out to see the country. Tourism mushroomed on the flat, practical, and efficient roadway, and drivers sustained the many mom-and-pop hotels, gas stations, and restaurants en route.

In 1956, President Eisenhower signed the Interstate Highway Act, designed to bring the Autobahn-style roads so popular in Europe to the United States. Since then, interstate highways have become ubiquitous and the more personal Route 66 a fading legend. Get a taste of what the journey was like in its heyday by visiting the precious few remaining institutions along this historic route.

---

sprang up across the region; bearing testament to this fact are the tiny ghost towns scattered along the backroads whose fate was sealed when the trains stopped coming.

When the ensuing world wars sent agricultural prices swinging, one group of risk-takers decided to strike out in a new industry. In 1921, local speculators completed their geological research, crossed their fingers, and drilled on ranchland, striking pay dirt when they hit oil and natural gas. Amarillo became the commercial center for this new industry. The Panhandle as a whole became so wild with greed that martial law was required to restore the peace. Cars and cheap fuel are conditions ripe for traveling, and the 1920s saw the construction of Route 66 (see opposite page) as well as many of the farm-to-market roads that crisscross the rural Panhandle, roads that served to link the economies of Texas, Oklahoma, and New Mexico.

While this newfound oil tempered the effects of the Great Depression for some, those still growing crops were devastated by the environmental conditions in the Panhandle, which were so severe they practically defined the Dust Bowl. Roosevelt's New Deal programs brought some relief, especially the Rural Electrification Project (page 37), which radically altered life positively and permanently when, in 1937, the lights came on in the Panhandle. These days, the economy remains a mix of agriculture and tourism.

The history of the Panhandle is fascinating, and the region has two remarkable vehicles for conveying it to visitors, both of which I highly recommend as essential elements of your visit: the Panhandle-Plains Historical Museum and the musical *Texas* (pages 182–183).

Start the route with a visit to the **Panhandle-Plains Historical Museum** in **Canyon**. This superb regional museum, located on the campus of the West Texas A&M University in an art deco building made of Texas limestone, is the state's largest history museum. It began as the pet project of a young visionary, Hattie Anderson, who moved to Canyon in 1920 to teach history and then set out to record the changing world around her. The historical society she founded collected stories, objects, artifacts, and art that represented the area's natural and cultural history and, by 1933, had completed the impressive task of building and opening a museum. Thoughtful and well-presented exhibits cover a remarkable range of topics, including

PANHANDLE-PLAINS HISTORICAL MUSEUM IN CANYON

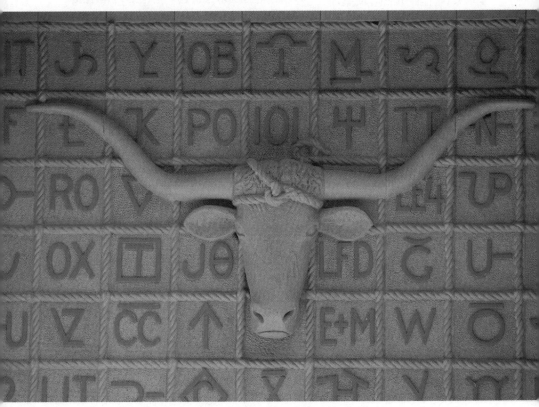

Texas art, dinosaur remains, fascinating photographs, weapons, furniture, and skillfully made Native American baskets. The museum is appropriate and engaging for both children and adults. You'll leave with a better understanding of the region, seeing it through different eyes as you proceed with your journey.

Canyon is a wonderful home base for exploring the region. The small town, really more of a suburb of Amarillo, is quiet, peaceful, and well located to several attractions on your itinerary. While lodging is limited, thankfully there is the **Hudspeth House Bed & Breakfast**. Built in 1910, the home was ordered as a kit from a Sears, Roebuck & Co. catalog; it boasts 8,000 square feet of living space, including 10 bedrooms and 10 bathrooms. The eight guest rooms have been refreshed with paint, trim, towels, and fixtures and are spotlessly clean. A restrained use of embellishments and antiques keeps the rooms open, airy, and extremely pleasant. Owned at one time by a Miss Hudspeth, a teacher at the university, the home is now under the stewardship of delightful owners Jill and Van, who welcome guests with genuine hospitality. The owners also let a roomy three-bedroom guest house for groups or families; check website for details.

ROOM AT THE HUDSPETH HOUSE IN CANYON

In the Plemons-Eakle Historic District of **Amarillo**, the striking **Heritage House Bed & Breakfast** was constructed as a private home in 1906, but has only recently opened as a bed and breakfast. The innkeepers are an attorney and former school teacher, which explains the "Courtroom" and "Classroom" themed rooms and the easy conversations lodgers enjoy at breakfast. The house has a vibrant history as the home of a prominent ranching and oil family and you can view some of their photos on loan and on display on the second floor. A well-kept and welcoming historic treat near downtown Amarillo. Other options in the region include camping or cabins in Palo Duro Canyon, a 10-minute drive from the town of Canyon, or booking a room in one of the many chain hotels that have sprouted up in the building boom along I-40 in Amarillo.

Sometimes small towns have an interesting mix of eateries, and that's certainly the case in Canyon. It's slim

Cattle Call

This is the part of Texas that cowboy legends are made of, and you'll still see plenty of cowboys around town. They're just riding their Ford pickup trucks instead of steeds, with cell phones at the ready instead of ropes. This is the heart of cattle-handling Texas, filled with blue jeans and muddy boots and all the other iconic images you'd expect. Learn more about the ranching industry by visiting the Amarillo Livestock Auction, held every Monday throughout the year, and enjoy an old-fashioned breakfast and lunch at the on-site Stockyard Café. The Panhandle is also a great place to take in a rodeo. The World Championship Chuckwagon Roundup is held in June, the Cal Farley's Boys Ranch Rodeo happens in September, and the World Championship Ranch Rodeo, in November, rounds out the year.

pickins here, but you can have your steak and eggs at the utilitarian **Ranch House Café**, a delicious spicy chicken curry or any number of Thai and Laotian dishes at **Sayakomarn's Thai & Lao Cuisine**, referred to locally as "Soccer Mom's," and a tasty lunch or dinner at **Feldman's Wrong Way Diner** on Fifth Avenue at 17th Street. While Feldman's may feel like any number of national franchises, the difference is it is local-owned and packed with people enjoying business lunches, family dinners, and birthday celebrations. The large menu includes the sorts of food you'd expect in this part of the state: huge and hearty stick-to-your-ribs steaks, fried chicken, and burgers, served with sides that are meals unto themselves elsewhere. Friendly service and a casual, lighthearted dining room means you really can't go wrong with Feldman's.

Canyon is the perfect jumping-off point into the captivating **Palo Duro Canyon**, just a 10-minute drive east along Fourth Avenue then TX 217. The second-largest canyon in the United States after the Grand Canyon in Arizona, Palo Duro was created by the movement of the Prairie Dog Town Fork of the Red River over the course of 240 million years. The river cut its way through the flat caprock of the Panhandle, eventually carving a canyon 120 miles long and between 6 and 12 miles wide. Water and wind erosion exposed the mesa walls, with their bands of red, orange, and brown rock, caves, and "hoodoos"—or spindly totem pole–like spires created by the wearing away of the edge of a plateau. The Spanish christened the canyon Palo Duro, or "hardwood," for the trees and shrubs growing at its base along with prickly pear cactus, yucca, and plenty of wildflowers.

The land here in the Panhandle is flat. So very, very flat that the discovery of the canyon and its lazy river must have struck Native Americans as nothing short of miraculous. Vegetation, game in the form of bison and

CABINS IN THE PALO DURO CANYON

mammoths, shelter, and, of course, water drew Native Americans to the canyon approximately 10,000 to 15,000 years ago. In more recent history, first the Apache, then the mounted Comanche and Kiowa, lived in the canyon, trading with groups in New Mexico. The first Europeans came to the region in 1541 as part of the Coronado expedition searching for Quivira, the fabled Native American settlement thought to possess large holdings of gold and silver. While they didn't find any treasure, they did stumble upon the Apaches, whose culture and livelihood revolved around the abundant buffalo grazing throughout the region. The US military arrived in 1852, searching for the headwaters of the Red River; within two decades they had put an end to the Native American presence in the Panhandle.

In 1876, after the government completed a full-scale survey of the area, Charles Goodnight drove his cattle into the canyon. In 1933, the state of Texas was able to purchase a portion of the canyon to develop into a park. The Civilian Conservation Corps built the road to the canyon floor and several cabins, and made other improvements that made the park accessible and enjoyable. As you explore the park, bear in mind that the vast majority of the southern part of the canyon remains private ranchland, unseen by many, a staggeringly large, remaining piece of cowboy country.

One of the best ways to learn more about local history, and experience the beauty of the Palo Duro Canyon is to see the "Official Play of the State of Texas," *Texas*. People come from all over to experience the performance, a must-see event in the region. The show is staged in the Pioneer Amphitheater, the outdoor venue built at the bottom of the canyon, performed by college students from all areas of the state, acting, singing, and dancing the history of the region. From the pioneers to the railroads and relations with the Native Americans, this high-energy musical hits all the highlights, disappointments, elation, and despair that were part and parcel of settling the West. The canyon itself plays a part. For instance, when the script calls for someone to ride in on horseback, you will hear the galloping hooves in the distance, then see dust and bobbing hats, as the mounted riders approach the stage.

No need to rush through dinner to get to the play on time; the **Big Texan** (page 185) hosts a barbecue beside the amphitheater each night the play is performed. Folks gather for dinner around 6 PM. The buffet tables are loaded down with fresh fruit, homemade potato au gratin, green salad, and steak, served with sweet tea and cobbler for dessert. (Buffet tickets are $16, less for children under 12, and are available at the amphitheater or online at www.paloducanyon.com). There is usually live music and dancing before the show starts at around 8:30. The most wonderful thing about the whole experience is the simple passage of time spent in this inspiring setting. You arrive in the canyon in broad daylight, dance at dusk, watch the last bits of

THE MUSICAL TEXAS IN THE PALO DURO CANYON

sun shimmering a burnt umber on the canyon wall, and gaze up at the stars as the show wraps up with an impressive fireworks display. The play and the barbecue are seasonal, running Tuesday through Saturday June through August, so please plan accordingly.

Whether you see *Texas* or not, count on spending another day just enjoying this spectacular natural area. There are plenty of ways to tour the canyon. Some folks drive in, taking in the sites from the comfort of their air-conditioned car, and others park and hike. Some enjoy the view from the saddle—both **Old West Stables** and **Palo Duro Stables** are happy to rent you a horse—and still more make reservations with **Elkins Ranch** for a guided tour. The folks at Elkins will take you into the canyon at daybreak and cook you breakfast cowboy-style. They'll cart you around in a jeep and explain the various natural wonders, historical facts, and cultural histories of the area. Heck, they'll arrange for Cookie, the camp cook, to whip up a chuck wagon dinner and treat you to some cowboy poetry, harmonica playing, and more Old West entertainment. Another option is to head out with a team of knowledgeable guides to trace the footsteps of the Native Americans who once called Palo Duro home. Basically, if you want to eat under the stars over an open fire and learn something new, the folks at Elkins Ranch have a tour for you. Call or visit; the ranch is located beside the entrance to **Palo Duro Canyon State Park**.

There are several **camping** options within the canyon, with designated areas for backpack and primitive camping, as well as spaces with electrical access. Even equestrian camping is offered for people who want to bring their horse along for the fun. If you like the outdoors but prefer some amount of creature comforts, consider renting one of the **cabins** built by the Civilian Conservation Corps in the 1930s. These stone structures are rustic, but have heat, air conditioning, and bathrooms inside and picnic tables and a charcoal grill outside. Those in the "Cow Camp" also have little refrigerators. Outstanding panoramic views and starry nights come standard with all cabins.

Quitaque

Clearly, part of Caprock Canyon State Park's appeal is its remoteness; those who seek it out tend to be well prepared. Whatever your recreational plans, please be sure to pack plenty of fresh water and snacks, and wear clothing and shoes appropriate for the season of your visit. Stop in Quitaque (pronounced KITTY-quay or KITuh- kway), the tiny hamlet on TX 86 near Caprock Canyons, for supplies.

There isn't anywhere for a substantial meal in Palo Duro Canyon, so it's a great time to head to Amarillo and put in an appearance at **Tyler's Barbeque**, the sort of place folks love to love. Opened by Amarillo native Tyler Frazer in 2010, the oak-fired pits here have delivered smoky, juicy, top-notch barbecue almost non-stop, winning statewide recognition along the way. The ribs sell out quick, but there's still pulled pork, chicken, brisket, several kinds of sausage, and homemade potato salad, slaw, beans, and peach cobbler to choose from. Get there early since you don't want to miss the opportunity to sample some of the best barbecue in the Panhandle.

You could easily drive right by **Coyote Bluff Café**, but if you are in the market for a fantastic hamburger, consider stopping. While the café may not look like much, looks can be deceiving. This spot has earned a growing following of devotees with their green chile cheeseburger, hickory burger with barbecue sauce, and a super spicy burger smothered with sauteed jalapeños, onions, tabasco and a special house sauce created to really turn up the heat.

The **Big Texan Steak Ranch**, as they are quick to remind you, "ain't no chain or franchise." This Amarillo institution on I-40 really is one of a kind, as unique as the lanky cowboy sign out front. Founded by R. J. "Bob" Lee in 1960, the Big Texan Steak Ranch was originally located along the old Route 66 in east Amarillo. As the new interstate was set to cut through the city, Bob had a hunch that the businesses on little Route 66 would suffer, so he moved his operation to its current location, bringing along the iconic cowboy sign by helicopter. And, true to its name, there's nothing small about the Big Texan. Whether it's breakfast, lunch, dinner, drinks, or desserts, the portions are huge, but the biggest of all is the 72-ounce steak, the "Texas King." If you can eat it along with all the side dishes in an hour, then it's yours for free. If you can't, the experience will set you back $72 and you'll have plenty of steak to take home for lunch tomorrow. The restaurant is a cavernous room with wood floors; deer heads on the wall complete the frontier theme. Part theme park, part movie set, and part old-time fun, the Big Texan is the place to come for a slice of imaginative, old-time Texas.

While the thoroughfare is no longer marked on modern maps, portions of Route 66 live on, such as a historic section of Sixth Avenue in Amarillo. Knickknack shops and biker bars stand shoulder to shoulder for several blocks in this historic district, of which the keystone is the **Golden Light Café**. The consummate greasy spoon, the Golden Light flips some of the best burgers in the area, served in red plastic mesh baskets along with a mound of fries. You just have to appreciate the unassuming attitude of this joint. The dining counter is shoved right up against the grill, the ceilings feel like they are barely 7 feet tall, and no one bats an eye at cold beers at midday. The chili for the Frito pie bubbles in a huge vat on the stove, and the burgers and buns seem to fly off the grill as orders are filled lickety-split. This place

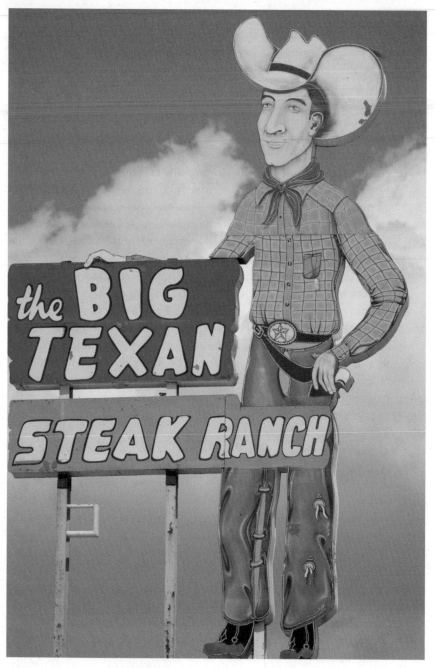

THE BIG TEXAN STEAK RANCH IN AMARILLO

is such a classic, it's on the National Register of Historic Places. A full roster of live music, from blues and country to singer-songwriters and rock, fills the café Thursday through Saturday evenings.

While you may or may not get any kicks on Route 66, you can definitely get one of the best pieces of pie you've ever sunk a fork into. From Amarillo, head west on I-40, where you will, 49 miles later, find yourself approaching **Adrian**. Exit 23A will put you right on Old Route 66, slightly north of the interstate, where you can't miss the **Midpoint Café** (and if you do, you will soon find yourself in New Mexico). While it may feel like the middle of nowhere, it is precisely the geomathematical mid-point of Route 66. Drive 1,139 miles east and you'll be in Chicago; 1,139 miles west and you'll be in Los Angeles. The Midpoint Café is pretty noticeable; it's practically the only thing in town. The restaurant is filled with retro chrome and Formica tables and plenty of "Route 66" signs. While the burgers are worth a mention, the pie is worth the drive. The Ugly Crust Pie hearkens back to a time before anyone counted calories or cholesterol and all that mattered was taste. The crust is marvelously crisp, a feat achieved by the use of pure butter. One forkful and the molten chocolate center oozes out, mixing with the ice cream, hot fudge sauce, and whipped cream. There's nothing halfway about the service or the great feeling you get here—of being just one of many who've stopped in for some sugar.

PIE AT THE MIDPOINT CAFÉ IN ADRIAN

Returning to Amarillo from Adrian is the perfect time to stop in and check out the bumper crop at **Cadillac Ranch**. Meant to represent the golden age of American automobiles, these ten caddies seem to have hit a bit of a rough spot in the road. Half-buried in the dirt and mud of a desolate wheat field alongside I-40, the cars have drawn a crowd since they were first planted. The collection was originally installed in 1974 several miles to the east by millionaire Stanley Marsh III with the help of some folks from the Ant Farm, a San Francisco art group. When growth around Amarillo threatened the desolation of the location, the whole shebang was moved to its current spot. The directions may sound somewhat imprecise, but you'll find it, just like thousands do every year. Cadillac Ranch is located along I-40, between exits 60 and 62. Take the frontage road on the south side of

I-40, park your car alongside the road, and enter the field through the hole in the fence. Visitors are encouraged, at least by each other, to spray-paint the cars, and if you didn't bring paint, folks are usually happy to share. Wacky, free, fun, and as iconic as they come.

Back in Amarillo, there are two niche museums that may be of interest, the **Kwahadi Kiva Indian Museum** and the **American Quarter Horse Hall of Fame and Museum**, both located along I-40. The Kwahadi Kivi Indian Museum represents one man's personal collection of artifacts and art relating to the cultures of the Native Americans of the region. The modest museum comes alive during performances of traditional Native American dances, performed by the Kwahadis, a talented group of local Boy Scouts who have danced in venues all over the world; contact the museum for performance dates. The American Quarter Horse Hall of Fame and Museum, on the other hand, is sleek and modern, with plenty of information on America's most popular horse. Amarillo is paradise for horse lovers traveling with their four-legged companions, and as you drive through town, you'll see lots of horse trailers, some headed to area equine shows and rodeos, others just for a jaunt on the miles of riding trails in the canyon.

If the wide open road has you itching for adventure, visit **Jack Sisemore Traveland RV Museum**. The museum, located at the Jack Sisemore RV dealership, is sure to put a smile on your face. This collection of vintage RVs dates as far back as the 1930s, many with original furnishings, accessories, and details. You'll get to explore classic teardrop trailers, vintage Airstreams, and the wonderful mix of Harley Davidsons are a bonus.

An hour-and-40-minute drive south of Canyon, **Turkey** is about as small and peaceful as towns come out here. What puts Turkey on the map is its most famous native son, Bob Wills. Diehard Wills fans—you know who you are—and the merely curious will enjoy a trip to this windswept Panhandle Plains town that Wills called home.

James Robert (Bob) Wills was born in Texas in 1905, and, after several moves, his family settled into a little community between the Little Red River and the Prairie Dog Town Fork of the Red River. There he learned to play the violin from his father, grandfather, and laborers in the cotton fields, and went on to play at local dances. In 1929, Wills moved to Fort Worth, playing for radio shows and organizing a band, the Light Crust Doughboys, so named for their sponsor, Light Crust Flour. In 1934, he moved to Tulsa, Oklahoma, expanding his radio audience and starting the band for which he would become famous, the Texas Playboys. Along the way, Wills pioneered an entirely new form of music, one deeply rooted in his home state of Texas: western swing. A synthesis of the depth of blues, the swing of jazz, and the expansive sound of big band, it was a style all its own, and Wills's compositions, most notably "San Antonio Rose," drew national attention. Wills, known as the King of Western Swing, won several awards and plenty of fame and recognition during his lifetime, and his unique contribution to American music has stood the test of time. Artists such as Asleep at the Wheel, George Strait, and countless others have covered many of Wills's originals to the delight of listeners. *For the Last Time: Bob Wills and His Texas Playboys,* recorded just before his death, is his best-selling album, a deserved Grammy winner, a classic for fans and a great introduction for newcomers. The **Bob Wills Museum** tells the story of his life, and the annual **Bob Wills Reunion** held in Turkey on the last

SCULPTURE OUTSIDE THE AMERICAN QUARTER HORSE HALL OF FAME AND MUSEUM IN AMARILLO

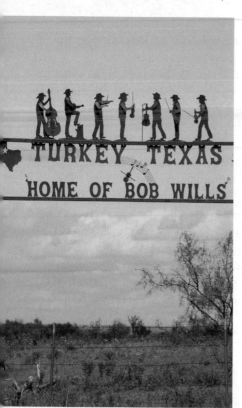
A TURKEY, TEXAS, WELCOME

Sunday in April is so popular that over 10,000 devotees routinely turn out.

For the rest of the year, however, Turkey may be just the ticket for those who like to get away from it all. Built in 1927, the **Hotel Turkey**'s current owners have set about renovating room by room, refinishing the original warm wood floors and doors, updating decor, and adding rugs, comforters, and period furniture. The hotel has a comfortable, lived-in, small-town feeling that seems hard to come by these days. Rocking chairs on the glassed-in porch are a great place to doze with an unopened book in your lap. The hotel restaurant serves breakfast daily, lunch every day except Monday, a fish dinner on Fridays, steak and shrimp on Saturdays, and they'll have pizza and wings for everyone Wednesday and Sunday evenings. It's a great place to unplug.

If you've fallen in love with the land here and want to see more, consider visiting **Caprock Canyons State Park**. Less developed and even more remote than Palo Duro, the canyon sits out on the pristine plains, rewarding visitors with its views of the sunset, flowers, wildlife, and the wide open sky. Like Palo Duro, Caprock Canyons was home to various communities of Native Americans for thousands of years, some of whom traded regularly with traders (*comancheros*) and buffalo hunters (*ciboleros*) from New Mexico. Artifacts found nearby are strong evidence of a *cibolero* camp in the area and detail the area's fascinating past. Today Caprock Canyons is home to the state's official bison herd, brought back from near extinction in the region, and the rarely seen golden eagle.

The park has campsites, picnic areas, a lake for swimming and fishing, horseback riding, and 90 miles of trails. While there are trails suitable for hikers of all levels, some are only appropriate for skilled outdoors people. Please be sure to assess your skills accurately, and check your plans with a park ranger. An audio tour of the park, available for a refundable $5 deposit, is particularly enjoyable for visitors who might like to view the park by car. Equestrians can make arrangements for guided or unsupervised horse rentals through **Quitaque Riding Stables**.

The two canyons of the Panhandle Plains have also become a mecca for mountain bikers, folks who want the physical challenge of a good ride and the thrill of wide-open wild spaces. In 1992, the park was gifted a 64.25-mile stretch of former railroad right-of-way, which has vastly increased the possibilities for recreation in the area. The **Trailway**, as the rail-to-trail conversion is known, crosses over 46 bridges and goes through one tunnel (Clarity Tunnel, home to a colony of Mexican free-tail bats) as it makes its way between the towns of South Plains and Estelline. Trail maps are available online at www.tpwd.texas.gov and at the park itself. You can reach Caprock Canyons State Park from Turkey by taking TX 86 west to CR 30, which becomes CR 29, and following signs to the park.

IN THE AREA

AMARILLO CONVENTION AND VISITOR COUNCIL, the Bivins Mansion, 1000 S. Polk Street, Amarillo, 79101. Call 1-800-692-1338. Website: www.visitamarillo.com.

AMARILLO LIVESTOCK AUCTION, 100 S. Manhattan Street, Amarillo, 79120. Call 806-373-7464. Website: www.amarillolivestockauction.com.

AMERICAN QUARTER HORSE HALL OF FAME AND MUSEUM, 1600 Quarter Horse Drive, Amarillo, 79104. Call 806-376-4811. Fee. Website: www.aqha.com.

BIG TEXAN STEAK RANCH, 7701 E. I-40, Amarillo, 79118. Call 1-800-657-7177. Huge steaks at this rambling and heavily-touristed steakhouse complex. Website: www.bigtexan.com. $$.

BOB WILLS MUSEUM, 602 Lyles Street, Turkey, 79261. Call 806-423-1253. Closed weekends. Website: www.bobwillsday.com.

CADILLAC RANCH, located in a pasture on the south side of eastbound I-40, between exits 60 and 62. Free.

CANYON CHAMBER OF COMMERCE, 1518 Fifth Avenue, Canyon, 79015. Call 806-655-7815. Website: www.canyonchamber.org.

CAPROCK CANYONS STATE PARK AND TRAILWAY, 850 Caprock Canyon Park Road, Quitaque, 79255. Call 806-455-1492. Fee. Website: www.tpwd.texas.gov.

COYOTE BLUFF CAFÉ, 2417 S. Grand Street, Amarillo, 79103. Call: 806-373-4640. Closed Sundays and Mondays. Hole-in-the-wall serving big, juicy burgers in the heart of cattle country. Website: www.coyotebluffcafe.com. Cash only. $$.

ELKINS RANCH, 11301 E TX 217, Canyon, 79015. Call 806-488-2100. Website: www.theelkinsranch.com.

FELDMAN'S WRONG WAY DINER, 2100 N. Second Avenue, Canyon, 79015. Call 806-655-2700. Fun decor and good food in a relaxed local eatery. Website: www.feldmansdiner.com. $–$$.

GOLDEN LIGHT CAFÉ, 2906 W. Sixth Avenue, Amarillo, 79106. Call 806-374-9237. No nonsense burgers, Frito pie, and live music keeps this diner hopping and humming. Website: www.goldenlightcafe.com. $.

HERITAGE HOUSE BED & BREAKFAST, 1620 S. Polk Street, Amarillo, 79102. Call: 806-220-2322. Two spacious rooms in a grand home in a historic district of Amarillo. Website: www.heritagehouseamarillo.com. $$.

HOTEL TURKEY, 201 Third Street, Turkey, 79261. Call 806-423-1151. Get away from it all at this friendly, casual hotel in the little town of Turkey. Website: www.hotelturkeytexas.com. $.

HUDSPETH HOUSE BED & BREAKFAST, 1905 Fourth Avenue, Canyon, 79015. Call 806-655-9800. Stylish rooms in a lovely historic home in the small town of Canyon. Website: www.hudspethhouse.com. $$.

JACK SISEMORE TRAVELAND RV MUSEUM, 4341 Canyon Drive, Amarillo, 79110. Call 888-702-0337. Closed Sundays. Website: www.rvmuseum.net.

KWAHADI KIVA INDIAN MUSEUM, 9151 I-40, Amarillo, 79118. Call 806-335-3175. Winter closed weekdays. Summer closed Mondays and Tuesdays. Fee. Website: www.kwahadi.com.

MIDPOINT CAFÉ, Historic Route 66, Adrian, 79001. Call 806-538-6379. One-of-a-kind location for burgers and "ugly pie." Website: www.route66midpointcafe.com. $–$$.

OLD WEST STABLES, 11450 Park Road 5, Canyon, 79015. Call 806-488-2180. Website: www.oldweststables.com.

PALO DURO CANYON STATE PARK, 11450 Park Road 5, Canyon, 79015. Call 806-488-2227. Fee. Website: www.palodurocanyon.com.

PALO DURO STABLES, 10160 TX 217, just outside Palo Duro Canyon State Park, Canyon, 79015. Call 806-488-2799. Website: www.paloduroriding stables.com.

PANHANDLE-PLAINS HISTORICAL MUSEUM, 2503 Fourth Avenue, Canyon, 79015. Call 806-651-2244. Summer closed Sundays. Winter closed Sundays and Mondays. Fee. Website: www.panhandleplains.org.

QUITAQUE CHAMBER OF COMMERCE, PO Box 48777, Quitaque, 79255. Call 806-455-1456. Website: www.quitaque.org.

QUITAQUE RIDING STABLES, FM 1065 beside the Trailway. Call 806-269-1209 or 806-455-1208. Website: www.quitaqueridingstables.com.

RANCH HOUSE CAFÉ, 810 23rd Street, Canyon, 79015. Call 806-655-8785. Straightforward meals in a no-frills diner. Website: www.theranchhousecafe .com. $.

SAYAKOMARN'S THAI AND LAO CUISINE, 419 16th Street, Canyon, 79015. Call 806-655-2698. Well-loved local favorite for Thai and Laotian cuisine on the square. Website: www.sayakomarns.com. $–$$.

TEXAS: **MUSICAL DRAMA IN PALO DURO CANYON,** 1514 Fifth Avenue, Canyon, 79015. Call 806-655-2181. June through August, Tuesday through Saturday nights. Fee. Website: www.texas-show.com.

TYLER'S BARBEQUE, 2014 Paramount Boulevard, Amarillo, 79109. Call 806-331-2271. Closed Sundays and Mondays. Outstanding barbecue, served hot from the pits until it's gone. Website: www.tylersbarbecue.com. $$.

10

THE BIG BEND

MARFA, SHAFTER, PRESIDIO, FORT LEATON, BIG BEND
NATIONAL PARK, LAJITAS, TERLINGUA, ALPINE,
MARATHON, FORT DAVIS, BALMORHEA

TOTAL DISTANCE: 200–300 miles

HIGHLIGHTS: Start your trip in **Marfa**, the funky modern-art outpost; from there
plan on visiting **Marathon**, with lovely lodging of its own, and **Alpine**. Use
any of these three old railroad towns as a jumping-off point into **Big Bend
National Park**, passing quirky **Terlingua** and historic **Fort Leaton**, while traveling **El Camino del Rio**, the River Road, along the Rio Grande. Head north
through **Fort Davis**, stopping to explore the town and **Fort Davis State Park**,
before pressing on to **Balmorhea Springs State Park** and its enormous and
refreshing natural spring-fed pool. Spend some time in a **ghost town**, keep
your eyes out for the **Marfa Lights**, and watch the huge sun rise and set over
this wondrous western landscape.

GETTING THERE: From San Antonio, take the 405-mile trip west to Marfa, via I-10,
or from Austin, take TX 71 through Johnson City (pages 35–38) and Fredericksburg (pages 39–42) to the intersection with I-10 for a total of 430 miles to
Marfa. Once on I-10, take exit 248 and follow FM 1776/US 67 56 miles south
to Alpine and an additional 26 miles west to Marfa. From Dallas/Fort Worth,
take I-20 approximately 500 miles west to exit 22, where you'll pick up FM
2903. Follow FM 2903 south to TX 17, which will take you through Fort Davis
and straight on to Marfa. Marfa is located 194 miles east of El Paso, by way of
I-10 and US 290.

If you start your route in Marfa, you'll take US 67 60 miles south to Presidio, FM 170 62 miles to Terlingua, passing Lajitas en route. From Terlingua,
head east to the intersection between FM 170 and TX 118, where you can
either turn north on TX 118 to Alpine (83.5 miles) or east on TX 118/Maverick
Drive to the Big Bend Visitor Center (30 miles). Should you press on into the
park, US 385 will take you to Marathon (87 miles).

US 67/US 90 runs between Marfa, Alpine, and Marathon. Marfa to Alpine

LEFT: CATTLE ON RANCHLAND BIG BEND COUNTRY

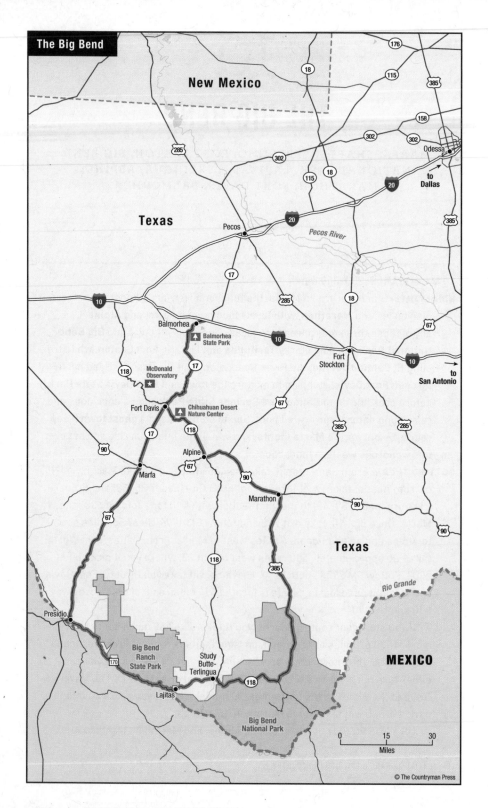

The Big Bend

New Mexico

Texas

Odessa

to Dallas

Pecos

Pecos River

Balmorhea

Balmorhea State Park

McDonald Observatory

Fort Stockton

to San Antonio

Fort Davis

Chihuahuan Desert Nature Center

Alpine

Marfa

Marathon

Texas

Rio Grande

Presidio

Big Bend Ranch State Park

Study Butte-Terlingua

MEXICO

Lajitas

Big Bend National Park

0   15   30
Miles

© The Countryman Press

is 50 miles and Alpine to Marathon is 30. You can reach Fort Davis from either Marfa (TX 17, 21 miles) or Alpine (TX 118, 24 miles), and from there it is a direct route 37 miles to Balmorhea on TX 17. Balmorhea is just south of I-10, making it a convenient ending point to the route.

To drive west in Texas is to drive straight to freedom. As you leave the congestion of the cities of Central Texas, super highways funnel into four-lane highways, which, by the time you reach the Big Bend region of West Texas, have become abbreviated two-lane country roads stretching out between huge swatches of fenced-in openness. When you look around it would be easy to feel lonely or vulnerable, with only a gas station or two for company, but the stunning views of the magnificent mountains ahead are fortifying. And while many people joke about the nothingness out here, a closer look at this part of the state quickly reveals both a vibrant ecosystem in the desert and lively culture in the towns within it.

There are several ways to approach the area; I suggest choosing a home base and fanning out to the various sites on day trips. There are two reasons for this. First, this region can get very remote, very quickly, and having a home base means easy access to any necessities you may need. Second, the weather can be unpredictable, and staying in one place will allow you to custom-tailor your day trips around the whims of Mother Nature.

WEST TEXAS CACTI

While the adventurous might enjoy staying in Big Bend National Park or one of the more far-flung lodging options outlined below, when it comes to amenities, it's hard to beat Marfa, though Alpine, Marathon, and Fort Davis are also very comfortable. For the purpose of outlining the route, let's start in Marfa.

Marfa is perched high on the Marfa Plateau, at an altitude of 4,830 feet; during a hot Texas summer, it's one of the coolest places in the state. But Marfa is cool altogether. With interesting architecture, lodging, gourmet food, and plenty of desert scenery, Marfa defines middle-of-nowhere chic.

Marfa, established in the 1880s as a stop on the railroad, has always been an outpost of sorts. Modest at the start, the original settlement was composed of three shelters: a one-room train station, a shack for gambling, and a tent with a restaurant inside. First known as Tank Town, Marfa was renamed at the suggestion of the railroad engineer's wife, who had seen the name in *The Brothers Karamazov*.

In 1911, the town became a station for the United States cavalry during the volatile Mexican Revolution. During Prohibition, "mounted watchmen" from Marfa patrolled the region to help curb alcohol smuggling, and later the United States Border Patrol did the same to stop the flow of illegal drugs. In the 1940s, Marfa was home to the Chemical Warfare Brigades, a prisoner-of-war camp, and an advanced flight training base. The military installation in town was known by various names, including Camp Albert, Camp Marfa, and Fort D. A. Russell. Deactivated in 1949, the base was put up for sale. In the 1970s, artist Donald Judd purchased the compound, sparking Marfa's transformation from a utilitarian West Texas town to an offbeat cultural outpost.

Marfa is a tiny town, with a customary Texas courthouse at its center and a railroad running through it. Most of the action is on San Antonio Avenue, otherwise known as US 67, and N. Highland Avenue, which runs north to the courthouse. Just a block south of their intersection, you'll find the **Marfa Visitor Center** where you can stop in and say hello.

There are few places to spend the night in town; fortunately several of them exceed expectations. The oldest newest addition to overnight accommodations in Marfa is the **Hotel Saint George**, built on the site and using some of the elements of its namesake, the original Hotel Saint George, constructed in 1886, damaged by fire in the 1920s, and closed in 1929. The hotel's most recent incarnation is sparse and sleek, with original well-worn concrete floors and brick walls offset by the 300 pieces of contemporary artwork of Marfa-connected artists on display for all to enjoy. Rooms are minimally decorated, with luxurious bedding and wonderful views of the town's landmarks, legendary sunsets, or stunning mountains. The hotel's fine dining restaurant, LaVenture, prepares luscious handmade pasta dishes and thick Black Angus ribeye steaks, but the shared dishes and inspired craft cocktails make for a fantastic evening.

All are welcome in the lobby, a public space that includes the **Marfa Book Company**. Founded in 1999, this pleasant bookstore is, in many ways, the town's meeting place. On the shelves, titles are very carefully chosen, and the selection, from fiction to travel, art to children's books, is admirable. From classics to the obscure, the Book Company, like many things in Marfa, is an epicurean treat.

The Hotel Paisano was built in 1930 as a hotel for cattlemen, who would spend hours in the lobby wheeling and dealing. When Hollywood breezed into Marfa to film the movie *Giant* in 1955, Elizabeth Taylor, James Dean, and Rock Hudson were all given rooms at the Paisano and quickly made themselves right at home. It's no surprise that the most popular room in the hotel is still the one Dean slept in.

While the hotel hit on some hard times in the years in between, it is now a heartwarming example of local landmark renovation. The courtyard centers around a bubbling fountain, with tables and chairs and window boxes lending a homey touch to an otherwise majestic entrance. With vintage tile work, cozy rooms—some even have balconies or enclosed patios—and plenty of historic detail, the Paisano is sure to appeal to guests who appreciate the individuality and quirkiness of older hotels. Since each room is different, be sure to check the website before you book and call with any questions.

If you are coming to West Texas to sleep under the stars, check into **El Cosmico**. You can bring a tent to pitch in one of their designated campsites, or spend the night tucked into a funky vintage trailer or white canvas yurt. The fenced-in, pedestrian-only camp includes outdoor showers, an open-air communal kitchen, and hammocks strung in a grove of trees. The brainchild of Liz Lambert, the Texas hotelier responsible for some of the coolest places to stay in Austin and San Antonio, El Cosmico is free-spirited and down to

THE HOTEL PAISANO IN MARFA

earth, a good balance for folks who like to go rustic without roughing it too much. Sure, you'll have to walk to the bathrooms in the middle of the night, but you'll do so by the light of the moon. Theme weekend getaways—cooking classes and music festivals—keep El Cosmico fresh and fun.

Marfa is a foodie's delight. There aren't many places to chose from, but the caliber belies the town's size, appealing to an urbanite's epicurean palate—and wallet. You'd almost have to make a spreadsheet to figure out what is open when, and those who aren't paying attention to operating hours may find themselves going hungry. At the very least, you can stop by the **Get Go**, Marfa's pricey gourmet food depot, to stock up on snacks.

Frama @ Tumbleweed Laundry is one of the precious few places in Marfa open every day for most of the day. They don't serve much—just coffee and ice cream—but their little shop is a good place to sit, meet some folks, and chat for a spell while your clothes spin in the massive machines of the attached Laundromat. Lunch is a bit easier. **Food Shark** works some Mediterranean-inspired magic inside their food truck. Order a Marfalafel and you'll get falafel wrapped with lettuce, tomato, cucumber, onions, tahini, yogurt, and a spicy harissa sauce in a flour tortilla. Falafel, hummus, and salads dominate the menu, and an eclectic mix of daily specials adds variety. They've served everything from carne guisada tacos and a warm maple-glazed ham sandwich on rye to *bahn mi* sandwiches—Vietnamese-

The Mystery of the Marfa Lights

One of the more confounding and fascinating phenomena in West Texas is the **Marfa Lights**, sometimes called the Marfa Mystery Lights or Ghost Lights. According to the lore, people have spoken of seeing the lights as early as the 1880s, but the first confirmed report dates only to 1957. Regardless of the decade or transmittance, the stories bear similarities. The lights are generally described as glowing orbs about the size of a soccer ball. They tend to appear only at night, organized in pairs or groups, and are said to be white, yellow, orange, red, and sometimes blue or green.

There seems to be no rhyme or reason for their appearance; they are seen with unpredictable infrequency throughout the seasons. The myriad explanations—temperature gradients, thermal expansion and contraction of quartz, headlights on nearby TX 67—add to the allure of this mystery. While no one knows what they are, folks agree that the lights do exist. The best place to have a look is at the Marfa Lights viewing platform on the south side of I-90, just east of town.

Every Labor Day, the town celebrates their local oddity with the **Marfa Lights Festival**, a long weekend of food, parades, music, and street dancing.

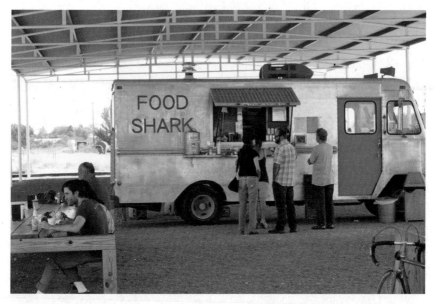

FOOD SHARK IN MARFA

spiced chicken or tofu on a baguette dressed with hoisin mayo and pickled vegetables—a hearty beef curry with rice, and a cucumber peanut salad. The desserts are always fresh and homemade. Order at the truck and find a seat at the super-sized outdoor picnic tables beside a railroad track. Good food and friendly folks make this place tick, though it can be tricky to get here in time to enjoy a meal. Only open for lunch Wednesday through Saturday (though they may serve food on Saturday if the mood strikes), so plan accordingly or hope to get lucky. **Squeeze Marfa** is a little café shoehorned into a building across from the courthouse with a tiny shaded patio tacked onto the side. The homemade yogurt, granola, and berry bowl is a nice breakfast, and the lunchtime panini sandwiches, made with fresh bread and various meats, vegetables, and spreads, are served hot from the grill.

Now that you've enjoyed breakfast and lunch, it's time to consider dinner. With so few places to eat in Marfa, consider waiting in line an inevitability. If waits don't bother you—after all, once you are in Marfa, you really don't have anywhere else to go, do you?—then just enjoy an evening spent on "Marfa Time." However, if you have your heart set on dinner at a particular place at a particular time, especially on a Friday or Saturday, make reservations to avoid disappointment.

One of the least complicated places to eat is the **Pizza Foundation**, a fun and funky pizzeria that doesn't suffer from any of the usual pizza complaints—too much cheese, soggy toppings, or an overly thick and chewy crust. The pizza here is crispy, yeasty, zesty, and tangy. Generous salads and a small selection of drinks round out the offerings at this inexpensive and

The Chinati and Judd Foundations

Minimalist sculptor Donald Judd and several artist friends purchased an old military compound in Marfa in the 1970s knowing it would make a perfect venue for their enormous permanent art installations. Coming from cramped New York, they found the unrestricted space in which to create liberating; Judd quickly filled the town with his art. Since his death in 1994, the caretaker of Judd's artwork and vision has been the Marfa-based **Chinati Foundation/La Fundación Chinati**. The foundation has an expansive collection of large-scale installations produced by various artists, each set against the stunning backdrop of West Texas. The rub is that visits are by guided tour only, so you'll need to plan ahead. The second Judd-related institution in Marfa is the **Judd Foundation**, which is dedicated to preserving the artist's studio and living spaces in Marfa and New York, totaling 15 in all. A quick walk around town and you're sure to spot many of them. The two foundations pair up each October for the annual **Chinati Weekend**, which offers visitors a weekend-long concentration of art in the form of concerts, readings, and exhibits. The Chinati Foundation regularly draws crowds of national and international art lovers, who happily cross Texas just to partake.

very casual spot. Open until orders overwhelm the oven's capacity, so get there early.

Cochineal, sparse and modern without seeming cold, serves a wide-ranging seasonal menu of creative cuisine. From the cold cucumber gazpacho and the bison tartar to quail medallions with blackberry sauce, the menu here is locally-sourced and universally delicious. The extensive wine list and fantastic desserts make it a stand-out. Cochineal is as delightful and tasty as any big-city bistro, just in the desert of West Texas.

From Marfa, it's an easy 60-mile drive south along TX 67 to Presidio, and along the way, you'll pass through the tiny, former silver-mining town of **Shafter**—nearly empty save the precious few homes and single white church huddled beside the mountains. In the 1890s, silver was discovered in northern Mexico, and cinnabar, of which mercury is a by-product, was found in Big Bend. A mining boom hit the region, with mining towns popping up around the countryside. Then, after a quick 20 years, it was all over; ghostly old towns like Shafter remain, stark and picturesque.

Nineteen miles later, the road brings you straight into **Presidio**, a little border town on the Rio Grande. Inhabited for centuries, this area is in fact the oldest continuously cultivated area in the United States, with archaeological evidence of farming dating back to 1500 B.C. The Spanish encountered Native Americans living here in organized communities in the 1500s;

Anglo settlers did not arrive until 1848. Today Presidio is a modest town, and most notably for this book, is the starting point of **El Camino del Rio (The River Road)**, the scenic 66-mile drive along FM 170 that hugs the Rio Grande and offers stunning views of the landscape shared by the United States and neighboring Mexico.

Leaving Presidio and turning eastward on scenic TX 170, in 3 miles you will come upon **Fort Leaton**, the private fort built in 1848 by Indian bounty hunter Benjamin Leaton, which he used as a lucrative trading post with the Apache and Comanche Indians. It is now preserved as a state park. Upon entering, coming from the relentless heat outside, visitors are immediately struck by the cool air and thick walls of the fort and can easily imagine its promise of safety. Take a look inside, where a particularly informative display of the region's history and a helpful park ranger await.

The fort is at the western entrance to **Big Bend Ranch State Park**, 300,000 acres of very remote and rugged land that includes deep canyons, waterfalls, and even an ancient extinct volcano. There are two main routes into the state park. One takes you northward along FM 169/Casa Piedra Road, and then east to a string of hiking trails, campsites, and scenic overlooks. The second, FM 170, also includes opportunities for camping and hiking, and ends at the **Barton Warnock Education Center**.

SHAFTER VIEWS

Nature lovers and the naturally curious will appreciate the center's interpretative, detailed displays of the five biological landscapes represented in this part of the Chihuahuan Desert. A stroll through its 2-acre botanical garden is also nice. The presentation "Una Tierra—One Land," a collaborative effort between the state and national parks in Big Bend and the Mexican states of Coahuila and Chihuahua just over the border, illustrates the two nations' shared ecological heritage. If you're camping or hiking, Big Bend Ranch requires a permit, which you can pick up here or at Fort Leaton along with maps and information.

Return to Presidio to continue the route. The distance between Presidio and the next stop is only about 50 miles, but you should plan on leaving at least an hour and a half for travel. Now is also a good time to purchase some water and

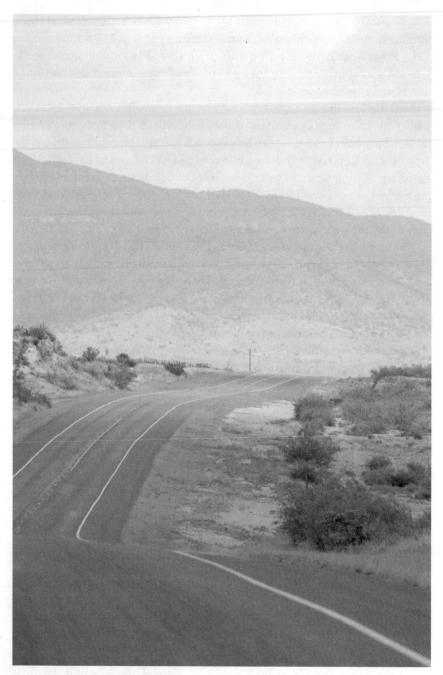

EL CAMINO DEL RIO—THE RIVER ROAD

snacks (see box below), and fill your gas tank before starting your journey, since you won't have the chance to do so again for quite some time.

On the road again, enjoy this gorgeous stretch of El Camino del Rio (TX 170), which follows the Rio Grande eastward as best it can, dipping and rising with the hills, and widening for scenic overlooks, all the way to **Lajitas**. Formerly a trading post for miners, ranchers, and smugglers, Lajitas was

An Ounce of Prevention . . .

Big Bend National Park is simply stunning. Hundreds of thousands of visitors come to the park each year, drawn to its remote location, quiet stillness, and wildness. You can stay overnight in the park or leave Marfa, Alpine, or Marathon in the cool of the early morning, take a scenic drive, and still be back by dinner.

First, a word of caution. Despite stories of exotic poisonous snakes and spiders, the leading cause of injury in Big Bend is much more commonplace: automobile accidents. Be extremely cautious of weather conditions, sharp curves, and unexpected wildlife in the roadway. Note that the speed limits within the park are low, and federal seat-belt laws are always in effect. Before you go, be sure your automobile is in good working order, with properly inflated tires and a full tank of gas.

The second most common problem is dehydration, a condition that can prove fatal. Avoid strenuous exercise in the heat of the day and use the more mild mornings instead for hiking or outdoor activity. You should plan on drinking at least a gallon of water per day to stay properly hydrated, so stock up before beginning your journey and remember that alcohol and soft drinks, while refreshing, are dehydrating.

In Big Bend, the summer is very hot and the winter very cold. Coupled with a propensity for storms and flash flooding, this makes the weather in Big Bend a force to respect. Bring along sunscreen and insect repellent, a blanket, a simple first aid kit, and snacks. Regardless of the season, wear long pants, a long-sleeved shirt, hat, and proper footwear for a hike. Before setting out on a trip into the park, let someone know where you are headed and your estimated time of return. You most likely will not be able to rely on your cell phone for communication.

These warnings are not meant to deter you, just advise you of the dangers so that you can best plan your trip. The National Park Service is the final word when it comes to conditions and safety within the park. Checking with its extremely informative website (www.nps.gov), as well as park rangers and staff, before you head out could quite literally save your life. Assess your skills realistically, take the time to become informed, and prepare properly in order to best enjoy exploring Big Bend.

transformed in the 1970s into a luxury resort. Located just yards from the Mexican border, parts of the resort have the look and feel of a frontier town, but the overall tone is of a country club in the desert, complete with a golf course, upscale restaurant, and private airstrip.

Mosey on down the road a stretch and you'll find yourself in the old mining town of **Terlingua**. Those who really like to get away from it all fall in love with Terlingua at first sight. At one time, 40 percent of the quicksilver mined in the United States originated in Terlingua. As with most other mining towns, the heyday of production was relatively short-lived. By 1942, the mine had closed and the population scattered, leaving the abandoned town to its solitude in the hot Texas desert. Fate smiled on the little ghost town when, in the 1960s and 1970s, a steady stream of tourists rolled through, stopping to marvel at its charms. A spicy annual chili cook-off earned it the nickname Chili Capital of the World. If you're around in November, be sure to try a bowlful; all the details are online at www.abowlofred.com.

The friendly folks at **High Sierra** serve burgers, steaks, salads, and Mexican standbys, but it's the frozen mugs of ice-cold beer and a chance to shoot the breeze with other customers in this ultra casual hangout that have them coming back. The **Starlight Theatre** was built in 1931 to bring a little culture to the hardscrabble town. The old-timey place is now a restaurant and bar, with dinner daily and live music on its three stages most nights of the week. The food ranges from stick-to-your-ribs chili and homemade tacos to a grilled filet mignon with garlic and mushrooms—their signature dish. Who says there's nothing to eat in the desert?

If you can't get enough of the scenery, the history, or the charm of Big Bend, then stop in at the **Terlingua Trading Company**. The store, at one time the largest general store in West Texas, now houses hundreds of regional specialty books and loads of memorabilia, making it the perfect spot to find a piece of Terlingua to take home with you.

Want to tour Big Bend, but nervous about being a novice? With all of Big Bend laid out in front of you, you might want to get outfitted for hiking, biking, or boating. Check in with the knowledgeable folks at **Angell Expeditions**, **Big Bend River Tours**, **Desert Sports**, or **Far Flung Adventure Center**—they'll help you assess your skills, offer suggestions, rent equipment, or accompany you as guides. They'll have you safely hiking, biking, off-roading, or rafting in a jiffy.

By now you've noticed that there certainly aren't many options when it comes to lodging; fortunately there is **La Posada Milagro**, which lets four lovely rooms, each decorated with sophisticated simplicity. Stucco, stone, straw, and splashes of color are tempered by crisp white linens and bright sunshine. Perched on a hill, the little historic inn enjoys its vantage point over the old town and stunning views of the Chisos Mountains.

From Terlingua it is just a few miles east until TX 170 dead-ends into

Desert Hot Springs

As hard as it may be to imagine a hot spring in the desert, there is one here. Folks have come for generations to take a dip in the curative 109-degree waters. **The Chinati Hot Springs** resort has expanded the springs' natural popularity by formalizing the experience. The resort takes a communal approach to desert hospitality, with the large kitchen available to all guests, and shared baths and hot tubs. Cabins are clean, cheerful, and creatively decorated, and camping is also an option. To reach the resort from Marfa, take US 67 to Presidio; then it's 36 miles to Ruidosa, where you will see signs. Alternatively, while TX 2810 to Pinto Canyon Road looks like a straight shot on the map, the road, while gorgeous, is rugged, only partially paved, and recommended only for vehicles with high clearance.

TX 118 at the settlement of **Study Butte**. Here you can either head north, following TX 118 83 miles to **Alpine,** or widen the route by taking TX 118 east to US 385 to Panther Junction, the headquarters of Big Bend National Park. The sojourn outlined thus far, from Marfa to Presidio, through Terlingua and back to Alpine, is a leisurely day trip totaling approximately 200 miles, taking you past stunning scenery and imparting a taste of the region's history. The route is easily navigated, and while you may enjoy times alone on the road, it is traveled enough that you are unlikely to find yourself isolated. Those heading on into **Big Bend National Park** should be sure to take the necessary precautions (see box on page 205). While the park's enormous size, remoteness, and rugged beauty give it an air of intrigue that has drawn visitors to the region for decades (see box on pages 208–209), these same factors mean that it is essential to plan your trip wisely and in advance. While you can visit the park as a day trip from Marfa or Alpine, many find Marathon to be a handy base for exploration, as US 385 will take you directly to the park's visitor center in Panther Junction.

Big Bend offers various sites for primitive camping as well as an RV park, but you'll find only one place to stay within its borders that has a traditional roof. The **Chisos Mountains Lodge** complex isn't fancy, but it's just right for a good night's sleep after you've spent the day hiking, horseback riding, or rafting. The rooms are reasonably priced; some, such as the Roosevelt Stone Cottages, are equipped with three double beds, perfect for large families or friends traveling together. The restaurant serves solid meals, and there is a store for provisions and a visitor center for those in need of maps and guidance.

Marathon is located just 30 miles southeast of Alpine on US 90, and when

The Big Bend

The Big Bend region is just over one million acres of vast West Texas wilderness, cradling a wide bend of the Rio Grande. Archaeological finds date back almost 9,000 years. Communities of Native Americans have lived in the region, crisscrossing its peaks, valleys, and riverbeds as they hunted and gathered.

The Spanish arrived in the 1500s and, despite ruling the region for centuries thereafter, left the mountainous area unsettled. When Mexico gained independence from Spain, Mexicans, too, largely avoided the region. Both the Spanish and the Mexicans referred to what we now know as Big Bend as *El Despoblado*, or "the uninhabited land." Not only did the rugged terrain resist settlement, the Mescalero Apache and the Comanche thoroughly controlled the hills, keeping intruders at bay for centuries.

After the end of the Mexican-American War in 1848, forts built to suppress Native Americans at the country's expanding boundaries and defend pioneers gained a foothold in the region. By the 1880s, sprawling ranches spread like patchwork across Texas. Both Big Bend National Park and Big Bend Ranch State Park are made up of former privately owned parcels of ranchland.

In the 1890s, silver and cinnabar were discovered in northern Mexico and Big Bend. A mining boom hit the region, then ended, leaving the deserted towns of Shafter (page 202) and Terlingua (page 206) in its wake.

By 1910, the Mexican Revolution had filled the Big Bend region with revolutionaries and bandits, including the legendary Pancho Villa. Things had quieted down by 1944, when Big Bend National Park was dedicated. Remote and rustic, the new park had no paved roads and was surrounded by far-flung ranches, a ghost town or two, but few people. In the 1960s, tourists started to get more adventurous, and Big Bend's reputation as a great place to hike, raft, bird-watch, and camp grew. The traits that attracted people for centuries— swift rivers, native plants, wildlife, and breathtaking sunsets—are the very things that attract visitors to the park today.

Big Bend is part of the enormous Chihuahuan Desert, which also takes in parts of central Mexico and southern New Mexico. The region includes desert, river, and mountain ecosystems, and displays an astounding amount of diversity. For example, with 65 species of cacti, Big Bend National Park has the most of any in the park system, some of them unique to the Chihuahuan Desert. Of course, this fascinating ecology, foliage, and wildlife extend into Mexico.

South of the Rio Grande, or Rio Bravo del Norte as it is called in Mexico, the Mexican states of Chihuahua and Coahuila have declared the hundreds of thousands of acres known as Maderas del Carmen and the Cañon de Santa

Elena as protected natural areas. While the idea of an international park with areas on both sides of the border has been circulating since the 1930s, the reality is two adjoining national parks, each country administering the land within its own boundaries. The net gain is the same—a piece of protected Chihuahuan Desert, unified as nature intended. You cannot visit the Mexican Park—border crossings within Big Bend are illegal—but it is nice to know that the land has been set aside for conservation.

For more details and suggestions, visit www.nps.gov and www.visitbigbend.com online.

you drive in, it seems the entire place is lined up enjoying the view, since most of the small town is built along the north side of the highway, and the mountains to the south are an unobstructed vista. Another twentieth-century railroad town, Marathon was a shipping point for cattle from surrounding ranches, silver and mercury from nearby mines, and a natural rubber made from a native desert plant called guayule. When Big Bend National Park opened in 1947, Marathon was declared the Gateway to the Big Bend, a designation it still carries with pride.

Marathon offers very pleasant, diverse lodging options. **The Marathon Motel & RV Park** is one of those family-friendly spots where memories are made. Located on 10 acres along an unhurried section of I-90 a half mile west of Marathon, the facility dates back to the 1940s and has the look and feel of historic Americana. Over the years, the motel fell into disrepair, and it might well have been condemned were it not for the imagination and vision of two retirees, John and Mary Hoover, who saw the hotel's charm beneath its many needed repairs. By 1999, the Hoovers had transformed the hotel into a place so charming that when Daniel Self from Austin saw a "For Sale" sign out front, he jumped at the chance. Since taking over, Self has added an adobe courtyard, complete with a fountain and fireplace, from which guests can enjoy the stunning view.

Down the street, the grand **Gage Hotel** has been sheltering weary travelers in style for decades. Built by a former cattleman as a hub of activity for ranchers and miners, the hotel opened in 1927. A fortunate and familiar tale by now, the neglected hotel was given a much-needed renovation by a Houston couple who saw a special something in the old building. The hotel is solidly built, with an impressive entrance, stately living room, handsome library, and well-appointed rooms. Some rooms in this historic hotel have shared baths, with separate ones for men and women. All maintain their old-fashioned charm. The hotel was expanded in the 1990s; the hacienda-style rooms in the Los Portales addition are filled with old-time details, artfully and individually arranged, and each room overlooks the lush courtyard. The

THE GAGE HOTEL IN MARATHON CELEBRATES ITS RANCHING ROOTS

hotel offers wide selection of dining in a town without much else. The hotel restaurant, **12 Gage**, has steaks, game, and seafood on the menu, a fireplace for atmosphere, and a fantastic courtyard for romantic evening dining. Or, sip a prickly pear margarita and enjoy a burger in West Texas style at the Gage's **White Buffalo Bar**. Start your morning off right, grab a light lunch, or pick up something for the road at **V6**, where you'll find a small, but hearty, menu of sandwiches, smoothies, and locally-roasted coffee.

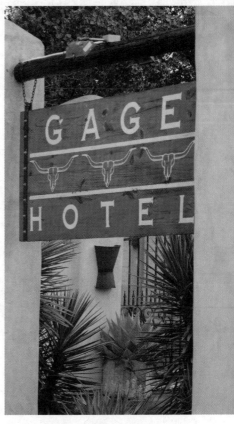

Pick up provisions at the **French Company Grocer**, a store that has been serving Marathon since 1900. Given Marathon's fairly remote location, it's no surprise that the Grocer is still a general store of sorts, with a little bit of everything and maybe just the thing you're looking for. Walk in on any given morning and you'll find anything from fresh banana bread to warm breakfast tacos on offer.

THE GAGE HOTEL IN MARATHON

Hop back on US 90 and travel 30 miles west to **Alpine**. While Alpine isn't blessed with quite the same views that Marathon enjoys, it is still a great place, full of West Texas character. Larger than either Marfa or Marathon, Alpine has services and shops that can be useful to travelers.

For years, Spanish, Mexican, and American traders passed through this area, camping near Burgess Springs (now called Kokernot Springs) for its steady supply of reliable water. In 1882, the railroad came, and since steam engines required water, Alpine became an important stop. A town took root, with restaurants, hotels, saloons, and shops springing up along both sides of the track. Now, surrounded by huge ranches, some in excess of 200,000 acres, and a jumping-off point into spectacular Big Bend, Alpine is a little town in the vastness of West Texas where folks just keep bumping into each other.

The heart and soul of Alpine may be the **Holland Hotel**, a sprawling building that takes up a solid city block right in the middle of town. The hotel was built in 1912, and more than one heroic owner has had a hand in the wonderful restoration you'll see when you arrive. The hotel has two dozen rooms,

A MURAL IN ALPINE

each well decorated and individualized along the same rustic, romantic, historic theme. All are well maintained and quite comfortable, and some have balconies. The downstairs common areas and sitting rooms are dramatic, with tile floors, wooden ceiling beams, and huge leather couches. The Holland Hotel has definitely captured and preserved the celebrated spirit of the Big Bend region. The Holland's sister property, the **Maverick Inn**, located across the busy main street from Sul Ross State University, is a completely renovated motor court packed with rustic charm. Adobe, clay tile, and plenty of wood details set the tone and the pool, fire pit, and outdoor breakfast patio add even more appeal. A no-fuss, pet-friendly, easy-going sort of place to unwind. Nearby, **Judy's Bread and Breakfast** serves breakfast and lunch, with freshly baked cookies, pastries, breads, and cinnamon rolls. This friendly, cozy place is a good spot for a midmorning snack. For an indulgent steak dinner, head straight to **Reata**; the Alpine outpost of this Fort Worth restaurant is the real deal. From the smoked quail with jalapeño cheddar grits and barbecue molasses glaze appetizer to the steaks and pork tenderloin plus warm pecan pie for dessert, Reata is gourmet cowboy cooking at its best. Despite its decadence, the menu includes nods to vegetarians and the health-conscious. Cap off an evening with live music and a drink at **Railroad Blues**, a funky West Texas original.

You'll see the distant hills grow steadily closer as you drive an easy 24 miles along TX 118 from Alpine (21 miles from Marfa on TX 71) to the town of **Fort Davis**. Forts were common in Texas, with many dotting the landscape from San Antonio to El Paso, and they played an essential part in the state's history. Fort Davis (the actual fort) was built in 1854 in a little community beside Limpia Creek known as Painted Comanche Camp. It provided both protection and a reliable water source for the thousands of migrants, wagon trains, pioneers, goods, and mail making their way west across Texas. The fort was used, abandoned, and pressed back into service several times, sustaining repeated attacks from raiders and Native American groups before finally being retired in 1891. In 1946, a Houston lawyer bought the old fort with hopes of restoring it. Unfortunately, he died in 1951 and the project lay dormant. In 1961, however, the fort was given national historic site status and the **Fort Davis National Historic Site** was opened to the public five years later. The historic site showcases five buildings with period decor and furnishings from the 1880s, but almost two dozen other structures and 100 ruins are found here in the protective shadow of the mountains. On holidays, spring break, and summer vacation, staff and volunteers don period dress to further the feel of the times. Spend the 15 minutes to watch the short film in the visitor center; it will give you the background needed to appreciate the site fully.

Four miles of hiking trails connect the Fort Davis National Historic Site to **Davis Mountains State Park**. To reach the park by car, leave Fort Davis, travel 1 mile north on TX 17 and 3 miles west on TX 118 to Park Road 3.

The Davis Mountains are one of the most extensive mountain ranges in Texas and are unusual for the large amount of rainfall they receive in comparison with the rest of West Texas. As a result, the mountains are home to

The Border

The stunning scenery that defines the 118-mile border between Texas and Mexico is shared by both countries. In fact, many of the sweeping vistas you'll enjoy on the US side are of distant mountains on the Mexican side. When you witness the Rio Grande slicing through this natural wonder, the fact that it is an international border can seem an afterthought. While the border is ever the subject of contentious debate and the brunt of social, political, and environmental stressors, it has been fairly permeable for a large portion of its history. As you travel near the border, please be aware that the National Park Service warns visitors of the possible presence of drug smugglers and illegal immigrants, the latter of whom may be in need of medical care due to exhaustion and dehydration. In all cases, the Park Service asks that you alert a ranger or dial 911.

a far greater variety of vegetation than the desert surrounding them. The higher you climb, the greener it gets, with Texas oak, black cherry, and yellow pine trees rising up to fill in the landscape.

The parkland was given to the state by a local family. In the 1930s, the Civilian Conservation Corps (CCC) arrived and built the jewel of the park, the newly-renovated **Indian Lodge**. The lodge is reminiscent of the southwestern Indian pueblos, with 18-inch-thick walls that keep the interior cool throughout the summer. There are campgrounds and trails for visitors who like to commune with nature, and modern amenities such as a full-service restaurant, the Black Bear, and swimming pool for those who just like to watch. Your cell phone may or may not work, and don't count on accessing the Internet; then again, no one comes here to catch up on email or phone calls. The reason most people come is for what *is* here—the mountain views, the warm, dry days and cool mornings and evenings, not to mention the awesome starry nights.

For a closer look at the sky, consider taking a drive to the **McDonald Observatory**. Built on Mount Locke in 1932, the observatory is part of the University of Texas and home to the Hobby-Eberly Telescope, one of the largest in the world. While there is plenty to do and see at the observatory during the daytime hours, the evening Star Party is really special; there is just nothing like the night sky out in rural West Texas. From Fort Davis, climb TX 118, 6,800 feet up, to enjoy a stellar view of both the heavens and the countryside.

Back in town, you can't miss the **Hotel Limpia** on Main Street. Built in 1912, the hotel has a decidedly Old World feel. In fact, staying at the **Hotel Limpia** feels a lot like staying at Grandma's house—in the best way possible. The carpets are a little worn from constant use and the linens are a tad faded from plenty of laundering, but the overall effect is of lovability. The lights are soft, the armchair cushions are concave from plenty of relaxing, and the wooden rockers and wicker patio sets practically beg guests to have a seat and put their feet up. The attached **Blue Mountain Bistro** is a good bet for coffee and pastries in the morning and more formal dining in the evening. The menu includes close to a dozen tapas to choose from; larger entrées include grilled shrimp with prosciutto and cream sauce, mocha-crusted pork tenderloin, and filet mignon.

Stone Village Tourist Camp offers a range of options in its old-school motor court. Unassuming and unfussy, the rooms are basic, yet quintessentially West Texas, and the entire "camp" has a communal, folksy feel. Exposed stone walls, campy lampshades, a modest pool, and wooden lounge chairs help guests loosen up a little. A stone's throw from the Davis Mountains, Stone Village is a good bet for easygoing guests who appreciate the charms of this Depression-era gem. Stop in **Stone Village Market** for snacks, supplies, or staples. This health-food convenience store is a good place to pick up sandwiches, since they make them to order as fresh as can be. **Fort Davis Drug Store** is a reliable stop for burgers and Blue Bell shakes. With its creaky floors, tall ceilings, and old-fashioned soda fountain, the Drug Store anchors State Street. From Fort Davis, it's another 37 miles north on winding TX 17 to **Balmorhea**, notable as the home of the San Solomon Springs and **Balmorhea State Park**, which is an oasis in the Texas desert.

BALMORHEA STATE PARK

In this arid region, water means life; not surprisingly, the San Solomon Springs have drawn people for centuries. In the mid-nineteenth century, the marshy springs were known as Mescalero Springs, named after the Mescalero Apache, who frequently brought their horses here for water. Mexican farmers channeled the springs' waters into irrigation ditches for their crops.

These days, however, the centerpiece of the springs is an enormous, almost 2-acre swimming pool constructed by the Civilian Conservation Corps in the 1930s. It's filled each day with 22 to 28 million gallons of pure artesian water fresh from the San Solomon Springs. A constant 74 degrees, the water takes a minute to get used to, but almost everyone who starts with a toe in ends up floating around with the fish. Yes, fish; consider bringing a pair of goggles for an underwater view. Arrive as early as you can since the park limits the number of visitors each day in order to protect the facilitites.

The park is popular with locals, and it's a frequent site of picnics and family reunions. Many of the people who come to take a dip also come to spend the night. The park has two types of accommodations: campsites and the hotel.

The newly-renovated **San Solomon Courts** is a Spanish colonial-style motel with white adobe walls and red clay tile roof. Also built by CCC workers, the hotel is modern enough, with heat, air-conditioning, and cable TV, but details such as exposed wood beams impart an air of nostalgia. The hotel is popular with families; picnic tables and grills outside each room

The Chihuahuan Desert Up Close

While it might seem a bit counterintuitive to come to the great outdoors only to spend time indoors, there are two educational centers in the Alpine area that are worth a quick visit. The **Museum of the Big Bend**, on the Sul Ross University campus in Alpine, has a large collection of artifacts that tell the stories of the Native Americans, Spanish, Mexicans, and Anglo-Americans who have lived in the region. While the museum will interest most, the on-site Discovery Center is geared specifically toward children. The Chihuahuan Desert Cactus Garden on the grounds gives a great visual overview of native cacti.

In addition, a visit to the **Chihuahuan Desert Nature Center & Botanical Gardens**, between Alpine and Fort Davis along TX 118, is a wonderful way to acquaint yourself with the flora and fauna of the desert. Botanical gardens and a greenhouse allow a close-up look, and several miles of nature trails provide a safe and easy way to explore the regional terrain.

ensure that evenings are spent eating, talking, and relaxing. All rooms have double beds and some have kitchenettes. People come here to slow down and just enjoy a summer day as it slips away behind the mountains.

The route ends here, conveniently close to I-10 for your return to the more populated parts of the state. As you drive and the mountains recede behind you, pause to consider that having made this trip, you've been let in on the secret of West Texas: precisely what everyone thinks of as just miles and miles of emptiness is actually miles and miles of the most living, breathing, precious land in the state.

IN THE AREA

ALPINE CHAMBER OF COMMERCE, 106 N. Third Street, Alpine, 79830. Call 432-837-4144. Website: www.alpinetexas.com.

ANGELL EXPEDITIONS. Call 432-229-3713 or 305-336-2787. Website: www .angellexpeditions.com.

BALMORHEA STATE PARK, 9207 TX 17, Toyahvale, 79786. Call 432-375-2370. Fee. Website: www.tpwd.texas.gov.

BARTON WARNOCK EDUCATION CENTER, 21800 FM 170, Terlingua, 79852. Call 432-424-3327. Fee. Website: www.tpwd.texas.gov.

BIG BEND NATIONAL PARK, Panther Junction Visitor Center, 79834. Call 432-477-2251. Fee. Website: www.nps.gov.

BIG BEND RANCH STATE PARK, Ranger Station, 1900 Sauceda Ranch Road, Presidio, 79845. Call 432-358-4444. Fee. Website: www.tpwd.texas.gov.

BIG BEND RIVER TOURS. Call 432-371-3033. Website: www.bigbendriver tours.com.

BLUE MOUNTAIN BISTRO, 100 Main Street, Fort Davis, 79734. Call 432-426-3244. Closed Wednesdays. Pleasant hotel restaurant with breezy patio dining. Website: www.hotellimpia.com. $$.

CHINATI FOUNDATION, PO Box 1135, 1 Cavalry Row, Marfa, 79843. Call 432-729-4362. Guided tour only Wednesday through Sunday. Check website for schedule. Fee. Website: www.chinati.org.

CHINATI HOT SPRINGS, Box 67 Candelaria Route, Marfa, 79843 (located near Ruidosa). Call 432-229-4165. Unwind in one of the pleasant cabins surrounding this hot spring in the desert. Website: www.chinatihotsprings .net. $-$$.

CHIHUAHUAN DESERT NATURE CENTER & BOTANICAL GARDENS, PO Box 905, Fort Davis, 79734 (4 miles south of Fort Davis on TX 118). Call 432-364-2499. Fee. Website: www.cdri.org.

CHISOS MOUNTAINS LODGE, Big Bend National Park, Basin Rural Station—Big Bend National Park, 79834. Call 432-477-2291. Comfortable accommodations inside the park. Website: www.chisosmountainslodge. com. $$-$$$.

COCHINEAL, 107 W. San Antonio Street, Marfa, 79843. Call 432-729-3300. Creative menu includes outstanding locally-sourced dishes served in a chic dining room. Website: www.cochinealmarfa.com. $$-$$$.

DAVIS MOUNTAIN INDIAN LODGE, PO Box 1707, Fort Davis, 79734. Call 432-426-3254. Newly renovated rooms in a vintage adobe lodge overlooking the mountains. Website: www.tpwd.texas.gov. $.

DAVIS MOUNTAINS STATE PARK, PO Box 1707, Fort Davis, 79734. Call 432-426-3337. Fee. Website: www.tpwd.texas.gov.

Train Whistle

While this region may seem wide open except for some cattle and a few cars, every once in a while a train will come speeding in from one horizon, bringing traffic to a halt, whistles blaring and wheels grinding, before disappearing into the other. Stay in just about any hotel in the area and chances are you'll hear numerous trains; it's just that the ones you'll remember will be the ones that woke you at night.

DESERT SPORTS, 22937 FM 170, Terlingua, 79852. Call 1-888-989-6900 or 432-371-2727. Website: www.desertsportstx.com.

EL COSMICO, 802 S. Highland Avenue, Marfa, 79843. Call 432-729-1950. Stay in a tent, yurt, tepee, or Airstream trailer. Website: www.elcosmico .com.$–$$.

FAR FLUNG ADVENTURE CENTER, Call 432-371-2633. Website: www.big bendfarflung.com.

FOOD SHARK, 909 W. San Antonio Street, Marfa, 79843. Call 432-207-2090. Closed Sunday through Tuesday. Delicious Mediterranean food and al fresco dining at communal tables. Website: www.foodsharkmarfa .com. $$.

FORT DAVIS CHAMBER OF COMMERCE, 100 Memorial Square, Fort Davis, 79734. Call 432-426-3015. Website: www.fortdavis.com.

FORT DAVIS DRUG STORE, 113 State Street, Fort Davis, 79734. Call 432-426-3929. Burgers and ice cream in the old drug store at the center of town. Website: www.fortdavisdrugstore.net. $$.

FORT DAVIS NATIONAL HISTORIC SITE, PO Box 1379, Fort Davis, 79734. Call 432-426-3224. Fee. Website: www.nps.gov/foda.

FORT LEATON STATE HISTORIC SITE, FM 170, Presidio, 79845. Call 432-229-3613. Fee. Website: www.tpwd.texas.gov.

FRAMA @ TUMBLEWEED LAUNDRY, 120 N. Austin Street, Marfa, 79843. Call 432-729-4033. Serving up coffee, ice cream, and laundry facilities. Website: www.tumbleweedlaundry.com. $.

FRENCH COMPANY GROCER, 206 N. Avenue D, Box 477, Marathon, 79842. Call 432-386-4522. Website: www.frenchcogrocer.com.

GAGE HOTEL, 102 I-90 W., Marathon, 79842. Call 432-386-4205. Mission-style hotel with historic details and luxurious touches. Website: www.gage hotel.com. $$$.

THE GET GO, 208 S. Dean Street, Marfa, 79843. Call 432-729-3335. Website: www.thegetgomarfa.com.

HIGH SIERRA, 100 Ghost Town Road, Terlingua, 79852. Call 432-371-3282. Hearty food, cold beer, and entertainment Terlingua-style. Website: www .highsierra.homestead.com. $$.

HOLLAND HOTEL, 209 W. Holland Avenue, Alpine, 79830. Call 432-837-2800. Historic hotel loaded with character and charm in downtown Alpine. Website: www.thehollandhoteltexas.com. $$–$$$.

HOTEL LIMPIA, 100 Memorial Square, Fort Davis, 79734. Call 432-426-3237 or 1-800-662-5517. Anchoring Fort Davis since 1912, this hotel retains a historic feel. Website: www.hotellimpia.com. $.

THE HOTEL PAISANO, 207 N. Highland Avenue, Marfa, 79843. Call 1-866-729-3669 or 432-729-3669. Lovely rooms in an historic railroad hotel in the center of Marfa. Website: www.hotelpaisano.com. $$–$$$.

INDIAN LODGE STATE PARK, PO Box 1458, Fort Davis, 79734. Call 512-389-8982 or 432-426-3254. Fee. Website: www.tpwd.texas.gov.

JUDY'S BREAD AND BREAKFAST CAFÉ, 113 W. Holland Avenue, Alpine, 79830. Call 432-837-9424. Try the freshly baked goodies—especially the cinnamon rolls—for breakfast and lunch. Closed Tuesdays. $.

LA POSADA MILAGRO, 100 Milagro Road, Terlingua, 79852. Call 432-371-3044. Understated luxury in Terlingua. Website: www.laposadamilagro.net. $$–$$$.

MARATHON CHAMBER OF COMMERCE, P.O. Box 163, Marathon, 79842. Call 432-386-4516. Website: www.marathontexas.com.

MARATHON MOTEL AND RV PARK, I-90, PO Box 141, Marathon, 79842. Call 432-386-4241. Simple, clean, and friendly lodging under the stars. Website: www.marathonmotel.com. $.

MARFA BOOK COMPANY, in the Hotel Saint George, 105 S. Highland Street, Marfa, 79843. Call 432-729-3700. Website: www.marfabookco.com.

MARFA CHAMBER OF COMMERCE, Hotel Paisano, 207 N. Highland Avenue, Marfa, 79843. Call 432-729-4942. Website: www.marfachamber.org.

MARFA VISITOR CENTER, 302 S. Highland Avenue, Marfa, 79843. Call 432-729-4772. Website: www.visitmarfa.com.

THE MAVERICK INN, 1200 E. Holland Avenue, Alpine, 79830. Call: 432-837-0628. Comfortable old-school motor court with plenty of charm and an outdoor pool. Website: www.themaverickinn.com. $.

McDONALD OBSERVATORY, Fort Davis, 78734. Call 432-426-3640. Fee. Website: www.mcdonaldobservatory.org. Reservations required.

MUSEUM OF THE BIG BEND, TX 90, Alpine, 79830. Call 432-837-8143. Closed Mondays. Free. Website: www.museumofthebigbend.com.

PIZZA FOUNDATION, 305 Spring Street, Marfa, 79843. Call 432-729-3377. Closed Monday through Thursday. Big slices of zesty NY-style pizza, ordered at the counter and served on paper plates. Website: www.pizza foundation.com. $.

RAILROAD BLUES, 504 W. Holland Avenue, Alpine, 79830. Call 432-837-3103. Closed Sundays, except holidays. Website: www.railroadblues.com.

REATA, 203 N. Fifth Street, Alpine, 79830. Call 432-837-9232. Closed Sundays. Upscale dining with gourmet cowboy cuisine. Website: www.reata.net. $$$.

SAN SOLOMON SPRING COURTS AT BALMORHEA STATE PARK, TX 17, Toyahvale, 79786. Call 432-375-2370. Undergoing renovations; scheduled to reopen in Spring 2019. Website: www.tpwd.texas.gov. $–$$.

SQUEEZE MARFA, 215 N. Highland Avenue, Marfa, 79843. Call 432-729-4500. Closed Mondays. Solid breakfasts and lunch sandwiches in a little outdoor alcove. Website: www.squeeze marfa.com. $–$$.

STARLIGHT THEATRE RESTAURANT & BAR, Terlingua Ghost Town, 100 Ivey Street, Terlingua, 79852. Call 432-371-4000. Dinner and Sunday Brunch only. Serving award-winning chili, grilled steaks and wild game, and plenty of local flavor. Website: www.thestarlighttheatre.com. $$.

STONE VILLAGE TOURIST CAMP AND MARKET, 509 N. State Street, Fort Davis, 79734. Call 432-426-3941. Comfortable rooms and health-conscious groceries in a laid-back renovated motor court. Website: www.stonevillagetouristcamp.com. $–$$.

TERLINGUA TRADING COMPANY, 100 Ivey Street, Terlingua, 79852. Call 432-371-2234. Website: www.ghosttowntexas.com.

12 GAGE, 102 I-90 W., Marathon, 79842. Call 432-386-4205. Fine dining in the Gage Hotel featuring entrees such as elk and buffalo meatloaf. Website: www.gagehotel.com. Reservations recommended. $$$$.

V6, 102 I-90 W., Marathon, 79842. Call: 432-386-4205. Gage Hotel coffee bar with delicious breakfast items, snacks, sandwiches and, of course, coffee. Website: www.gagehotel.com. $.

11

TEXAS FRONTIER

WACO, CLIFTON, ABILENE, BUFFALO GAP, SAN ANGELO, FORT McKAVETT, SAN SABA

TOTAL DISTANCE: From Waco to San Saba is approximately 400 miles.

HIGHLIGHTS: Visit Magnolia Market, Waco Mammoth National Historic Site, and the Dr. Pepper Museum in **Waco** and head north to explore nearby artsy, creative **Clifton**. Intersect with the route outlined in Chapter 3 at both Hico and Dublin as you head west to **Abilene**, where museums and steakhouses co-exist in this can-do city. Drop down to **Buffalo Gap**, spend an hour or two exploring a heritage village, then kick the evening off with a memorable steak dinner in the country. Cruise into the college town of **San Angelo**, where a former fort, bordello, and repurposed chicken farm and community art museum all have out the welcome mat. Take a U-turn and head back east, detouring to **Fort McKavett** if you're inclined, and ending the route **San Saba**, where you can sample pecans, sip wine, or buy cowboy boots, all on the same few blocks. From here you can continue on back to Waco, follow the route outlined in Chapter 3, or drive a little farther to meet up with the routes outlined in Chapters 1 and 2.

GETTING THERE: Waco is located on I-35, about an hour and 45 minute drive from either Austin or Dallas/Fort Worth. To begin the route, from Waco, take US 84 west out of town, then TX 6 north approximately 35 miles to Clifton and continue on another 34 miles to Hico. Stay on TX 6 until it crosses I-20 and then take 1-20, following signs to Abilene, approximately 115 miles from leaving Hico. From Abilene, it's a scenic 15 miles to Buffalo Gap on Buffalo Gap Road/FM 89. Leaving Buffalo Gap, take Buffalo Gap Road/FM 89 to US 277 and follow it to San Angelo, 67 miles to the south. From San Angelo, follow US 87 south out of town, pick up US 190, and head east for a total of 130 miles to San Saba. From San Saba, it's another 126 miles back to Waco on US 84.

LEFT: A STORM MOVES IN OVER THE TEXAS FRONTIER

Texas has had its share of border disputes, many of them fought near the present-day center of the state in an area known as the Forts Region, where today you'll find reminders of this turbulent past. As you will see on this route, borders weren't the only boundaries being contested in this region. The limits of the culture, law, ingenuity, creativity, and a sense of community, were forced to expand as they evolved on this unstable frontier.

Waco, located on I-35, is an easy hour and a half drive from either Austin, Dallas, or Fort Worth and three hours from Houston, making it a great jumping off point from which to explore the Texas Frontier. Alternatively, you can pick up the thread at any point, in particular the intersections with Chapter 3.

These days, Waco embodies a can-do, re-use, re-purpose, re-imagine sort of pioneer spirit. Decades of collaborative efforts have come to fruition and Waco has been designated a "Main Street City" for its preservation, restoration, and community-building. Clearly, Waco is a city with a lot to offer, but the below are some highlights to hit as you start your route.

Since Waco is a university town, it's no wonder there are plenty of Inns to accommodate. Just a few blocks from Magnolia Market, **Miguel House** is a stunning Mediterranean-inspired bed and breakfast, with luxurious rooms and a private bowling alley in the basement. Utterly unique. A little more casual, but not lacking for historic details, **The Cotton Palace** makes believers out of first time guests. It's hard to know which is more charming, the 1910 Arts and Crafts home or it's amiable hosts. On the edges of town, **The Bed and Breakfast on White Rock Creek**, enjoys a rustic wooded setting. Spacious rooms, tubs, and porches mean plenty of room relax. Close to everything, yet far enough away that the only noise you'll hear is that of singing birds.

The folksy appeal of Chip and Joanna Gaines' HGTV show *Fixer Upper* made them popular, but their marketing brilliance and knack for brand expansion have made their latest project, **Magnolia Market at the Silos**, a destination unto itself. Just a quick stop off I-35, this family-friendly complex includes grain silos transformed into showrooms, a garden shop bursting with style, and an enormous grassy lawn (actually artificial turf) where everyone is encouraged to run around to their heart's content. Home decor, DIY tips, and design inspiration aside, the real draw here for the traveler are the bakery and food trucks dotting the property offering everything from tacos to barbecue to pizza, and plenty of hot and cold drinks. Because of their wide appeal and easy access to I-35, the Silos are almost always crowded, although somewhat less so in the early morning.

Waco is also home to Baylor University, the oldest continuously-operating university in Texas, and host of the **Mayborn Museum Complex**, featuring natural science, cultural history and, in particular, a nice overview of the excavation of the **Waco Mammoth National Historic Site**.

Texas Frontier

In 1978, two local men decided to poke around the banks of the Bosque River for arrowheads and fossils and ended up stumbling upon an enormous bone. Knowing a bit about paleontology, they took it to scientists in the natural history museum at Baylor University who identified it as the femur bone of a Columbian mammoth. The museum quickly organized an excavation and by 1997 they had successfully uncovered the previously undisturbed remains of two dozen Mammoths, a Western camel, dwarf antelope, American alligator, giant tortoise, the tooth of a saber-toothed cat, and the bones of an unidentified animal. This scientific cache has yielded a huge amount of information about the animals' lives, but little about their deaths, which appear to have happened at different times and in different circumstances. The Waco Mammoth National Historic Site joined the National Park System by presidential proclamation in 2015. Showcasing the discovery of the remains of a herd of Columbian mammoths—thought to have lived approxi-

THE POPULAR MAGNOLIA MARKET AT THE
SILOS IN WACO

mately 67,000 years ago—it is the only site of its kind in North America.

Waco is the birthplace of Dr. Pepper (page 60) and the **Dr. Pepper Museum and Free Enterprise Institute** here keeps growing and growing. The facility is divided into two parts: a gift shop and soda fountain on one side, and a museum with all kinds of artifacts tracing the history, bottling, and marketing of being a Pepper on the other. The daily Liquid Lab demonstrations of the science of soda are particularly enlightening. Just a mile away **The Texas Ranger Hall of Fame & Museum** honors the unique branch of local law enforcement. The Rangers began as a scrappy group of frontiersmen, each paid roughly $1.25 a day, but required to supply their own horse, weapons, ammunition, and rations. As you can imagine, the museum has plenty of old weapons, but they also have art, sculpture, and a section on the Lone Ranger.

History comes alive through art, craft, and agriculture at **Homestead Heritage**, an intentional non-denominational Christian community dedicated to simplicity and sustainability. The spacious complex is made up of nineteenth-century structures brought to the site, tucked under huge shade trees, beautifully landscaped, and given new life as the workspace for blacksmiths, weavers, woodworkers, and any number of other artisans. Unlike similar living history museums, this enterprise does not claim to be historic or a museum, but rather a community dedicated to preserving and perfecting the elegance and efficiency, the art and craft, of what we might consider "endangered" skills. The community offers classes and workshops and the property is free and open to the public. **Café Homestead**, the very popular on-site restaurant, is lovely and the food is delicious. There aren't any surprises on the menu, which features burgers, sandwiches, and soups, but the attention to quality and detail makes it something special.

There are plenty of places to eat in Waco, but some home-grown originals stand out. **George's** has been feeding Waco classic Texas dishes since 1930 and has long been a favorite. The chicken-fried steak, fries, and macaroni and cheese just seem tastier eaten in the rambling, character-filled atmosphere of the place. Consider how thirsty you are before ordering a "Big O," 18 ounces of beer served in heavy, goblet-like glasses that a waitress once christened "Big Oranges." For something spicier, try **Cajun Craft**, a cute, casual Cajun eatery with fun outdoor seating. Diners love the boudin balls, crab-stuffed bacon-wrapped jalapeños, crawfish poutine, fried chicken jambalaya, and the list goes on. For something lighter, **Lula Jane's**

AN ARTISAN DEMONSTRATES THEIR CRAFT AT HOMESTEAD HERITAGE IN WACO is an oasis of sweet serenity. Pies, cookies, scones, and a delicious version of baked oatmeal have customers in love with this lovely spot. Lunch specials vary, according to the owner's whims.

A leisurely 35 miles north from Waco on TX 6, you'll come to **Clifton**, the "Norwegian Capital of Texas," which has earned the special designation as a Cultural District by the Texas Commission on the Arts and the State of Texas. Cited several times as one of the top small art communities in the nation, rural Clifton boasts an unusually high level of enthusiasm for and support of the arts and much of that is channelled through the **Bosque Arts Center**. Housed in the former Main Hall of Clifton College, the center hosts shows, exhibits, and workshops in the visual and performing arts. The renown **Bosque Art Classic** is an annual juried and judged art show and purchased pieces are on rotating view at the Center's **Roland Jones Memorial Gallery**.

Forts and Missions

In an early attempt to control what is now Texas, French explorer Robert de la Salle established Fort Louis in 1685 in an attempt control the mouth of the Mississippi, only to find out later that erroneous maps and directions in the little-known area had actually placed him closer to what is now Inez, Texas, near Matagorda Bay in the Gulf of Mexico. Located so far off its intended mark and meeting with strong resistance from Native Americans, the fort lasted only a few years.

The seventeenth and eighteenth centuries ushered in the rise of the Spanish *misiónes*, religious outposts developed under the guidance of Catholic Dominicans, Jesuits, and Franciscans and protected by the *presidio* (fort). Native Americans in this newly Spanish-controlled region of Texas were viewed as Spanish subjects, in need of indoctrination in the ways, language, customs, and beliefs of the Spanish crown. During this period, the region was host to twenty-six missions, many of which are still standing and open to visitors, the Alamo Mission in San Antonio, or "The Alamo," being one of the most well-known.

Mexican rule of Texas between 1821 and 1836 seemed to only fan the flames of discontent between Anglo "texians" and the government to the south, tensions which boiled over into the Texas Revolution and ultimately the creation of the Republic of Texas in 1836. Annexed by the United States in 1845, disputes over borders flared again and with Anglo-American pioneers pushing westward into the region, the Texas Rangers, and later, Buffalo Soldiers, were brought into help protect the settlements from Native Americans, who for their part, were seeking to maintain control over lands historically considered theirs.

Originally named Cliff Town for the limestone cliffs in the vicinity, Clifton was founded in the winter of 1852–53. A year later, the first Norwegian pioneer, Cleng Peerson, arrived and was followed by so many Norwegian immigrants that Clifton has been officially designated the Norwegian Capital of Texas. This very specific history makes a visit the **Bosque Memorial Museum** particularly interesting. From the log cabin out front to the photos of everyday immigrant life in Bosque County, pieces of Texas primitive furniture, and artifacts and ephemera from medical and educational practices on the frontier, the collection gives you a sense of what life was like in early days of immigrant settlement in the region. The Horn Shelter Exhibit, named for excavation of the burial site of a man and child found nearby, will take you back over 11,000 years.

THE SCREEN DOOR INN IN CLIFTON

In the center of town, the original restored blue screen doors greet you at the front of the **Screen Door Inn** on Avenue D. In fact, you'll find plenty of screen doors throughout the inn, a throwback to the days before air conditioning, but still during mosquitoes. Part of the historic Brooks Block, named for the turn-of-the-century Brooks Building, the inn has breathed new life into an old space. Polished pine floors, beadboard, exposed brick, and a claw-foot tub or two set the tone in this lovely boutique inn. Lodgers can enjoy basic breakfast of eggs, sausage, and homemade biscuits at the **Corner Drug Café**, a former pharmacy a few doors down which offers nostalgia you can taste. Bygone lunch staples such as crispy fried chicken served with mashed potatoes, green beans with bits of bacon, and cornbread are still served at here. There are also quiches, soups, salads, sandwiches, and plenty of homemade cookies, cakes, muffins, and pies.

If you are looking for something a little more unusual, consider checking yourself into jail and spend the night in **The Cell Block**. Tucked into the Clifton Art Alley, this tiny city jail was actually in use quite a bit, as local lore emphasizes, to sleep off a little too much drinking or maybe play a few

THE CORNER DRUG CAFÉ IN CLIFTON

friendly games of dominoes. The place still doesn't have a television and the train still rumbles by a few blocks away, but these days this fantastic little spot only houses overnight guests looking for a stylish place to relax. Efficient, rifle with design details, and capped off with a rooftop deck, The Cell Block is as unique as they come. Owned by the same folks, the farm-to-table restaurant **Sinclair** also pairs an urban sensibility with small town intimacy. Start with a Texas cheese sampler, move on to Lockhart quail served with homegrown pomegranate, and follow up with a slice of jalapeño cheesecake with candied jalapeño and local spiced honey drizzle. Fine dining in the shadow of the town's grain elevator.

People love poking around Clifton's antique shops and the **Bosque County Emporium** is a favorite and the **Norwegian Country Christmas Tour** (www.visitclifton.org) held the first Saturday of December, featuring Norwegian crafts, food, and tours of homes and buildings reminiscent of the early settlers, is a big draw.

Back on TX 6, it's another 34 miles to **Hico**, and the intersection of the route detailed in Chapter 3. Stop for lunch or a look around the Billy the Kid Museum then continue north on TX 6 and then take 1-20 to Abilene, a drive of approximately 115 miles. Incidentally, Abilene is roughly 150 from Fort Worth.

Abilene is when the west starts to feel a little wild. Home to approximately 110,000 residents, Abilene has a tangible sense of "can do" community enthusiasm. From non-profits to the arts, Abilene is dynamic and really delivers for visitors. This doesn't mean the offerings are extensive—the downtown core is rather compact—but they are well-designed and engaging.

A great place to start is **Frontier Texas!**, the visitor information center for the Texas Forts Trail, one of 10 Texas Heritage Trails designated by the Texas Historical Commission. Wander through the exhibits featuring Native Americans, cattle trails, pioneers, outlaws, and the prairies they shared. Well-staffed and stocked with copious amounts of information about the region.

Downtown is home to the city's museums, within easy walking distance to one another. **The Grace Museum**, housed in a historic early-1900s hotel, has a lovely art collection with a distinctly Texas twist. The museum came about through a series of folks taking the reins. In the 1980's, the Abilene Preservation League and the Abilene Fine Arts Museum joined forces to save the hotel building, which had been neglected and fallen into disrepair. After extensive renovations, the building is now on the National Register of Historic Places. The Grace is a unique museum due in part to the wide range of items on display. There are 5,000 pieces of artwork and 12,000 historically significant objects, curated in exhibits to highlight the creativity, ingenuity, and beauty of life in West Texas.

"TESTING THE TEXAS WIND," A BRONZE HOLLOW-CAST BULL BUFFALO IN FRONT OF FRONTIER TEXAS! CONTAINS A BRONZE HEART, PLACED INSIDE THE PIECE BY ITS SCULPTOR T. D. KELSEY

It may come as a surprise that **National Center of Children's Illustrated Literature** (NCCIL, commonly referred to as "the nickel") is located in Abilene, but the roots of how it came to be are also unexpected. In 1993, the mayor of Abilene, Dr. Gary McCaleb, was invited to read a brand new children's book titled *Santa Calls* to local school children. So taken that the story had been set in Abilene, McCaleb reached out to the author, William Joyce. As it turns out, Joyce had never visited Abilene and had no special reason for picking the city other than wanting to pick a locale to justify the fact that one of the characters in the tale wears a cowboy hat. Through this chance encounter, the two men struck up a friendship, and the seeds of the NCCIL began to germinate. Opened in 2000, the organization honors the artwork of children's picture book illustrators and curates new exhibits every three months so there is always something inspiring to see. The story explains why there is a statue of Santa Claus out front and, summing up the whole whirlwind experience, Joyce has said "How was I supposed to know Abilene was a city of cock-eyed optimists and dreamers?" It is heartwarming to see the whimsical and poignant illustrations of children's literature so lovingly displayed as the artwork they are.

Innkeeper and descendent of West Texas pioneers, Terry Browder has spared no detail restoring the sumptuous **Sayles Landmark Bed and Breakfast**. Built by Judge Henry Sayles in 1886, only five years after the town of Abilene was established, this elegant house was home to Mr. Sayles, his wife, and their ten children. Each of the inn's six rooms are unique, some are spacious with Victorian beds and antique crystal chandeliers and others with cozy with beadboard, leather chairs, and framed vintage photographs. Mr. Browder also owns the **Sayles Ranch Guesthouses**, a collection of roomy, beautifully decorated, and well appointed luxury accommodations scattered throughout Abilene.

The Beehive garners consistent kudos for juicy steaks, succulent rack of lamb, and crisp chicken-fried steaks served alongside tall Mason jars of their signature Long Island iced tea. Many consider the very popular and generously-sized pulled pork-filled avocado appetizer large enough for a meal. Since its beginnings in the 1980s, the restaurant and saloon has become iconic, due in large part to the diligence, friendliness, and warmth of its owners, brothers who immigrated to the United States from Iran and fit

Fort Griffin

In fact, tiny **Fort Griffin State Historic Site** (north of Albany) became so notorious that many of the gunfighters of the Old West, such as Wyatt Earp and Doc Holliday, passed through to spend a raucous night or two. An active defensive fort between 1867 to 1881, only stone remnants remain now, but it's enough to give you an idea of the size, scope, and isolation of the operation. In fact, the fort is surrounded by so much ranchland that there is minimal light pollution, so one benefit of camping is a view of the Milky Way. Feel like you're not alone out here? You aren't. Fort Griffin is home the approximately 250 cattle in the Official State of Texas Longhorn herd.

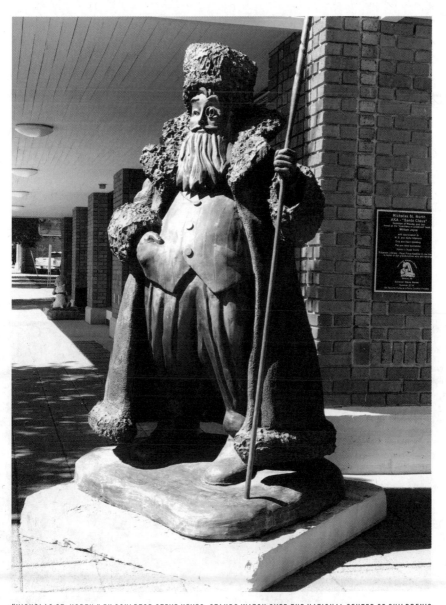

"NICHOLAS ST. NORTH," BY SCULPTOR STEVE NEVES, STANDS WATCH OVER THE NATIONAL CENTER OF CHILDREN'S ILLUSTRATED LITERATURE IN ABILENE

right into the Texas frontier, which has a history of welcoming anyone who can prepare a perfect steak. Speaking of perfect steak, make a reservation for **Perini Ranch Steakhouse** (pages 235–236) in Buffalo Gap, 25 minutes south of Abilene, for an outstanding steakhouse experience.

Vagabond Pizza has moved into fill a gap for wood-fired gourmet pies in downtown Abilene. Once a food truck, Vagabond has found a home in a cavernous former jewelry store, where the rustic chic atmosphere pairs well with the menu. Depending on the size of your appetite, folks tend to order a salad for themselves and split hot-out-of-the-oven pizzas. Although some order a whole pie with no intentions of sharing, especially when the toppings are unique as fire-roasted quail with chimichurri sauce.

Immensely popular for its chicken salad with grapes and cashews served with two slices of homemade zucchini bread, the **Hickory Street Café** is located in a charming older home with a tea room atmosphere. The Café has been serving lunch in Abilene for over 30 years.

Greek immigrants Nick and George Vletas opened the doors to **Vletas Candies** in Abilene in 1912 and through wars, depressions, recessions, and the wild pendulum swings of the oil business, the family has continued to make chocolates. Located in a repurposed railroad depot across from NCCIL, the confectioner makes all kinds of chocolates, fudge, brittles, and

TAYLOR COUNTY HISTORY CENTER/BUFFALO GAP HISTORIC VILLAGE IN BUFFALO GAP

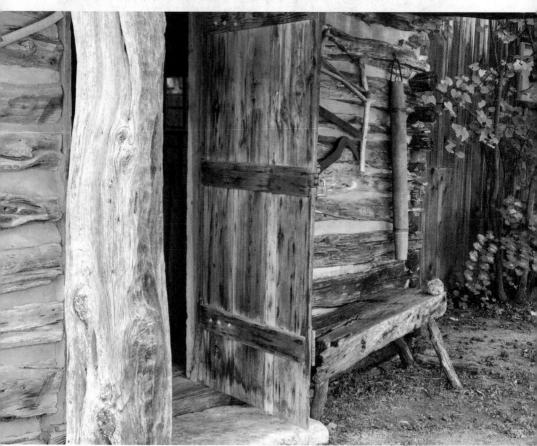

dipped fruits with high quality ingredients and lots of love. The smells alone are worth the stop.

Heading south on Buffalo Gap Road for 25 miles, you'll leave the edges of Abilene behind and drive through open country before arriving at the tiny frontier town of **Buffalo Gap**. Once a watering hole for buffalo, it may be hard to imagine that in 1874, Buffalo Gap was declared the county seat. The decision makes more sense when you discover it was the the *only* town in Taylor County at the time. Six years later, the settlement had 1,200 inhabitants and all the trappings of a community, including a drugstore, jail, blacksmith's shop, saloon, grocery stores, and the beginnings of a college. But, when the Texas and Pacific Railway chose Abilene as its headquarters in 1883, folks packed up and moved north to the "big city." Between 1890 and 1980, the popula-

THE HEARTH IN THE DINING ROOM OF THE PERINI RANCH STEAKHOUSE IN BUFFALO GAP

tion at Buffalo Gap fluctuated between 250 and 400. In the 1950s, as the town diminished, several townsfolk stepped forward to help preserve some of the community's more historically significant buildings and today you can visit the collection at the **Taylor County History Center/Buffalo Gap Historic Village**. Enter through the Mercantile to purchase tickets, then wander the grounds. Take a peek into the limestone building used as both the jail and courthouse, the little post office, a wagon barn, homes, and a church. The wide view of the fields and distant hills across the street makes it that much easier to imagine how remote Buffalo Gap must have felt to it's early citizens.

Perini Ranch Steakhouse is a reason to make Buffalo Gap a destination all on its own. Thick ribeyes, strips, and filets seared over mesquite flames and plenty of hospitality earned this steakhouse a James Beard Foundation shout out in 2014 as an "American Classic" for "timeless appeal" and cuisine which "reflects the character of their community." The restaurant's roots are quite a bit deeper, when, in 1983, amid depressed cattle and oil prices, rancher Tom Perini decided to try his luck in the kitchen and converted a hay barn on his property into a Texas roadhouse. The gamble paid off and folks have been coming to enjoy steaks served with green chile hominy, garlic potatoes, and whisky bread pudding ever since. Reservations recommended. Stroll through the adjacent Perini Ranch Market or pick up a copy of their cookbook.

Leaving Buffalo Gap, it's another 67 miles south to **San Angelo**, the city that sits on the fault line of the frontier, having been claimed by Spain, Mexico, The Republic of Texas and, in 1846, the United States.

The current city was founded alongside the newly-formed Fort Concho in 1867 by a settler who named the new community after his wife, Angela, calling it "Santa Angela." Years of use shortened the name to "San Angela" and the US postal service stepped in 1883 to edit it to "San Angelo," which is grammatically correct in Spanish. As with many settlements in the area, San Angelo had plenty of saloons, brothels, and gambling, but hardly any enforced laws. A county seat, railroad hub, and destination for tuberculosis sufferers in the early 1900s, San Angelo grew quickly, for better or worse.

One of the very best legacies of this era is the San Angelo City Park system, put in place in 1903 and well-connected to the heart of historic San Angelo, is spread out along the Concho River. The 10-mile stretch of riverfront parkland makes San Angelo more pedestrian friendly than many other Texas cities its size. The **San Angelo Convention & Visitor Bureau**

Fort McKavett

You'll need to make a slight detour to visit **Fort McKavett State Historic Site**, but most who visit report the drive to be well worth it. Originally named Fort San Saba, the outpost served as a waystation for travelers making their way to California. Perched on a hill and surrounded by 80 acres of wilderness with mile-long views, it's easy to imagine how remote the site must have felt when it was first established in March 1852. Abandoned in 1859, the site was reopened almost a decade later as Fort McKavett after post-Civil War immigration increased tensions with resident Native Americans, specifically the Comanche, who viewed the fledgling fort as an unwelcome intrusion on their territory. With a foothold in the region, the fort served from 1868 through 1883 as an outpost and supply chain as the expanding United States sought to map, understand, and gain control over its expanding borders. You'll find over a dozen well-preserved limestone structures, many of which furnished with period items, and visitors are welcome to take a look around. Officer's quarters, barracks, a hospital, school house, and large vegetable gardens bring to life the forts' efforts sustaining a small community on the frontier and the on-site museum provides plenty of historical context. See www.texasfortstrail.com for details sits on the edge of the river, with paths leading down to the water and alongside the shore.

Nearby, the **Fort Concho National Historic Landmark** offers a glimpse back in time through its recently renovated complex. It is a little difficult to appreciate with modern life swirling around, but Fort Concho's location was chosen due to its proximity to the nearby Concho River and long views of uninterrupted prairie. Built in 1867, the fort was constructed to protect established settlers, wagon trains, stagecoaches, trade routes, and the US mail service. By the late nineteenth century, the railroad had reached West Texas and goods, services, and people were able to travel without the protection of forts. On July 20, 1889, a small group of soldiers lowered the American flag, retiring it and themselves to San Antonio the next morning. If your travels have taken you to the Texas Hill Country (Chapters 1 and 2), you may recognize the architecture at Fort Concho. A little more refined than that of other regional forts, the buildings here were constructed by German masons from nearby Fredericksburg, who brought with them a knowledge and expertise working with locally-quarried sandstone and native pecan lumber.

FORT CONCHO NATIONAL HISTORIC LANDMARK IN SAN ANGELO

A few blocks away, you'll spot the distinctive curved roof—reminiscent a saddle or Conestoga wagon—of the the **San Angelo Museum of Fine Arts**. While the collection is diverse, the emphasis here is on Texas artists, particularly on pieces created since World War II, and on the ceramic arts. Exhibits are constantly changing and range from "Folk Art of the Concho Valley" to "A Voyage Across Cultures: The Enduring Fascination of Chinese Export Porcelain." Ceramic artists come from all over the nation for the San Angelo National Ceramic Competition and the San Angelo Ceramic Invitational Exhibition, both of which feature tremendous talent. The EnPleinAirTEXAS, a national juried painting competition, has become a popular October event and a chance to meet artists and watch them work. Concerts by the West Texas Jazz Orchestra, a group comprised of public school band directors, Angelo State University music professors, and other area musicians, are especially popular. The museum's mission includes outreach to both

San Angelo and the rural communities of the Concho Valley, making it a dynamic arts and cultural resource in West Texas.

The Texas frontier wasn't just known for pushing boundaries—it pushed the limits of public morality in more ways than one. Throughout the nineteenth century, male immigrants outnumbered females, and a large number of residents were criminals or fugitives from the law, who chose the territory specifically for its loose restrictions and lack of law enforcement. Smuggling, gambling, drinking, and prostitution flourished on the frontier and the story of the Hattons illustrates what a way of life it had become. In 1902, Mr. and Mrs. Hatton purchased 18 Concho Street, running a saloon on the ground floor and entertaining on the second. The couple divorced and, in an interesting move, Mr. Hatton received the first floor of the building and Mrs. Hatton took ownership of the second, which had its own entrance. What followed was 50 years of prostitution at Miss Hattie's in the heart of what was known as The Concho, or "vice district." Though illegal for most of its tenure—the Mann Act was passed to end prostitution in 1910—Miss Hattie's brothel operated with the knowledge of both the police and the sheriff before a raid by the Texas Rangers in 1952 finally closed its doors for good. **Miss Hattie's Bordello Museum** came about in the 1970s when the

THE SAN ANGELO MUSEUM OF FINE ARTS IN SAN ANGELO

building's owner found original furniture and accessories packed away and decided set them back in place in vignettes for the public to view. One of the most interesting features of the building are the tunnels connecting the brothel to the nearby banks and bar.

Around the corner and up a block or two is **M. L. Leddy's Boots**. In 1922, M. L. Leddy left the cotton farm of his youth, purchased a saddle and boot shop in the small town of Brady, and set about building a business. In the process, Mr. Leddy built a reputation, and quickly became known for making high-quality custom boots for customers who appreciated his personal touch. By 1936, Leddy's had outgrown Brady, moved to San Angelo, and, in 1941, opened a second location in the Fort Worth Stockyards. These days, Leddy's is run by the fourth generation of Leddy's family and has

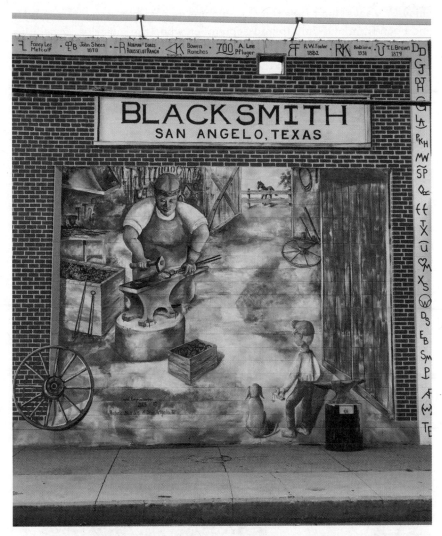

"THE BLACKSMITH SHOP," BY ARTIST CRYSTAL GOODMAN, IS LOCATED ON THE CORNER OF CONCHO AVENUE AND OAKES STREET IN DOWNTOWN SAN ANGELO. READ MORE ABOUT THE HISTORIC BACKGROUND OR ACCESS AN AUDIO TOUR OF THE CITY'S MANY STREET MURALS AT WWW.HISTORICMURALSOFSANANGELO.ORG

expanded to offer Western wear, hats, belts, buckles, jewelry, and clothing in addition to its legendary boots and saddles. Stop by the shop in San Angelo where you can still see bookmakers hand-piecing each boot using the time-tested tools and techniques of the craft.

On a pretty day, take a look at the world-renown **International Waterlily Collection**, designated by the International Waterlily & Water Gardening Society as a premiere collection. Ken Landon is the gardener behind the effort and rotates ½ to 1 percent of the collection's vast store of waterlilies through the viewing area at San Angelo's Civic League Park for the public to enjoy. Ken says that to see the most blooms as possible, visit between 9 AM and noon from mid-July to mid-September, when the majority of the lilies are opening and nearing their peak size.

Art gallery lovers flock to the **Chicken Farm Art Center**, a 3-acre chicken farm repurposed in 1971 by three local potters as a community for artists to live and work. Home to 15 studios and host to numerous musical events

STEP INTO M. L. LEDDY'S BOOTS IN SAN ANGELO TO SEE JUST HOW BOOTS ARE MADE AND MARVEL AT THE FINAL PRODUCT

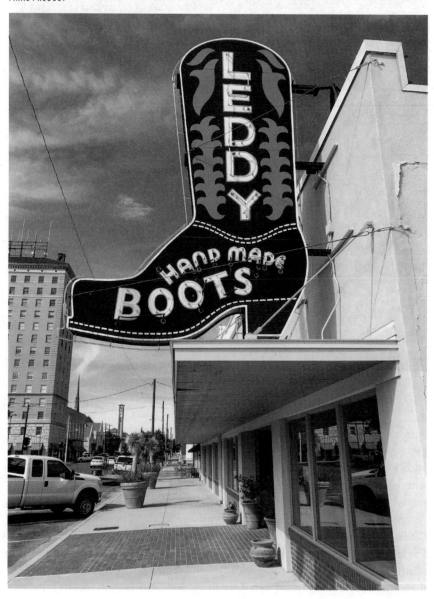

and art demonstrations, including art-filled First Saturdays, Second Thursday Concert in the Yard, which starts at 6:30 PM, the Annual Open House in November, and the biannual Ceramic Weekend competition in April. Events tend to be free and all showcase local West Texas talent.

The Art Center is home to one of the most unique lodging options in this book, the **Inn at The Art Center**. Tucked into two grain silos, the six rooms in this rambling bed and breakfast are chock-full of all kinds of whimsical details, including tile mosaic, murals, beautifully polished natural wood, and artwork. The showers, linens, and bedding are all on point and you'll find fresh-out-of-the-oven baked goods in the communal kitchen each morning. The lovely innkeepers are a wealth of information and fun stories about the Chicken Farm and its artists.

In a silo beside the inn, the **Silo House Restaurant** offers a menu of dishes such as grilled ribeye with creamy polenta and caramelized brussel sprouts or lamb chops with jalapeño peach glaze served with risotto. The restaurant doesn't have a liquor license, but diners are welcome to bring their own.

Downtown, the **Zero One Ale House** serves pints and pub food, including an interesting mix of burgers, tacos, curries, seared tuna, barbecue pork nachos, and a side dish called "twice baked fried potato balls," which diners report taste great. Tours of the on-site brewery are available one Saturday a month and the $10 registration fee includes a flight of the house brews of your choice.

Over the river and just under a mile south of Fort Concho is the **Concho Pearl Ice House**. The pink to purple-hued concho pearl is unique to West Texas, found only in freshwater mussels in the region's lakes and rivers. This concho pearl is a former gas station now painted a light lemon chiffon color, with blue and green accents. Diners love the spicy "cannonball burger"—a burger topped with melted pepper jack cheese, a few bacon-wrapped jalapeños, and buffalo sauce. The brisket-stuffed avocado and "cowboy sushi" are also favorites. Lots of longnecks, plenty of picnic tables, and a playground complete the relaxed ice house vibe.

Heading southwest, the **Cork and Pig Tavern** is a popular place to dine near San Angelo State University. The deviled eggs with bacon crisps, meaty pizzas, marinated grilled ribeye, and key lime pie are favorites, supplemented by the wine list, drafted beers, and cocktails.

After leaving San Angelo and heading east 120 miles, you'll arrive in **San Saba**, the "Pecan Capital of the World." Founded in 1854 along the San Saba River, San Saba is part of the northern edge of the Texas Hill Country (see Chapters 1 and 2). The town has had a burst of civic enthusiasm and has been putting some elbow-grease into its historic main streets.

For example, **The Dofflemyer Hotel** is a stylishly renovated boutique hotel in the former San Saba National Bank building, constructed in 1913

NATIVE GRASSES ALONG THE BACKROADS OF THE TEXAS FRONTIER

by W. C. Dofflemyer. While the downstairs housed the bank, the upstairs was home to the San Saba Club, a gentlemen's social club, a space which has since been transformed into the hotel's five guest rooms and one suite. Gorgeous wood floors, vintage-style bathroom tile, stone walls, tin ceilings, and pecan-themed art give this hotel plenty of character. Spend a few minutes perusing the photographs in the lobby, they offer a peek into San Saba's past.

The Dofflemyer is connected, by location and ownership, to **Oliver and**

Co., the café next door. A nice spot for a light lunch, Oliver's has a menu of big salads, jalapeño pimento cheese sandwiches, grilled paninis, soups, muffins, and freshly-brewed coffee. They also have plenty of pecans, artisan chocolates, and homemade ice cream to eat in or take home.

Need more pecans? Visit the **Great San Saba River Pecan Company**, where you can buy everything from award-winning pecan preserves to unbelievably rich chocolate pecan pies. You can even pick your own pecans in their orchard from November through January.

Wrap up the route with a visit to **Wedding Oak Winery**, a tasting room located in a beautifully restored building on East Wallace Street, or spend some time poking through the shops such as long-time purveyor of cowboy boots **Harry's Boots**.

From here you can continue back to Waco or meet up with the routes outlined in Chapters 1, 2, or 3.

IN THE AREA

BED AND BREAKFAST ON WHITE ROCK CREEK, 267 Ruby Dell Lane, Waco, 76705. Call 254-799-9783. Wonderfully spacious accommodations in a wooded setting. Website: www.whiterockcreek.com. $–$$.

THE BEEHIVE, 442 Cedar Street, Abilene, 79601. Call 325-675-0600. Popular steakhouse known for quality food and generous portions. Website: www.beehivesaloon.com. $$–$$$.

BOSQUE ARTS CENTER, 215 S. College Hill Drive, Clifton, 76634. Call 254-675-3724. Website: www.bosqueartscenter.org.

BOSQUE COUNTY EMPORIUM, 121 N. Avenue D Avenue, Clifton, 76634. Call 254-675-8133. Find them on Facebook.

BOSQUE MEMORIAL MUSEUM, 301 S. Avenue Q, Clifton, 76634. Call 254-675-3845. Website: www.bosquemuseum.org.

CAFÉ HOMESTEAD, 608 Dry Creek Road, Waco, 76705. Call 254-754-9604. Closed Sundays. Wholesome, hearty, and homemade meals at Homestead Heritage. Website: www.cafehomestead.com. $–$$.

CAJUN CRAFT, 601 S. 11th Street, Waco, 76706. Call 254-754-3869. Closed Sundays. Casual Cajun eatery with fun outdoor seating. Website: www.cajun craftwacotx.com. $–$$.

TEXAS CATTLE GRAZING ON THE FRONTIER

THE CELL BLOCK, 120 Clifton Art Alley, Clifton, 76634. Call 254-227-5656. Very stylish digs in the former city jail. Website: www.stayatthecellblock .com. $$$–$$$$.

CHICKEN FARM ART CENTER, 2505 Martin Luther King Drive, San Angelo, 76903. Call 325-653-4936. Website: www.chickenfarmartcenter.com.

THE CONCHO PEARL ICEHOUSE, 1605 S. Chadbourne, San Angelo, 76903. Call 325-617-7909. Burger, barbecue, and beer in a casual ice house environment. Website: www.theconchopearl.com. $$.

CORK & PIG TAVERN, 2201 Knickerbocker Road, San Angelo, 76904. Call 325-227-6988. Wood-fired pizzas, grilled steaks, and a stand-out key lime pie make this pub-style eatery popular. Website: www.corkandpig.com. $$–$$$.

CORNER DRUG CAFÉ, 102 N. Avenue D, Clifton, 76634. Call 254-265-7737. Closed Mondays and Tuesdays. Light and tasty breakfast and lunch fare in a renovated drug store in the middle of town. Website: Find them on Facebook. $–$$.

THE COTTON PALACE, 1910 Austin Ave, Waco, 76701. Call 254-753-7294. This 1910 Arts and Crafts home is just as lovely as its hosts. Website: www.thecottonpalace.com. $$–$$$.

DR PEPPER MUSEUM AND FREE ENTERPRISE INSTITUTE, 300 S. 5th Street, Waco, 76701. Call 254-757-1025. Fee. Website: www.drpeppermuseum.com.

FORT CONCHO NATIONAL HISTORIC LANDMARK, 630 S. Oakes Street, San Angelo, 76903. Call 325-481-2646. Fee. Website: www.fortconcho.com.

FORT McKAVETT STATE HISTORIC SITE, 7066 FM 864, Fort McKavett, 76841. Call 325-396-2358. Fee. Website: www.texasfortstrail.com or www.thc.texas.gov.

FORT GRIFFIN STATE HISTORIC SITE, 1701 US-283, Albany, 76430. Call 325-762-3592. Fee. Website: www.texasfortstrail.com or www.thc.texas.gov.

FRONTIER TEXAS!, 625 N. 1st Street, Abilene, 79601. Call 325-437-2800. Free. Website: www.texasfortstrail.com.

GEORGE'S RESTAURANT, 1925 Speight Avenue, Waco, 76706. Call 254-753-1421. Closed Sundays. Bustling local favorite for Texas classics. Website: www.georgesrestaurant.com. $–$$.

THE GRACE MUSEUM, 102 Cypress Street, Abilene, 79601. Call 325-673-4587. Fee. Website: www.thegracemuseum.org.

THE GREAT SAN SABA RIVER PECAN COMPANY, 234 West Hwy 190, San Saba, 76877. Closed Sundays. Website: www.greatpecans.com.

HARRY'S BOOTS, 403 E. Wallace Street, San Saba, 76877. Call 325-372-3636. Website: www.harrysboots.com.

HICKORY STREET CAFÉ, 644 Hickory Street, Abilene, 79601. Call 325-675-0465. Lunch only; Closed Saturdays and Sundays. Charming café, with a healthy menu of tearoom favorites. Website: www.hickorystreetcafe.com. $–$$.

HOMESTEAD HERITAGE, 608 Dry Creek Road, Waco, 76705. Call 254-754-9600. Free. Website: www.homesteadheritage.com.

INN AT THE ART CENTER, 2503 Martin Luther King Boulevard, San Angelo, 76903. Call 325-659-3836. Website: www.innattheartcenter.com. $$–$$$$.

INTERNATIONAL WATERLILY COLLECTION, 2 S. Park Street, San Angelo, 76901. Call 832-274-3377. Free. Website: www.internationalwaterlilycollection.com.

LULA JANE'S, 406 Elm Street, Waco, 76704. Call 254-366-0862. Closed Sundays. Sweet and savory treats in a lovely spot. Website: www.lulajanes.com. $

M.L. LEDDY'S, 222 S. Oakes Street, San Angelo, 76903. Call 325-653-3397. Website: www.leddys.com.

MAGNOLIA MARKET AT THE SILOS, 601 Webster Avenue, Waco, 76706. Call 254-235-6111. Website: www.magnoliamarket.com.

MAYBORN MUSEUM COMPLEX, 1300 S. University Parks Drive, Waco, 76706. Call 254-710-1110. Fee. Website: www.baylor.edu/mayborn.

MIGUEL HOUSE BED AND BREAKFAST, 1425 Columbus Avenue, Waco, 76701. Call 254-523-6611. Stunning Mediterranean-inspired building with a bowling alley in the basement. Website: www.migelhouse.com. $$$$.

THE NATIONAL CENTER FOR CHILDREN'S ILLUSTRATED LITERA-TURE, 102 Cedar Street, Abilene, 79601. Call 325-673-4586. Fee. Website: www.nccil.org.

PERINI RANCH STEAKHOUSE, 3002 FM 89, Buffalo Gap, 79508. Call 325-572-3339. Reservations required. Outstanding destination steakhouse on a ranch outside of tiny Buffalo Gap. Website: www.store.periniranch.com. $$–$$$.

RAILWAY AND HERITAGE MUSEUM OF SAN ANGELO, 703 S. Chadbourne Street, San Angelo, 76903. Call 325-486-2140. Fee. Website www.railwaymuseumsanangelo.homestead.com.

SAN ANGELO CONVENTION & VISITOR BUREAU, 418 W. Avenue B, San Angelo, 76903. Call 325-655-4136. Website: www.discoversanangelo.com.

THE SAYLES LANDMARK INN, 642 Sayles Boulevard, Abilene, 79605. Call 325-670-9402. Six wonderfully unique rooms in a turn of the century inn on lovely Sayles Boulevard. Website: wwww.sayleslandmark.com. $$–$$$.

SAYLES RANCH GUESTHOUSES, 1001 Sayles Boulevard, Abilene, 79605. Call 325-669-6856. Beautifully decorated and well appointed accommodations throughout the city. Website: www.saylesranch.com. $$$$.

SINCLAIR, 215 W. 3rd Street, Clifton, 76634. Call 254-675-8888. Closed Monday through Wednesday. Fine dining at this small town farm-to-table restaurant. Website: www.sinclairrestaurant.com. $$–$$$.

TAYLOR COUNTY HISTORY CENTER/BUFFALO GAP HISTORIC VILLAGE, 133 North William Street, Buffalo Gap, 79508. Call 325-572-3365. Closed Mondays. Fee. Website: www.taylorcountyhistorycenter.com.

TEXAS RANGER HALL OF FAME & MUSEUM, 100 Texas Ranger Trail, Waco, 76706. Call 254-750-8631. Fee. Website: www.texasranger.org.

VAGABOND PIZZA, 1056 North 2nd Street, Abilene, 79601. Call 325-268-4321. Closed Sundays and Mondays. Wood-fired pizzas in the heart of Abilene. Website: www.vagabondpizza.com. $–$$.

VLETAS CANDIES, 1201 N. 1st Street, Abilene, 79601. Call 325-673-2005. Website: www.candiesbyvletas.com.

WACO MAMMOTH NATIONAL HISTORIC SITE, 6220 Steinbeck Bend Drive, Waco, 76708. Call 254-750-7946. Fee. Website: www.nps.gov/waco.

WEDDING OAK WINERY, 316 E. Wallace Street, San Saba, 76877. Call 325-372-4050. Website: www.weddingoakwinery.com.

ZERO ONE ALE HOUSE, 20 W. Beauregard Avenue, San Angelo, 76903. Call 325-653-5123. Brewery with pints and an interesting array of pub food. Website: www.zeroonealehouse.com. $$.

SUNSET OVER RAY ROBERTS LAKE STATE PARK

12

NORTH TEXAS

McKINNEY, BONHAM, DENISON, WHITESBORO,
PILOT POINT, NOCONA, DENTON

TOTAL DISTANCE: 130 miles

HIGHLIGHTS: Stroll the historic **McKinney** town square, taking in restaurants, shops, and the county museum. Continue onto **Bonham** and **Denison** and explore their connections to politicians Sam Rayburn and President Dwight Eisenhower. Visit the several heritage villages to get a glimpse of what life was like in yesteryear. Spend some time in nature, at one of several state parks, two lakes, and a wildlife preserve. Enjoy the tiny towns; have a burger in an old gas station in **Pilot Point** and a piece of pie in **Whitesboro**. Spend some time in the vibrant college town of **Denton**, where food, history, and live music are easily enjoyed.

GETTING THERE: McKinney and Denton are each located approximately 35 miles north of Dallas and Fort Worth, respectively.

To begin the route, from McKinney, take TX 121 40 miles north to Bonham and from there an additional 15 miles on TX 56 and 13 miles farther on US 69 to Denison. From Denison, follow US 75 south, US 82 west, and US 377 south for a total of 30 miles to Whitesboro. From there, it's an additional 23 miles south on US 377 to Pilot Point. From Pilot Point, it's 30 more miles, using US 377 and FM 428, to Denton. Alternatively, in Whitesboro, you could continue along US 82 to connect with I-35 in Gainesville and take I-35 south to Denton, along the westside of Lake Ray Roberts.

It used to be you could hunt doves, quail, and pheasants in North Texas all season long, but those birds have long since flown the region. Big-city bustle and development have devoured the land, eating up farms and ranches and replacing country roads with highways. That said, this route is special. Leave the busy Dallas/Fort Worth metro area behind and head out for a day trip or weekend getaway. You may need to look a little more closely to be sure not

to miss the great details. There are still hamburgers, ice cream, local history museums, town squares, and sunsets to enjoy if you know where to look. But times are changing quickly, so be sure to get out into the country while there is still country to get out into.

Incorporated in 1859 and once a small agricultural and railroad community, the population of **McKinney** has grown as the Dallas-Fort Worth Metroplex has expanded its reach. Between 2000 and 2017 alone, the population more than tripled to over 175,000. Despite its growth, however, the historic downtown remains compact, walkable, and full of shops, restaurants, and cultural events; it's the perfect homebase from which to explore the region.

Start your visit off at the **Collin County History Museum**, located just a block off the square, where you'll learn a bit about Collin McKinney, the city's namesake. A New Jersey native, Mr. McKinney arrived in Texas via Kentucky, and was a delegate representing the Red River Colony to the Convention of 1836, during which Texas announced its intention to declare independence from Mexico. He was one of five to draft, and the oldest to sign, the Texas Declaration of Independence and served on the committee charged with the writing of the Constitution of the Republic of Texas, all at the age of 70. The museum is housed in a 1911 Italianate post office building; be sure to ask about the secret passages.

STATELY ENTRANCE TO THE COLLIN COUNTY HISTORY MUSEUM IN McKINNEY

Several blocks south of the square, you'll find **Chestnut Square**, a collection of historic homes and buildings maintained by the The Heritage Guild of Collin County. The grounds include a 1920's-era store and a mid-1800s home used as an inn where you could stay, have your clothes washed, and enjoy a hot breakfast, all for 25 cents a night. The Faires House, built in 1854 and featuring a hand-chiseled door crafted by Mr. Faires himself, is thought to be the oldest standing house in McKinney. While the complex is sandwiched between a busy road and downtown development, it's still possible to get a sense of history meandering among the buildings at this shady spot.

Judging from the sidewalk, **Patina Green Home and Market** doesn't look like a café, but wander in and toward the back of the shop and you'll find

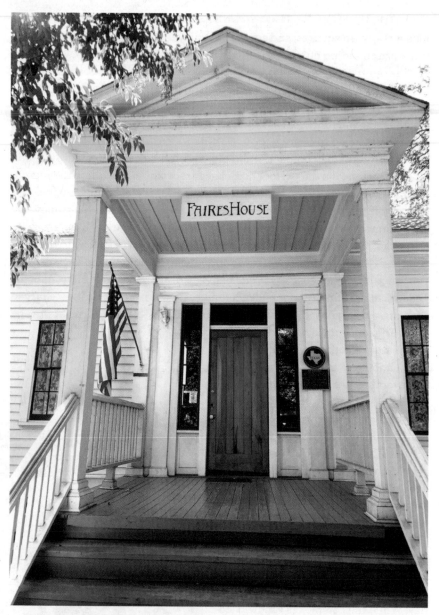

THE FAIRES HOUSE, CONSIDERED THE OLDEST STANDING HOUSE IN McKINNEY, WAS ORIGINALLY LOCATED ON SOUTH TENNESSEE STREET, BUT IS NOW PART OF THE CHESTNUT SQUARE COLLECTION OF HISTORIC BUILDINGS

the culinary goodness. While the entire seasonal menu is impressive, folks single out the "brisket on a biscuit" for praise, and the little sandwich delivers. Get there early to get a taste, since the moist brisket on a smoked cheddar biscuit with a dollop of jalapeño blackberry jelly is almost always sold out by 1 PM.

Around the corner, **Hugs Café**, a restaurant specially designed to train and employ adults with special needs, offers delicious lunches and a standing invitation for free hugs. The turkey sandwich with cheese, bacon, lettuce, and homemade peach chutney is a favorite, as are the chicken salad, daily soup specials, and the wedding cake cookies drizzled lightly with icing. Casual, cheerful dining in support of some wonderful young people.

Barbecue aficionados won't want to pass up the chance to taste some meat directly from the pits at **Hutchins BBQ**, frequently mentioned on statewide "Best of" lists. The all-you-can-eat meal might seem a little pricey, at almost $20, but it just might be the best deal since it allows you to sample the whole range of specialties—from brisket and broccoli slaw to sausage and bacon-wrapped jalapeños—and you'll certainly walked away stuffed.

Back on the square, **Harvest Seasonal Kitchen** features farm-to-market specialities which are as fresh and flavorful as can be. The creamy deviled eggs with a candied pecan, candied mustard seed, and a sprinkling of marigold petals on top are a must-try to start. While the menu evolves with the seasons, the cayenne-laced fried chicken and the locally-sourced chicken fried steak (dinner only) are both outstanding mainstays. A polished dining room, covered patio seating, desserts like lemon goat cheese icebox pie, and a very well-priced lunch menu make Harvest a great taste of McKinney.

HARVEST SEASONAL KITCHEN IN McKINNEY

Tucked into the former law offices of nineteenth-century Texas Governor James Throckmorton, and popular for its casual atmosphere paired with an outstanding seasonal menu, **Rye Craft Food and Drink** is a terrific spot to unwind. The goat cheese stuffed piquillo peppers with preserved lemon, the smoked gouda macaroni and cheese served in a small skillet, and the miso-braised pork belly with crispy sweet potatoes are all stellar starters, perfect alongside with a craft cocktail or Texas beer.

McKinney's quiet, leafy neighborhoods make a nice homebase, and **McKinney Bed & Breakfast** is a particularly pleasant place to stay. You can't miss the red rocking chairs on the porch on this 1880's Victorian house, where guests have three pristine and tastefully decorated rooms to choose from. Innkeepers Wayne and Vicki Hill outdo themselves with gourmet breakfasts and baked goods, including biscotti baked fresh daily.

Head northeast for 40 miles on TX 121 and you'll find yourself in **Bonham**. The community grew around a wooden two-story blockhouse fort built in 1837 and known as **Fort Inglish** for its builder, Bailey Inglish. The "Fort Inglish" you'll notice driving into town is actually a replica, built as the county's bicentennial project in 1976. Clustered together with several log cabins dating from the 1830s, a buggy, and a military wagon, it makes for a quick historical stop. Originally called "Bois d'Arc," the town was eventually named in honor of James Bonham, who died defending the Alamo. Get a glimpse of Mr. Bonham as you pass by the courthouse, where a statue of him, created by Texas sculptor Allie Tennant, is on display. There are plenty more local facts, artifacts, and historic details at the **Fannin County Museum of History**, where you'll get to take a look back at a vibrant and emerging North Texas in the nineteenth and twentieth centuries.

The town's most "famous" native son is likely Sam Rayburn, the legendary Texas politician. **Sam Rayburn** (1882-1961) may not be a household name now, but he was a fixture in the U.S. House of Representatives for close to half a century. Elected in 1912 as a Democrat from Texas' 4th congressional district, Mr. Rayburn served almost 50 years in public service, including 17 years as Speaker of the House, the longest tenure in U.S. history. Putting that in context, Mr. Rayburn entered Congress when President Woodrow Wilson entered office and served until he passed away in 1961 at the start of President Kennedy's term. Known for personal integrity, fairness, and an insistence paying his own way and refusing all reimbursement, Rayburn has been called "the most impressive person in Congress" and was posthumously awarded the Congressional Gold Medal.

The **Sam Rayburn House State Historic Site** is open to the public, just as it was when Rayburn lived there. In fact, the politician extended an open invitation to his constituents to drop by his home whenever they'd like. Like many in the area, the home did not have running water until 1917, and Ray-

Babe's Chicken

Cruising through Sanger, just off 1-35 between Gainesville and Denton, stop in at **Babe's Chicken** for fried chicken, mashed potatoes, corn, biscuits, and a slice of meringue pie. There are several Babes's scattered throughout the greater Dallas area, but very little advertising and historic, not highway, locations give each a hometown feel. Details at www.babes chicken.com.

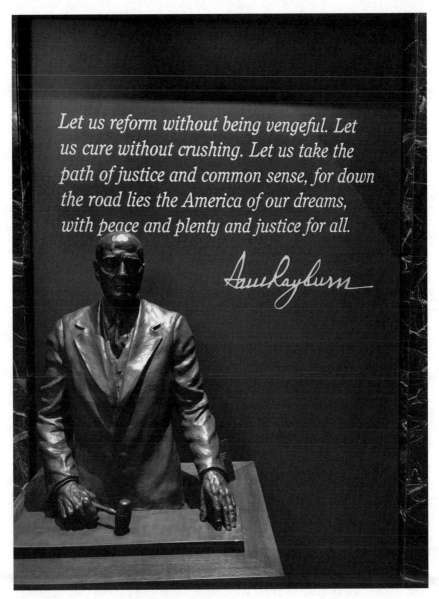

Let us reform without being vengeful. Let us cure without crushing. Let us take the path of justice and common sense, for down the road lies the America of our dreams, with peace and plenty and justice for all.

Sam Rayburn

THE SAM RAYBURN LIBRARY AND MUSEUM IN BONHAM

burn himself paid to bring electricity to the building in 1935. His sense of practicality extended to his public service and didn't go unnoticed by his fellow congressmen. A token of their appreciation is parked in Bonham: a 1947 Cadillac Fleetwood, known as "Mr. Sam's Cadillac." During a rare time when Rayburn was not Speaker, he was also without the use of the congressionally-funded Cadillac. His colleagues couldn't stand the thought of him without a car, but knew he would never accept a gift over $25. So, 142

Democrats and 50 Republicans donated $25 apiece to purchase him the car. Rayburn was embarrassed, but appreciated the sentiment. To avoid the perception of conflict of interest, he personally thanked each Republican donor while returning their gift.

Remembered for his ability to work across party lines with a strong sense of parliamentary procedure, Rayburn earned the respect of many and a visit to the impressive **Sam Rayburn Library and Museum** helps to put his efforts in historical context. Now owned by the University of Texas at Austin and a division of the Dolph Briscoe Center for American History, the free-standing library is relatively small, but stately, with marble floors, an exact replica of the office Rayburn used while Speaker, and his wide collection of books. The eight striking "Gold Medallion" presidential portraits painted by Victor Lallier, the most well-known portrait painter in twentieth-century Texas, are a touching tribute to the breadth and depth of Rayburn's service. Knowledgeable docents have lots of stories to share, so don't be shy about asking.

If you plan to stop for lunch, **Muddbones** is the burger joint locals swear by and one you'll find on "Best Burger" lists statewide. Big, hand-formed patties cooked your way and served with all the fixin's, a can of Coke, and a bag of chips. It's a no-frills eatery, with picnic tables and friendly service.

Follow TX 56 and US 69 for 33 miles to **Denison**, which many people visit because of an interest in President Dwight D. Eisenhower and the **Eisenhower Birthplace State Historical Park**. While Dwight David "Ike" Eisenhower was born in 1890 in a neat-as-a-pin white house on Lamar Avenue in Denison, his family returned to their home state of Kansas in 1892.

A towering figure of the twentieth century, Eisenhower attended West Point and graduated in 1915, a member of the "class the stars fell on," so called because over a third of the graduates became generals. During World War II, five-star General Eisenhower served as Supreme Allied Commander of the Allied Expeditionary Force and later went on to become President of Columbia University and the Supreme Commander of NATO before, reluctantly, running for President of the United States. In 1952, citizens confirmed "I like Ike" was a popular sentiment; Eisenhower won by a landslide, and duplicated the feat in 1956. As the 34th President of the United States, Eisenhower's terms spanned 1953–61, a time when the Korean War, civil rights, the arms race, the space race, and McCarthyism topped the public's list of concerns. A visit to Eisenhower's humble beginnings help put this era in context, and the friendly, informative staff and interesting memorabilia bring the site to life. If the visit piques your interest, consider visiting President Eisenhower's family farm, now the Eisenhower National Historic Site (www.nps.gov/eise), in Gettysburg, Pennsylvania or the Dwight D. Eisenhower Presidential Library, Museum and Boyhood Home (www.eisenhower.archives.gov) in Abilene, Kansas.

Step a little further back in time with a visit to the **Grayson County Frontier Village**, nestled under shade trees just west of US 75. Created during the Great Depression when the Civilian Conservation Corps moved over a dozen historic buildings circa 1840-1900 to this spot, the village is fairly basic, but offers a nice opportunity to appreciate the workmanship and scale of buildings of this era. Since it's a self-guided tour, but sure to pick up information before meandering through. Frontier Village is located at the entrance to **Loy Lake Park** and near the **Eisenhower Veterans Monument**, a veterans memorial plaza featuring an enormous bust of Eisenhower.

East and back over US 75, **Huck's Catfish** brings a taste of the Delta up the Red River, serving moist and flakey filets of farm-raised catfish battered and fried "Mississippi style" and perfectly paired with garlic coleslaw, hushpuppies, red beans, black-eyed peas, fried okra, or creamed spinach. Wash it down with sweet tea and consider leaving room for a scoop of apple, peach, or pecan cobbler. The restaurant is tucked onto a side street and looks a bit like an office building, but the blue catfish painted on the front are reassuring. It's first come, first served, and often crowded.

A CATFISH DINNER AT HUCK'S CATFISH IN DENISON

Round out the vintage feel of this route with a trip to **Watson's** for a burger, onion rings, and a milkshake. What began as a root beer stand in the 1950s quickly became a drive-in burger joint, fuelled be hungry teens who attended what was then the high school across the street. While times have changed, you can still pull into Watson's and get a hot meal delivered directly to your car window with a smile.

Denison was founded in 1872 at the intersection of the Missouri-Kansas-Texas railroad—the "MKT," which became shortened to "Katy"—and the Red River. Commercial activity hummed around the Katy Depot on the riverbanks, attracting folks such as Doc Holliday, who came to set up a dental practice, but left to pursue gambling and gunfighting, including one famous bout at the O.K. Corral.

These days, the Katy Depot is home to **The Red River Railroad Museum**. Not just for train enthusiasts, this little local museum is packed with railroad memorabilia illuminating the social and cultural impact of this bygone era and includes the chance to peek inside some original MKT locomotives.

Press northward to **Eisenhower State Park** for a view of Lake Texoma. The park runs along the shores of the lake, with camping, screened shelters, and trails along the shady bluffs and a sandy beach for swimming and piers for fishing. It's pretty, well-maintained, and a lovely spot to watch a sunset.

Detour to the **Hagerman National Wildlife Refuge**, which hugs the southern shore of the Big Mineral Arm of Lake Texoma, an offshoot of the Red River between Texas and Oklahoma. The refuge provides a large swath of native habitat—a mix of wetlands, tallgrass prairie, and riverine bottomland hardwood forest—that migratory birds favor for eating, resting, and nesting. Each year, over 270 bird species are found living or passing through the refuge as they make their way along the Central Flyway twice a year. Meadowlarks, mockingbirds, mourning doves, warblers, neotropical songbirds, geese, and even bald eagles all frequent the refuge, making it one of the best bird-watching destinations in North Texas. The visitor center is especially informative, with information on the Red River Valley habitats and ecosystem and an indoor viewing area overlooking the water complete with benches, references materials, and telescopes.

STOP IN FOR SOMETHING SWEET AT LOVEJOY'S ON MAIN IN WHITESBORO

Leaving the parks behind and heading west, it's hard not to fall in love with **Lovejoy's on Main**, the boutique gift shop, cafe, and soda fountain in tiny **Whitesboro**. Owned and operated by high school sweethearts Rita and Hank Lovejoy, Lovejoy's is the perfect spot for a light lunch, pie, ice cream sundae, or a float, served with a side of small town friendliness and a dash of nostalgia. Stroll up and down the quiet Main Street for more.

At this point, you can head south on US 377 toward Lake Ray Roberts and Pilot Point, en route to Denton or even back to McKinney, or continue along US 82 west for 50 miles to **Nocona**.

The little town of **Pilot Point** got its name from a tall cottonwood tree, growing well above a surrounding grove of oak trees; it was so distinctive that Native Americans, Texas Rangers, and early settlers all used it as a landmark. Things kicked off with a bang in 1854 when settlers began to arrive, followed by a post office, school, several churches, a telegraph line, and finally a railroad. The Civil War and Reconstruction created social tensions and violence, and the town's proximity to the frontier meant it was vulnerable to cattle rustling and lawlessness. In the 1890s, German Catholic immigrants, encouraged by *empresarios*, began to move to Pilot Point, creating yet another social shift in the community.

These days, folks driving through Pilot Point make a point to stop at **Magnolia Station**, which serves Cuban pulled pork pressed sandwiches, burgers cooked with blackened spices and bleu cheese, and a smoked meatloaf club special everyone loves, all cooked in a Depression-era gas station. Patio seating only.

Approximately 10 miles north of Denton, you'll come to Lake Ray Roberts, an almost 30,000-acre reservoir with **Ray Roberts Lake State Park** spread out over part of both the north and south shores. There are three distinctly developed sites in the park: the Johnson Branch Unit on the north shore, the Isle du Bois Unit on the southern shore, and the Jordan Unit just northeast of Isle du Bois. Both Johnson and Isle du Bois units have tent camping (some with water views) hiking, fishing, boating, kayaking, and swimming. For those who don't want to rough it, the **Lone Star Lodge and Marina** built high on a ridge at the Jordan Unit may be the perfect compromise. The rooms here are simple, clean, and comfortable, but you may not spend much time in yours as long as the lake and trails beckon. The lodge, built of rustic stone and wood, with plenty of windows, a patio, and gazebo overlooking the water, is a popular venue for weddings and special events.

If you are traveling with your horse in order to enjoy the 27 miles of the park's equestrian trails, Texas Parks and Wildlife is ready to host you both overnight at one of their equestrian campsites or at the lodge, which offers both indoor and outdoor stalls to choose from.

A migratory hotspot in its own way, **Denton** attracts over 45,000 students who come to attend the University of North Texas and Texas Woman's University. This city of just over 100,000 leverages big-city cultural events, small-town charms, and youthful energy, making it a popular day trip destination. And the folks at the **Discover Denton Welcome Center** are always happy to greet visitors. While Denton isn't a small town, strolling its historic square is an easy way to appreciate the offerings. Pull into a parking spot beside the courthouse and leave your car behind as you explore the historic district on foot.

As with most small towns in Texas, Denton has a large courthouse in the center of its square. Though the county itself was formed in 1846, the court actually held proceedings first under a tree and then in a log cabin. In 1857,

Nocona

The town of Nocona and the craft of boot-making have a long lineage together, but the story begins with the Justin Boots brand. Founded in 1879 in Spanish Fort, Texas, near the Red River, the boot company was well positioned to offer cowboys custom-fit boots as cattle drives made their way through the region. When the railroad laid track in nearby Nocona in 1887, the company founder H. J. "Joe" Justin moved as well to better move his product. Joe's daughter, Enid, began learning the trade when she was just 12 years old. When her father passed away and the rest of the family decided to move the operation and equipment to Fort Worth, she stayed behind, borrowed

THE NOCONA BREWERY IN NOCONA

$5000, and founded Nocona Boots. The new company enjoyed a run of popularity when oil was discovered nearby and their 16-inch lace-up boot became a durable favorite of oil field workers. In 1981, however, Nocona Boots' path wound its way back to Justin Boots. The companies merged and in 1999 moved to El Paso; the once thriving factory in the company's namesake town has sat vacant for years.

Recently, however, Nocona is staging a comeback. The town has received funds to develop the original Justin Leather Goods Building, a former eyesore at 100 Clay Street, into a community center and farmer's market. In the spirit of giving back, a local entrepreneur has opened the **Nocona Brewery** and the **Old Nocona Boot Factory**, breathing new life and functionality into the legacy buildings. Open, airy, and industrial, Nocona Brewery makes, pours, and distributes its craft brew from this spot, often alongside live music. You can oogle over or purchase classic Nocona boots on the retail side of the complex, where the smell of leather harkens back to the old days. Details at www.noconabeer.com and www.theoldnoconabootfactory.com.

MAGNOLIA STATION IN PILOT POINT

the very county completed a new, wooden two-story courthouse, which was subsequently destroyed in a fire on Christmas Eve, 1875. Two years later, the county replaced it with a brick courthouse, one of the first brick buildings built in Denton. This building was struck by lightning and in a saga too long to tell here—including the possible bribing of a county commissioner, a stone cutter's strike, and cost overruns in the thousands of dollars—the courthouse was completed on May 21, 1897.

These days, the building houses the **Courthouse on the Square**

Museum, one of three Denton County museums within walking distance to one another. There is quite a bit at the Courthouse on the Square Museum, from farming tools and dolls to Denton County pottery and pecan folk art. It's well-worth a visit, particularly for the insights into African American, Hispanic, and Native American heritage. The **Denton County African American Museum** and **Bayless-Shelby House Museum** are in nearby **Denton County Historical Park**. The small but powerful Denton County African American Museum, housed in a modest and sparsely furnished home built in 1904, depicts life at the time without sugarcoating the unrelenting racism faced by African Americans. The Queen Anne-style Bayless-Shelby House, built in 1898, presents quite a contrast. Docents bring the history to life through details, stories, and plenty of background knowledge.

You'll need to drive a few minutes to serene **The Little Chapel in the Woods**, located on the grounds of Texas Woman's University. Built during the Great Depression and dedicated by First Lady Eleanor Roosevelt in 1939, the chapel was designed by Texas architect O'Neil Ford. Ford was born in Pink Hill, Texas in 1905, and moved to Denon to attend North Texas State Teachers College in 1917, but financial hardship forced him to leave after completing two years of study, and he went on to earn an architectural certificate by mail. Ford was so widely regarded in his time that in 1974 he was declared a National Historic Landmark, the only person given that title. Ford was a master of mixing the wood, brick, stone, and other materials of the American Southwest with a sense of European modernism and elegance. Ford designed buildings which were beautiful both inside and out. From the curb, his designs are wonderfully proportioned and seem nestled in the landscape around them. Once inside, nature seems to take center stage as huge windows and soaring ceilings showcase the outdoors. Take a moment to admire the individually-designed stained glass windows of the chapel, each depicting "Women Ministering to the Human Needs."

Back on the square, **Recycled Books, Records, and CDs** stands out as a shining example of what has become an endangered species: the independent bookstore.

COURTHOUSE ON THE SQUARE MUSEUM, HOUSED IN THE HISTORIC DENTON COUNTY COURTHOUSE IN DENTON

Muenster

German roots run deep in parts of Texas (see Chapters 2 and 4). Tiny **Muenster** (pop. just over 1,500) was originally established as a German Catholic colony by the Flusche brothers who, in 1889, acquired 22,000 acres of land along the newly laid Missouri-Kansas-Texas Railroad line and invited like-minded folks to join them. Through recruitment, they wooed twenty five men, seven women, and six children to the site by December 1889, a fact they celebrated with the Feast of the Immaculate Conception and their first Mass in their new home. A year later, the community was able to construct a school for the price of $1,000 which, amazingly, served Muenster students for almost a century until it closed in 1987. While people no longer speak German around here, many vestiges of German heritage remain. Stop by **Rohmer's Restaurant** for a taste of German comfort food favorites, including Wiener schnitzel, kraut and fried potatoes. Details at www.rohmersrestaurant.com.

Filled to the brim with books, magazines, CDs, and even vinyl, the bookstore occupies Wright's Opera House, built by a retired rancher on the site of the old Denton courthouse which was destroyed by lightning in 1894. The advent of motion pictures silenced the opera music in 1913 and the building was used as a theater, department store, and office supply store until Recycled Books, Records, and CDs moved in in 1990. It's a great place to go offline and fall in love with browsing all over again.

Across the street, **Barley and Board** has taken over the first floor of a cavernous brick building and brought up-market brew-pub fare to Denton. While the menu is impressive, they've earned high praise for their basic burger—a hot and juicy patty served with melted cheese, grilled onions, housemade pickles and a special sauce on a brioche bun. This, plus the wide inventory of craft beers on tap, makes Barley and Board and a good choice for everything from lunch, brunch, dinner, or just a happy hour drink and a few appetizers.

Across the square, **LSA Burger Co.** is a mash-up of huge burgers, non-burgers, queso, salads, beers, desserts, cocktails, music, and a rooftop deck for fun. Kitschy and fresh, it's easy to see why this two-story place is always crowded. Moving away from the square, barbecue, burgers, and beer rule the menu at **Rooster's Roadhouse**. Fun-loving and walking a line between raucous and laid-back, Rooster's is understandably pretty popular. A block or two farther, **Boca 31** crafts hot, homemade empanadas and fills individual tacos to order at its relaxed spot a few blocks off the square. Friendly service, super fresh ingredients including well-seasoned meats, flavorful sauces, and heaps of shredded cabbage and pickled onions, and a

HOMEMADE EMPANADAS AT BOCA 31 IN DENTON

refreshing daily *aguas frescas* special. Order as few or as many as you'd like at the window.

When **Beth Marie's** opened in 1998, they hoped that their dozens of flavors of premium ice cream would entice folks to stop by Historic Courthouse Square for a cone. The customers did come, and this ice cream parlor quickly became a Denton favorite. The ice cream is made 10 gallons at a time in a circa-1927 ice cream machine. Locally-inspired flavors include Texas Honey Whiskey, Shiner Bock, and Texas Doctor, which is Dr. Pepper ice cream studded with bits of praline pecan. Nearby, **Atomic Candy** hit the sweet spot when they opened their candy shop in Denton in 2011. Most people find they come for the sweets and stay for the nostalgia. Fun fact: the Chick-O-Stick and peanut butter bars are made by the Atkinson Candy Co. in the East Texas town of Lufkin. Turns out you can feel like a kid in a candy shop at any age.

Denton has a vibrant live music scene, and there are plenty of places to catch a set or two. **Harvest House** is a good place to start. Located right off the square, Harvest House serves beer, cocktails, and fresh-squeezed juices in their spacious indoor/outdoor hybrid space. There's fire pits, sofas, pool tables, dogs, resident food trucks, and, of course, live music. All that, plus the relaxed atmosphere and diverse clientele means there's something for everyone.

Denton plays host to plenty of happenings throughout the year; two big ones include the **North Texas State Fair and Rodeo** (www.ntfair.com/) in August and the **Denton Arts and Jazz Festival** (www.dentonjazzfest.com/) in April. If you want to spend the night, since Denton marches to a different drummer, the perfect place to stay is somewhere a little unusual. **Old Irish Bed and Breakfast**, located on Patricks Pastures Alpaca Ranch, has charmed many of its clientele with its cozy cottages and delightful group of resident alpacas. Situated about 15 minutes east of downtown Denton, Old Irish enjoys an enthusiastic following of guests who can't seem to get enough of the owners' hospitality and the alpacas toothy grins. Breakfasts—small treats on the weekdays and homemade spreads on the weekends—are delivered to your door in the morning.

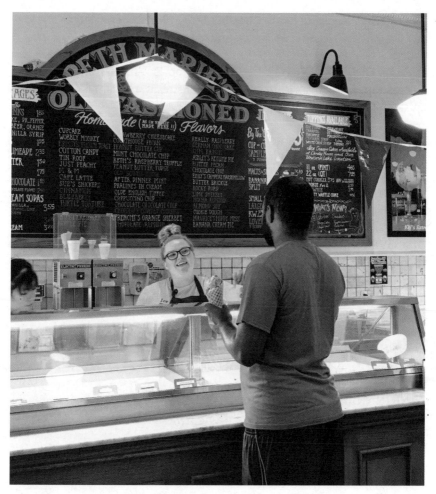

SERVING ICE CREAM AT BETH MARIE'S IN DENTON

IN THE AREA

ATOMIC CANDY, 105 W. Hickory Street, Denton, 76201. Call 940-383-3780. Website: www.atomic-candy.com.

BARLEY AND BOARD, 100 W. Oak Street, Denton, 76201. Call 940-566-3900. Up-market brew-pub fare, but they've earned high praise for their basic burger. Website: www.barleyandboard.com. $$.

BETH MARIE'S, 117 W. Hickory Street, Denton, 76201. Call 940-384-1818. Homemade ice cream in a wide range of flavors. Website: www.bethmaries .com. $.

CHESTNUT SQUARE, 311 S. Chestnut Street, McKinney, 75069. Call 972-562-8790. Free. Website: www.chestnutsquare.org.

COLLIN COUNTY HISTORY MUSEUM, 300 E. Virginia Street, McKinney, 75069. Call 972-542-9457. Free. Website: www.collincountyhistorymuseum.org.

COURTHOUSE ON THE SQUARE MUSEUM, 110 W. Hickory Street, Denton, 76201. Free. Website: www.dentoncounty.com.

DENTON COUNTY HISTORICAL PARK, 317 W. Mulberry Street, Denton, 76201. Free. Website: www.dentoncounty.com.

DISCOVER DENTON WELCOME CENTER, 111 W. Hickory Street, Denton, 76201. Call 940-218-1815. Website: www.discoverdenton.com.

EISENHOWER BIRTHPLACE STATE HISTORIC SITE, 609 S. Lamar Avenue, Denison, 75021. Call 903-465-8908. Fee.

EISENHOWER STATE PARK, 50 Park Road 20, Denison, 75020. Call 903-465-1956. Fee. Website: www.tpwd.texas.gov.

FANNIN COUNTY MUSEUM OF HISTORY, 1 N. Main Street, Bonham, 75418. Call 903-583-8042. Fee. Website: www.fannincountymuseum.org.

FORT INGLISH, TX-56 & Chinner Street, Bonham, 75418. Call 903-583-3943. Fee. Website: www.tshaonline.org.

GRAYSON COUNTY FRONTIER VILLAGE, 111 R C Vaughan Road, Denison, 75020. Call 903-463-2487. Fee.

HAGERMAN NATIONAL WILDLIFE REFUGE, 6465 Refuge Road, Sherman, 75092. Call 903-786-2826. Fee. Website: www.fws.gov.

HARVEST HOUSE, 331 E. Hickory Street, Denton, 76201. Call 940-218-6148. Part beer garden, juice bar, and coffee shop, with great live music to boot. Website: www.dentonharvesthouse.com. $–$$.

HARVEST SEASONAL KITCHEN, 112 E. Louisiana Street, McKinney, 75069. Call 214-726-0251. Farm-to-market specialities; the deviled eggs are a must. Website: www.harvesttx.com. $–$$.

HUCK'S CATFISH, 2811 Trail Drive, Denison, 75020. Call 903-337-0033. Closed Sundays and Mondays. Popular for its farm-raised catfish, battered and fried "Mississippi style." Website: www.huckscatfish.com. $–$$.

HUGS CAFÉ, 224 E. Virginia Street, McKinney, 75069. Call 469-301-6900. Delicious deli food with a purpose. Website: www.hugscafe.org. $–$$.

HUTCHINS BBQ, 1301 N. Tennessee Street, McKinney, 75069. Call 972-548-2629. Some of the best barbecue in the area; the all-you-can-eat buffet allows you to graze to your heart's content. Website: www.hutchinsbbq.com. $$–$$$.

LITTLE CHAPEL IN THE WOODS, 415 Chapel Drive, Denton, 76209. Call 940-898-3516.

LONE STAR LODGE RESORT AND MARINA, 2200 FM 1192, Pilot Point, 76258. Call 940-686-0261. Simple, clean, and comfortable rooms at the state park near lake. Website: www.lonestarlodgeresortandmarina.com. $–$$.

LOVEJOY'S ON MAIN, 138 E. Main Street, Whitesboro, 76273. Call 903-564-3685. Sweet treats and sandwiches courtesy of high school sweetheart owners. Website: www.lovejoysonmain.com. $.

LSA BURGER, 113 W. Hickory Street, Denton, 76201. Call 940-383-1022. Burgers anchor the place, but there are plenty of other options; the rooftop deck is a big draw. Website: www.lsaburger.com. $–$$.

MAGNOLIA STATION, 110 E. Liberty Street, Pilot Point, 76258. Fantastic food cooked in a Depression-era gas station; patio seating only. Call 940-686-2060. Website: www.magnoliastationii1.treetopscafe.com or find them on Facebook. $–$$.

McKINNEY BED & BREAKFAST, 406 Parker Street, McKinney, 75069. Call 214-808-6727. Delightful Victorian inn with red rockers on the porches outside and fresh self-serve biscotti inside. Website: www.mckinneybedand breakfast.com. $–$$.

MUDDBONES, 1701 TX 121, Bonham, 75418. Call 903-583-5385. Burgers with all the fixin's in a no-frills eatery. Website: www.muddbonestx.com. $.

NOCONA BREWERY, 915 US 82, Nocona, 76255. Call 940-825-7238. Craft microbrewery, with live music. Website: www.noconabeer.com. $–$$.

OLD NOCONA BOOT FACTORY, 901 US 82, Nocona, 76255. Call 817-513-2586. Website: www.theoldnoconabootfactory.com.

PATINA GREEN HOME AND MARKET, 116 N Tennessee Street, McKinney, 75069. Call 972-548-9141. Come for the home decor ideas, stay for the "brisket on a biscuit." Website: www.patinagreenhomeandmarket.com. $–$$.

RAY ROBERTS LAKE STATE PARK, 100 P W 4137, Pilot Point, 76258. Call 940-686-2148. Fee. Website: www.tpwd.texas.gov.

RECYCLED BOOKS, 200 N. Locust Street, Denton, 76201. Call 940-566-5688. Website: www.recycledbooks.com.

THE RED RIVER RAILROAD MUSEUM, 101 E. Main Street, Denison, 75021. Call 903-463-5289. Fee. Website: www.redriverrailmuseum.org.

ROOSTER'S ROADHOUSE, 113 Industrial Street, Denton, 76201. Barbecue with a side of Texas decor. Website: www.roosters-roadhouse.com. $$.

RYE CRAFT FOOD AND DRINK, 111 W. Virginia Parkway, McKinney, 75069. Call 214-491-1715. Fantastic craft cocktails and all kinds of noshes. Website: www.ryemckinney.com. $$.

SAM RAYBURN HOUSE STATE HISTORIC SITE, 890 TX 56, Bonham, 75418. Call 903-583-5558. Fee. Website: www.thc.texas.gov.

SAM RAYBURN LIBRARY AND MUSEUM, 800 W. Sam Rayburn Drive, Bonham, 75418. Call 903-583-2455. Free. Website: www.cah.utexas.edu.

WATSON'S, 631 W. Main Street, Denison, 75020. Call 903-465-4669. 1950s drive-in burger standby. Find them on Facebook. $–$$.

Index